MICHIGAN PAPYRI XVI
A GREEK LOVE CHARM FROM EGYPT
(P. MICH. 757)

AMERICAN STUDIES IN PAPYROLOGY

Editors
L. Koenen, M. Haslam, A. E. Hanson

Number 30
P. MICHIGAN XVI

A GREEK LOVE CHARM FROM EGYPT
(P. MICH. 757)

Edition and Commentary
by
D.G. Martinez

P. MICHIGAN XVI

A GREEK LOVE CHARM FROM EGYPT
(P. MICH. 757)

Edition and Commentary
by
David G. Martinez

Scholars Press
Atlanta, Georgia

P. MICHIGAN XVI
A GREEK LOVE CHARM FROM EGYPT (P. MICH. 757)

Edition and Commentary
by
D.G. Martinez

Library of Congress Cataloging in Publication Data

University of Michigan. Library. Manuscript. P. Mich. 757. English & Greek.
P. Michigan XVI : a Greek love charm from Egypt (P. Mich. 757) / edition and commentary by David G. Martinez.
p. cm. -- (Michigan papyri ; 16) (American studies in papyrology ; no. 30)
Includes index.
ISBN 1-55540-547-9
1. Magic, Greek 2. Charms-- Egypt. 3. Love--Miscellanea.
4. Manuscripts, Greek (Papyri) 5. University of Michigan. Library.
Manuscript. P. Mich. 757. I. Martinez, David G. (David Grey)
II. Title. III. Series. IV. Series: American studies in papyrology
; v. 30.
PA3305.M5 vol. 16
[BF1622.G8]
133.4'3'0938--dc20 90-47007
CIP

Printed in the United States of America
on acid-free paper

For Meredith

ὡϲ ἐφίληϲεν ἡ Ἶϲιϲ τὸν Ὄϲιριν

καθὼϲ καὶ ὁ Χριϲτὸϲ ἠγάπηϲεν τὴν ἐκκληϲίαν

Table of Contents

List of Figures and Plates

Figures:

Plate:

PREFACE

This study is an extensive revision of my University of Michigan dissertation, *P. Mich. 6925*: *A New Magical Love Charm*, accepted by the Department of Classical Studies in August, 1985. The text, translation, and a brief commentary, based on the dissertation and early proofs of the present work, have recently been published by R.W. Daniel and F. Maltomini in *Supplementum Magicum* (see bibliography, p. 130). There are divergences between my edition and that of Daniel-Maltomini, some of which are discussed in the commentary.

I wish here to clarify the method by which I present in the following pages *P. Mich.* 757 and the five "parallel" documents (see below p. 6). The text of the former is given in full on p. 22 as it appears on the tablet, preceded and followed by transcripts of its individual sections. After the translation of §§ J and K, each of the various divisions of the commentary begins with the appropriate passage of *P. Mich.* 757 followed by the corresponding portions of the parallel texts. Here and in the *lemmata* I normalize the spelling of the Michigan tablet to provide a standard; the readings of the parallels are presented without normalization. Important advances have recently been made in establishing the texts of the parallels by D.R. Jordan (*ZPE* 72 [1988] 245ff.; a new edition of the first Wortmann tablet with corrections for two others) and R.W. Daniel and F. Maltomini (*Supplementum Magicum*, already mentioned). Daniel and Maltomini kindly allowed me access to the galleys of their editions which I utilized in the final corrections to this volume. Points at which the reader should consult the addenda (pp. 119-121) are marked by an asterisk (*).

I could not have completed this volume without generous financial assistance from various funding agencies of the University of Colorado at Boulder, namely, the Council on Research and Creative Work, the Council on University and Scholarly Publications, and the IMPART program. I am especially grateful to the first mentioned organization for the Jr. Faculty Development Award which allowed me to spend the summer of 1988 in Ann Arbor, where much of the important work of revision was done.

Ancient magic has commanded the attention of a number of distinguished scholars past and present, and the pages which follow will sufficiently reveal my debt to them. I would like here to mention a few who have directly contributed to my work by way of conference and/or correspondence, namely H.D.Betz, W.M. Calder III, R.W. Daniel, C.A. Faraone, D.N. Freedman, J.F. Gannon, A.E. Hanson, M.W. Haslam, A. Henrichs, D.R. Jordan, P. Keyser, R. Kotansky, F. Maltomini, K.A. Mathews, B.M. Metzger, L. Miller, C.R. Phillips, K. Rudolph, P.J. Sijpesteijn, E. Schütrumpf, G. Schwendner, M. Smith, Ch. Witke. These have generously shared with me their erudition but have no part in the remaining mistakes, which are my responsibility. I am grateful to Margret Koenen for her superior work in composing the camera-ready copy of a frustrating manuscript and for her patience in working with an even more frustrating author. S. Adler has proofread the galleys twice and saved me from many errors. My parents, Angel and Robbie Martinez, and my parents-in-law, Thomas and Irma Longley, have on several occasions provided much-needed moral support.

Among all who have helped me in this project I must make special mention of two. L. Koenen, who directed my dissertation, has continued to encourage and assist me as a friend and scholarly mentor. Most of what is said here that is of any value is either directly or indirectly a result of his influence. My wife Meredith has done far more than merely tolerate an academic's idiosyncrasies and work habits. She has created a familial atmosphere which is both loving and compelling, an ideal place to live and work. I dedicate this book to her with affection and appreciation.

Boulder, Colorado
May, 1990

D.G.M.

Editorial Sigla

The editorial *sigla* employed in this study are those commonly used in editions of papyri.

[ ]	lacuna in text
( )	resolution of an abbreviation or symbol
{ }	superfluous letter or letters
\` ´	additions above the line
⟦ ⟧	deletion in the original
< >	omission in the original

A dot placed beneath a letter indicates that the letter is doubtful. Within square brackets dots indicate the estimated number of missing letters.

I. INTRODUCTION

P. Mich. 757 (inv. no. 6925) is one of many magical spells inscribed on lead tablets from the 3rd/4th century A.D.[1] In this document a certain Ailourion, son of Kopria, by means of magical names and formulae[2] invokes the chthonic deities and *daimones* to bring him his beloved, whose name, as it happens, is also Kopria.[3] The plate is well preserved and, aside from a crack slightly off center to the left, undamaged. Sand and calcium deposits obscure very little of the writing in parts of the lower edge and upper right hand side. The creases running vertically at regular intervals indicate that the tablet was rolled up.[4] The script resembles W. Schubart's P. Berol. 43a (4th cent. A.D.) and the hand of the Bodmer Menander texts (3rd/4th cent. A.D.; cf., e.g., the specimens of *Dyskolos* in R. Seider, *Palaeographie der griechischen Papyri* II # 51, pl. XXVI). As is usual in lead documents, the reverse is blank.[5]

---

[1] The handbook version of this charm in *PGM* IV 296ff. (see below p. 8ff.) more specifically designates it as a φιλτροκατάδεϲμοϲ, "erotic binding spell." The 3rd/4th century date is based solely on paleographic grounds.*

[2] Such formulae take various shapes; e.g., the palindrome (a word or name which reads the same from the beginning as from the end, often with a central converging point, as in our text §§ A, C, J 1; cf. below pp. 21, 23, 24); the *Schwindeform/Schwindeschema* ("diminishing" word, as §§ A, C, D, E, F); the *logos*, i.e., a group of magical words or names which commonly occur together (such as the *φωκενϲεψ-logos* § J 3, the *βαρβαριθα-logos* § J 16; some *logoi* consist of a single long and often palindromic word, such as the *ιαεω-logos* [§ A] and the *αβεραμεν-logos* [§ J 1]). This meaning of *logos* is not to be confused with the more general sense, "spell," "incantation" (cf. below p. 8).

[3] For Κοπρία and Copronyms in general, see P. Perdrizet, *Revue des Études Anciennes* 23 (1921) 85-94; S.B. Pomeroy in *Studies in Roman Law in Memory of A. Arthur Schiller*, edd. R.S. Bagnall and W.V. Harris (Leiden 1986) 147-62.

[4] Among the parallels to our text (see below p. 6), cf. the photograph of L in Kambitsis' edition (pl. XXXI).

[5] The two Wortmann texts (see List of Abbreviations s.vv. W_1 and W_2) are exceptions.

Lead in Magical Documents

It is well known that specific metals were regularly prescribed for certain objects used in magical rites.[6] In this context, lead became a standard writing surface for various kinds of forceful, practical spells, generally termed *defixiones*, including love charms and cursing spells.[7] Audollent's collection[8] of over 300 such documents, dating from the 5th century B.C. to the 4th century A.D.,[9] contains only 21 examples of tablets made from other materials.[10] The instructions of

---

[6] E.g., one must use a bronze sickle or scythe to cut magical herbs (Ovid *Met.* VII 227; Verg. *Aen.* IV 513 [with R.G. Austin's commentary *ad loc.*] and cf. Macrobius' discussion of this passage in *Sat.* V 19. 8-14); iron is specifically forbidden for this purpose (Pliny *NH* XXIV 12 and 103). The clashing of bronze (less frequently iron) cymbals or implements prevents the moon from being drawn down or eclipsed (Plut. *Mor.* 944b; Ovid *Met.* VII 207f.; Tib. I 8.21-22; Juv. 6.442f.; Livy XXVI 5.9; Stat. *Theb.* VI 686f.; Mart. XII 57.16f.; Tacit. *Ann.* I 28; cf. J.E. Lowe, *Magic in Greek and Latin Literature* [Oxford 1929] 27-28) and wards off harmful deities and spirits (Theoc. 2.36 and Gow's note *ad loc.*; Lucian *Philops.* 15; Ovid *Fasti* V 441f.). Bronze was also frequently used for needles in magic (Ovid *Fasti* II 577f. with J.G. Frazer's commentary *ad loc.* [vol. II p. 451f.]; *PGM* IV 321f. [see below p. 9]; VII 442; XXXVI 236).

[7] In general see Aud. pp. xlviiff.; Kagarow 9f.; Hopfner, *OZ* I § 608; Jordan, "Well" 226f. By "practical" I mean spells prepared by magicians for the actual use of clients as opposed to handbook recipes (see below pp. 6ff.). "Forceful" magic is that which seeks to influence the attitudes, actions, or circumstances of one against his/her will; thus love charms fit this category. They generally demand that the beloved endure great misery until he/she fulfills the lover's desires. This point is well illustrated by our text (e.g., §J 9-10, 23; see below pp. 24ff.) and by the sympathetic process delineated in *PGM* IV 296ff. (below pp. 8f.). The latter prescribes the constructing of two effigies, the one a bound, kneeling female figure, representing the girl to be charmed, the other an armed image of Ares, threatening the girl with a sword. Next follow instructions to write magic words on the female doll, pierce it with needles, and bind both figurines to a lead tablet inscribed with a love spell similar to ours. Thus the term *defixio*/κατάδεcμοc applies to any spell which has the *binding* of a victim as its intent.

[8] See List of Abbreviations s.v. Aud. Audollent's volume, which comprises Attic and non-Attic Greek tablets as well as Latin tablets, was designed to supplement the earlier edition of exclusively Attic *defixiones* by R. Wünsch (List of Abbreviations s.v. Wünsch). For Greek *defixiones* which do not appear in these two corpora, see now the exhaustive survey by D.R. Jordan in *GRBS* 26 (1985) 151-97. For Latin tablets not in Audollent, see Jordan, *op. cit.* 151-52 nn. 3 and 4. The best general treatments of these documents are K. Preisendanz in *RAC* VIII 1-29 and Kagarow (see List of Abbreviations s.v.).

[9] See Audollent's chronological table, p. 556. Some tablets date from as late as the 6th cent. A.D. (Jordan, "Well" 227).

[10] Aud. p. xlviif.: 11 ostraka; 4 mica; 2 bronze; 2 gold; 1 tin; 1 marble.

magical handbooks, such as *PGM* X 36f., provide further evidence: λαβὼν λάμναν ἢ πέταλον μολιβοῦν ἀπὸ ἡμιόνων γράφε τὰ ὑποκείμενα ὀνόματα.[11] Most magical lead tablets are not nearly so lengthy or complex as our text. Many, in fact, preserve only a list of names of those to be cursed or a single name.[12] The ancients also used lead for other kinds of writing, both religious (e.g., oracular questions, amulets) and secular (private letters, identification tags).[13]

Practical considerations probably helped establish the use of lead for spells. It is soft, pliant, and easy to roll up or fold. Other properties, such as its relative worthlessness (Lucian *Sat.* 20), coldness (Plutarch *Mor.* 567c, 691b), pallid, death-like color (Pliny *NH* XI 274),[14] and weight,[15] contribute to the general im-

---

[11] Cf. *PGM* IV 328ff. (see below pp. 9f.); V 304ff.; VII 397f., 432f.; XXXVI 1f. (=*P. Oslo* I 1.1f. on which see S. Eitrem's n.); *ibid.*, 231f. On magical handbooks, see below pp. 6-8.

[12] List of names: Wünsch 2-17, 19-26, 28-31, 33-39; Aud. 46, 53, 57-59. One name: Wünsch 1, 18, 27, 32. Audollent (pp. 107ff.) includes in the latter category the horde of 499 lead strips from Styra, each bearing one name. D.R. Jordan, however, advises me that two points militate against the identification of these documents as *defixiones*: their extremely early date and their uniformity of size and shape, which suggests mass production for a specific purpose (cf. the Attic cavalry tablets, next note). On these tablets see also Miller, *Studies* 8, who cites L.H. Jeffery, *Local Scripts of Archaic Greece* (Oxford 1961) 86. Professor Jordan also informs me that the 38 tablets which Audollent (pp. 80ff.) describes as being from the Piraeus actually belong to the group from Styra.

[13] For the principal bibliography on the Dodonean oracular lead strips, see H.W. Parke, *The Oracles of Zeus* (Oxford 1967) 126 nn. 2 and 18; cf. *ibid.* 259-73, where Parke has printed and translated some of the texts. The lead amulets are late and of Jewish-Christian origin; see Jordan, "Well" 227 and n. 12. K. Braun (*MDAI*, Ath. Abt. 85 [1970] 198ff.) discusses and catalogues 574 lead strips from a well in the Athenian Kerameikos which identify horses of the Attic cavalry as to color, brand, price, and owner's name. J.H. Kroll (*Hesperia* 46 [1977] 83ff.) treats 111 similar documents from a well in the Athenian Agora. For the private letters, see Miller, *Studies* 9-16 and Jordan, "Well" 226 with n. 9. The fullest general account known to me of different kinds of documents written on lead is that of Miller, *Studies* 1-29; Jordan's later survey ("Well" 226-29) both summarizes and supplements her material. See also the older discussions by Dziatzko in *RE* III 1.564f. s.v. Bleitafeln and by Besnier in *Dictionnaire des antiquités grecques et romaines* IV 1.514Bf. s.v. Plumbum.

[14] Pliny here attributes to Aristotle the opinion that one who has a *plumbeus color* will die young. Coldness is also associated with death (cf. LSJ s.v. ψυχρός I).

[15] For the heaviness of lead as a chthonic property, see Aud. 98.2ff.: *sic comdi* (i.e., *quomodo*) *[pl]um[b]um subsidet, sic Sintonem et Martialem Sint[onis] et Adiutorium Sintonis --- defero ad infero(s). Subsidet* = "sinks," *pace* Audollent. It is well known that many lead tablets have been found in wells, springs, cisterns, etc. (see D.R. Jordan, *Hesperia* 54 [1985] 207 n. 3 for a list of these). Although the

pression of the chthonic quality of the metal and its appropriateness for forceful magic.[16] This may be illustrated by the following sympathetic formulae[17] from Wünsch's collection of *defixiones*: ὡς οὗ[το]ς ὁ μόλυ[βδ]ος ψυχρὸς καὶ ἄ[θ]υμος[18] [οὕτως καὶ τὰ τῶν ἐνταῦθα γεγ]ραμμένων ψυχρ[ὰ καὶ ἄθυμα ἔςτω] καὶ ἔπη καὶ ἔργα κτλ. (105b.1-2); καὶ ὡς οὗτος ὁ μόλυβδος ἄχρηςτος, ὣς ἄχρηςτα εἶναι τῶν ἐνταῦθα γεγραμμένων καὶ ἔπη καὶ ἔργα (106b.1-2).[19]

Also important in this regard is the fact that astrological speculation associated lead with Kronos/Saturn; e.g., according to Proclus (*Ad. Tim.* 14b=vol. I 43, 5ff. Diehl), the emanations of the planets produced the various metals on earth:

---

above-cited text is not in this category, it seems nevertheless to allude to the practice of submerging *defixiones*, which W.S. Fox (*AJP* 33 [1912] 301ff.) explains as a sympathetic ritual against the enemy, competitor, etc. (i.e., as lead sinks, so should the victim sink or, as in Aud. 98, be offered to the *inferi*). A similar idea is probably implicit in the famous passages in the *Iliad* where Zeus weighs the κῆρε of the Greeks and Trojans (VIII 68ff.) or of Hektor and Achilleus (XXII 208ff.). In both cases it is the owner of the heavier κήρ who is doomed to failure or destruction. Scholiasts on both passages (see W. Leaf's commentary *ad locc.*) and Plutarch *Mor.* 17a cite Aeschylus' Ψυχοςταςία, in which Zeus weighs the souls of Achilleus and Memnon. Cf. also Soph. *OC* 1508, where Oedipus describes his imminent death as the "sinking point of life" (ῥοπὴ βίου; for parallels see R.C. Jebb's commentary *ad loc.*). The image of the sinking lead tablet inscribed with the victim's name belongs to the same sphere of Greek religious feeling as the older image of the ill-fortuned κήρ or ψυχή sinking in the scales.*

[16] In general see Aud. p. xlix; Wünsch p. 8; Kagarow pp. 9f.

[17] The general type of spell which follows, usually termed *similia similibus*, is well described and illustrated by C.A. Faraone, *ZPE* 72 (1988) 280-82.

[18] For ψυχρός cf. the imprecations which occur in several *defixiones* discovered in a well in the Athenean Agora; e.g., κραταιὲ Βετπυ, παραδίδωμί coι τὸν δεῖνα, ἵνα καταψύξῃς αὐτόν, and ὡς ταῦτα τὰ ὀνόματα ψύχεται, οὕτως ψυχέςθω ὁ δεῖνα (D.R. Jordan, *Hesperia* 54 [1985] 236, 238). Jordan (*op. cit.*, 207 and 241f.) explains these formulae as the coldness of the lead (and perhaps also of the water in the well) sympathetically transferred to the victim. He cites, among other parallels, Aud. 155b.20ff.: ὁρκίζο --- ἁγίους χ[αρα]κτῆρες οὕςπερ γεγραμμένους ἐν τούτῳ τῷ πετάλῳ τῷ ψυχρωφώρῳ, εἵνα --- καταψύξητε τ[ὴν] ἰς[χύν] τοὺς μυαλοὺς κτλ.

ἄθυμος is probably a mistake (or misreading?) for ἄτιμος in the light of the closely similar 107a.4f.: καὶ ὡς οὗτος ὁ βόλυβδος (i.e., μόλυβδος) ἄτιμος καὶ ψυχρός, οὕτω --- τὰ ἐκε(ί)νω ἄτιμα [κ]αὶ ψυχρὰ ἔςτω. ἄθυμος usually means "spiritless" or "despondent" rather than "lifeless."

[19] In general, cf. also Wünsch 97 (= Dittenberger, *Syll.* III 1175) 21ff.: ἡ γ[λ]ῶςςα αὐτῶν καὶ ἡ ψυχὴ μόλυβδος γένοιτο καὶ μὴ δύναιντο φθένγεςθα[ι] μηδὲ ποῆςαι.

λέγεται γοῦν Ἡλίου μὲν ὁ χρυϲόϲ, Ϲελήνηϲ δὲ ὁ ἄργυροϲ, Κρόνου δὲ μόλυβδοϲ καὶ Ἄρεωϲ ὁ ϲίδηροϲ. ταῦτα δὴ οὖν γεννᾶται μὲν ἐκεῖθεν, ὑφίϲταται δὲ ἐν γῇ καὶ οὐκ ἐν ἐκείνοιϲ τοῖϲ τὰϲ ἀπορροίαϲ ἀφιεῖϲιν (cf. Hopfner, OZ I § 605).

Other planet/metal lists consistently connect lead to Saturn,[20] which, significantly, is often described as an ill-boding planet of harmful or evil influence, both in literature (*stella nocens*, Lucan I 652)[21] and in magical texts (e.g., *PGM* XIII 1026ff.: πειρῶ δὲ καταϲκευάζειν αὐτὸν ⟨ϲελήνηϲ⟩ οὔϲηϲ ἐν ἀνατολῇ καὶ ϲυναπτούϲηϲ ἀγαθοποιῷ ἀϲτέρι ἢ Διῒ ἢ Ἀφροδίτῃ, καὶ ἐπιμαρτυροῦντοϲ μηδενὸϲ κακοποιοῦ, Κρόνου ἢ Ἄρεωϲ[22]). Also, an astrological treatise (*CCAG* VIII 2.149) advises that on the first hour of the seventh day, the hour and day in which Saturn rules, ποιήϲειϲ βλάβην τοῦ ἐχθροῦ.[23]

In a recent correspondence, D.R. Jordan suggested to me that a distinction might be made between an earlier period, when practical considerations established lead as the medium for *defixiones*, and a later period, when chthonic properties and astrological significance were ascribed to the metal as a more meaningful rationale for its almost exclusive use.[24] Indeed, the astrological material is late; but given that sympathetic formulae based on lead's "negative" qualities appeared quite early in these documents[25] and that prescription of certain metals for spe-

---

[20] Such lists are given by Hopfner, *OZ* I § 606; Roscher in Roscher III 2.2533-34 s.v. Planeten. Cf. also *CCAG* II 161.15f. Saturn, like lead (cf. above pp. 3, 4), is called "cold": *frigida Saturni --- stella*, Verg. *Georg*. 1.336; cf. Lucan I 651f.; Cic. *de Nat. Deor.* II 119 and A.S. Pease's commentary *ad loc.* (vol. 2 p. 850).

[21] Cf. *grave Saturni sidus in omne caput*, Prop. IV 1(b), 84; *haec tamen ignorat quid sidus triste minetur Saturni*, Juv. 6.569-70; similarly, Persius 5.50; Hor. *Od.* II 17. 22f. Cf. also *CCAG* II 160.5ff.: τὸν Κρόνον φαϲὶ --- βαϲκανίαϲ ποιητήν, τύφου τε καὶ μερίμναϲ καὶ μονοτροπίαϲ καὶ ὑποκρίϲεωϲ, φειδωλίαϲ, αὐϲτηρίαϲ, μελανειμοϲύνηϲ, αὐχμηρίαϲ, κακοπαθείαϲ, κτλ.

[22] With this text cf. esp. Cic. *de Div.* I 85 and for further parallels A.S. Pease's commentary *ad loc.* (*University of Illinois Studies in Language and Literature* VI [1920], no. 2 and 3, pp. 246f.). In general, for good and evil planets, see Gundel, H.G., *Weltbild* 48-52; Roscher in Roscher III 2.2530 s.v. Planeten.

[23] On the general topos of planets as day- or hour-rulers, cf. W. Hübner, *ZPE* 49 (1982) 53ff. and literature cited in n. 1.

[24] C.A. Faraone will in fact argue for such a distinction in the forthcoming Oxford press book, *Ancient Greek Magic and Religion*, edited by him and D. Obbink.*

[25] Wünsch 107, cited above p. 4 n. 18, is dated by Wünsch to the beginning of the 4th cent. B.C.

cific magical objects was a long and well-established tradition, I suspect that lead became integral for reasons beyond the merely practical at a very early date.

The Parallels: Handbook and Tablet

The spell of *P. Mich.* 757 (hereafter abbreviated M) closely resembles that of five other magical texts (collectively referred to as "parallels"), one a magical papyrus (*PGM* IV 296-433, abbrev. P), the others lead tablets (abbrev. C, L, W_1, W_2). For publication data, provenances, and dates of these documents, see List of Abbreviations, below pp. 131f. *PGM* IV (3274 lines) and certain other of the longer papyri in Preisendanz's collection (e.g., I, II, III, VII, XII, XXXVI) are considered magical handbooks, i.e., the working copies from which professional magicians transcribed incantations on lead tablets or other objects for their clients.[26] Among the ancient references to such handbooks[27] is the account in NT Acts 19.19 of the Ephesian sorcerers who renounced their art in response to their conversion under Paul: ἱκανοὶ δὲ τῶν τὰ περίεργα (= *artes magicas*) πραξάντων cυνενέγκαντεc τὰc βίβλουc κατέκαιον ἐνώπιον πάντων.[28] In a different vein, Lucian (*Philops.* 31) relates how a certain Arignotos purges a haunted house by reciting formulae from Αἰγύπτιαι βίβλοι.[29]

The handbooks contain spells for every occasion and often provide optional wordings for the same recipes;[30] e.g., a prescription (πρόγνωcιc, *PGM* III 479) is followed by "another copy" (ἄλλη ἀντ[ιγραφή], 483) and then "another" (ἄλλη,

[26] Cf. A.D. Nock, *JEA* 15 (1929) 220f. (*Essays* I 177ff.); K. Preisendanz, *Gnomon* 2 (1926) 191f.

[27] See A. Dieterich, *Jahrbücher für klass. Philol., Suppl.* 16 (1888) 751 (*Kleine Schriften* [Leipzig/Berlin 1911] 3).

[28] See the commentaries by E. Haenchen (Göttingen 1965; Eng. Oxford 1971) and F.F. Bruce (Grand Rapids 1951). Cf. Paul. *Sent.* V 23.18 (*Fontes Juris Romani Antejustiniani* II p. 410): *Libros magicae artis apud se neminem habere licet: et penes quoscumque reperti sint, bonis ademptis, ambustis his publice, in insulam deportantur, humiliores capite puniuntur.* Cf. also Augustus' burning of over 2000 soothsayers' books (Suet. *Aug.* 31). In general, for the prohibition and destruction of magical books among pagans and Christians, cf. W. Speyer, *Büchervernichtung und Zensur des Geistes bei Heiden, Juden und Christen* (Stuttgart 1981) 54 and n. 60; 130ff.; 169ff.

[29] Cf. *ibid.* 12: a Babylonian *magus* summons snakes, ἐπειπὼν ἱερατικά τινα ἐκ βίβλου παλαιᾶc ὀνόματα ἑπτά.

[30] Cf. esp. M. Smith, *Atti del XVII Congresso Internazionale di Papirologia* (Naples 1984) II 683ff., on the three versions of *The Eighth Book of Moses* in *PGM* XIII. See also A.D. Nock, *JEA* 15 (1929) 220-21 (*Essays* I 177-78).

489).[31] The fact that a handbook could offer a number of variations on a single spell is significant for our purposes, since, as we shall see, our five tablets differ considerably from P and from each other. Discerning textual relationships among them (and among other *defixiones*) is extremely difficult, since the magical books functioned as practical guides rather than fixed exemplars to be reproduced faithfully, and thus a *magus* in preparing a tablet could modify the handbook spell on the authority of the book itself or at his own initiative.[32]

One of the most common stylistic features of the handbooks is their use of vague, generic terminology[33] which permitted the *magus* to tailor a spell to the specific needs of his client. The following parallel passages from P and M illustrate: κατάδηcον· ἄξον τὴν δεῖνα, ἣν ⟨ἔτεκε ἡ⟩ δεῖνα, ἧc ἔχειc τὴν οὐcίαν, φιλοῦcάν με τὸν δεῖνα, ὃν ἔτεκεν ἡ δεῖνα (P 350f.); κατάδηcον Κοπρίαν, ἣν ἔτεκε μήτηρ Ταῆcιc, ἧc ἔχειc τὰc τρίχαc τῆc κεφαλῆc, Αἰλουρίωνι, ᾧ ἔτεκε μήτηρ ὀνόματι Κοπρία (M § J 7f.). This process of course led to errors; e.g., W_1 20f.: ἧc ἔχιc τὴν οὐcία⟨ν⟩ — ἑ τρίχεc τῆc [κεφ]αλῆc αὐτῆc — ταύτην. Here it seems that the magician copied from his handbook the generic τὴν οὐcίαν and then, realizing his mistake, ungrammatically filled in the specific substance to be used before he wrote ταύτην.

We also find that material could be abbreviated or augmented in accordance with the situation; e.g., in the command to the spirit of the dead as to where it should go to seek the beloved, all the texts have the three items εἰc πάντα (or πᾶν) τόπον, εἰc πᾶν ἄμφοδον, εἰc πᾶcαν οἰκίαν. W_1 19 and W_2 19 add εἰc πᾶν καπηλεῖον, on which Wortmann (p. 71) remarks that either the *magus* knew the girl to be a prostitute or he was simply trying to cover every possibility.

---

[31] See also ἄλλωc, e.g., in *PGM* IV 29, 463, 465, 1300; X 36; XIII 270; etc. (cf. *PGM* vol. 3 s.v.); this word often signals an optional phrase, name, *praxis* (see below p. 8), or entire spell, which may be used instead of the previously mentioned. Similarly in Egyptian magical texts, we often have, e.g., "a spell ...," "another one ...," "likewise another one ...," Borghouts, *AEMT* 14-17 and *passim*. Cf. ἄλλο in medical literature for suggesting optional cures (e.g., Galen, περὶ εὐποριcτῶν, vol. 14 p. 382 Kühn; *P. Oxy.* VIII 1088 (Marganne, pp. 240-44), col. iii 52, 56; *SB* XIV 11964.11; others in Preisigke, *Wörterbuch* I 59 s.v. ἄλλοc) and ἄλλο/ἄλλη in alchemy (*Les Alchimistes Grecs* I [Paris 1981], ed. R. Halleux, pp. 97-101, 107-108, and *passim*).

[32] On this point in general, see also below p. 12 n. 50 (on κοινόν) and p. 113; more specifically on the two Wortmann tablets, p. 19.

[33] For a similar usage of generic terms in business and civic documents, cf., e.g., *P. Mich.* II 122, pp. 81ff. (practice drafts for drawing up grapheion reports).

The distinctive formats of handbooks and tablets become more clearly defined when we understand the basic scheme of magical spells. It is to this point that we now turn.

The Parallels: *Logos* and *Praxis*

A magical ceremony often comprises two elements: *logos* (the "incantation" or "spell" addressed to the underworld deities and spirits, urging them to perform the wishes of the spell-operator) and *praxis* (the "act" accompanying the *logos*). For example, in Dido's magical rite (*Aeneid* IV 504ff.) she lays on the altar some of Aeneas' personal belongings and an effigy of him to be burned (*praxis*), after which the Massylian priestess *ter centum tonat ore deos, Erebumque Chaosque tergeminamque Hecaten, tria virginis ora Dianae*, 510-11 (*logos*). Similarly, Horace relates that the witches Canidia and Sagana, having performed a ceremony involving the blood of a black lamb and two effigies (*Sat.* I 8.23ff.), utter invocations to Hekate and Tisiphone (33-34).[34] In Theoc. 2, Simaitha burns barley, bay leaves, bran, wax effigies, etc. (18-63), and then, in what may be called a romanticized *logos*, addresses to Selene a long lament concerning how she lost Delphis (64-166).[35]

Our five tablets, designed for the practical use of their respective clients, contain only the *logos*. These should be compared with the handbook version of P, which, serving the needs of the *magus*, presents the full scheme of *praxis* and *logos*. The text and translation, which I have keyed to the synopsis on pp. 15f., are as follows:[36]

(I.A 1) Φιλτροκατάδεσμος θαυμαστός· λαβὼν κηρὸν ⟨ἢ πηλὸν⟩ | ἀπὸ τροχοῦ κεραμικοῦ πλάσον ζῴδια δύο,[37] ἀρρεlνικὸν καὶ θη-

[34] Cf. Hor. *Epod.* 5: Canidia and Sagana perform a *praxis* (15ff.); the former then utters an invocation to Nox and Diana in order to revive Varus' love (49ff.).

[35] The *praxis* itself may include *logoi*, often *similia similibus* (see above n. 17), to facilitate the sympathetic power of the ceremony; e.g., also in this poem Simaitha, during her *praxis*, says χὼς αὕτα λακεῖ μέγα καππυρίcαcα --- οὕτω τοι καὶ Δέλφιc ἐνὶ φλογὶ cάρκ' ἀμαθύνοι 24-26; cf. 28-31 and Gow's comments *ad loc.*; cf. also Verg. *Ec.* 8.77ff. and P 321ff.

[36] I print the text of Preisendanz with a few minor changes, some of which I treat in the nn. below.

[37] With the two effigies, cf. esp. Delatte/Derchain 330 (discussed below pp. 107f. on § A). Cf. also Hor. *Sat.* I 8.30-33, Verg. *Ec.* 8.80f., and C.A. Faraone's analyses of these texts in a recent article (*Class. Phil.* 84 [1989] 294ff.). For further exam-

λυκόν· τὸν μὲν ἄρσενα ὡς Ἄρεα | καθωπλισμένον ποίησον τῇ
ἀριστερᾷ χειρὶ || κρατοῦντα ξίφος, καταπλήσσοντα αὐτῆς εἰς
τὴν | κατακλεῖδα τὴν δεξιάν, αὐτὴν δὲ ὀπισθάγγωνα | καὶ
ἐπὶ τὰ γόνατα καθημένην, καὶ τὴν οὐσίαν[38] | ἐπὶ τῆς κεφα-
(I.A 2) λῆς ἄψεις ἢ ἐπὶ τοῦ τραχήλου. | γράψον δὲ εἰς τὸ πλάσμα τῆς
ἀγομένης· ἐπὶ μὲν || τῆς κεφαλῆς· ἴσεη Ιαω ιθι ουνε βριδω |
λωθιων Νεβουτοσουαληθ· ἐπὶ δὲ τῆς δε|ξιᾶς ἀκοῆς· ουερ μη-
χαν· ἐπὶ δὲ τῆς εὐωνύ|μου· λιβαβα ωϊμαθοθο· ἐπὶ δὲ τῆς ὁ-
ρά|σεως· αμουναβρεω· ἐπὶ δὲ τοῦ δεξιοῦ ὀφθαλ||μοῦ· ωρορμο-
θιο αηθ· ἐπὶ δὲ τοῦ ἄλλου· | χοβουε· ἐπὶ δὲ τῆς δεξιᾶς κλει-
δός· αδετα | μερου· ἐπὶ δὲ τοῦ δεξιοῦ βραχίονος· | ενε ψα
ενεσγαφ· ἐπὶ δὲ τοῦ ἄλλου· μελ|χιου μελχιεδια, ἐπὶ δὲ τῶν
χειρῶν· || μελχαμελχου αηλ· ἐπὶ δὲ τοῦ στήθους τὸ | ὄνομα τῆς
ἀγομένης μητρόθεν, ἐπὶ δὲ τῆς | καρδίας· βαλαμιν Θωουθ· καὶ
ὑπὸ τὸ ὑπογάστριον· | αοβης αωβαρ· ἐπὶ δὲ τῆς φύσεως· βλιχι-
ανεοι | ουωϊα· ἐπὶ δὲ τῆς πυγῆς· πισσαδαρα· ἐπὶ δὲ || τῶν πελ-
(I.A 3) μάτων τοῦ μὲν δεξιοῦ· ελω· τοῦ δὲ ἄλλο[υ]· | ελωαιοε. καὶ
λαβὼν δεκατρεῖς βελόνας | χαλκᾶς[39] πῆξον α′ ἐπὶ τοῦ ἐγ-
κεφάλου λέγων· | "περονῶ σου, ἡ δεῖνα, τὸν ἐγκέφαλον·" καὶ
β′ εἰς τὰς ἀκοὰς | καὶ β′ εἰς τοὺς ὀφθαλμοὺς καὶ α′ εἰς τὸ στό-
μα καὶ β′ || εἰς τὰ ὑποχόνδρια καὶ α′ εἰς τὰς χεῖρας καὶ β′ |
εἰς τὰς φύσεις καὶ β′ εἰς τὰ πέλματα καθ' ἅπαξ λέ|γων·
"περονῶ τὸ ποιὸν μέλος τῆς δεῖνα, ὅπως μη|δενὸς μνησθῇ πλὴν
(I.B 1) ἐμοῦ μόνου, τοῦ δεῖνα." καὶ λα|βὼν πλάτυμμα μολυβοῦν γρά-
(I.B 2) ψον τὸν λόγον τὸν || αὐτὸν καὶ δίωκε καὶ συνδήσας τὸ πέτα-
λον τοῖς | ζῳδίοις μίτῳ ἀπὸ ἱστοῦ ποιήσας ἅμματα τξε,[40] | λέ-

ples of magical figurines, see H.S. Versnel, *ZPE* 72 (1988) 288ff., and Faraone's contribution to the forthcoming *Ancient Greek Magic and Religion* (see above p. 5 n. 24).

[38] i.e., the "substance" or "property" of the one to be charmed, such as hair, clothing, etc.; cf. below p. 56 and D.G. Martinez, *Classical Journal* 84 (1989) 169f.

[39] For bronze as a standard metal for needles and other objects used in magic, see above p. 2 n. 6.

[40] Cf. Ovid *Fasti* II 575, where a witch, as part of a *praxis*, says *cantata ligat cum fusco licia plumbo*. R. Wünsch (*Rh. Mus.* 56 [1901] 403) argues that if *plumbo* here meant "lead tablet," Ovid would have described it in greater detail; he thus understands by it a lead effigy which is wrapped with magical thread, comparing it with an object in his private collection. In P, effigies and tablet are wrapped together, but there are examples of a doll wrapped without a tablet (Verg. *Ec.* 8.73-75) and of a tablet without a doll (*PGM* VII 452ff.). *Pace* Wünsch, I think that the Ovid

(I.B 3) γων, ὡς οἶδας· "Αβραcαξ, κατάσχες." τίθεσαι Ι ἡλίου δύνοντος παρὰ ἀώρου[41] ἢ βιαίου θήκην, παραΙτιθῶν αὐτῷ καὶ τὰ τοῦ καιροῦ ἄνθη.[42] λόγος ὁ γραΙΙφόμενος καὶ διωκόμενος·

(II.A) παρακατατίθεμαι[43] Ι ὑμῖν τοῦτον τὸν κατάδεσμον, θεοῖς χθονίοις Ι υεσεμιγαδων καὶ Κούρῃ Περσεφόνῃ Ερεσχιγαλ Ι καὶ Ἀδώνιδι τῷ βαρβαριθα, ⟨καὶ⟩ Ἑρμῇ καταχθονίῳ Ι Θωουθ φωκενταζεψευ αερχθαθου μιΙΙσονκταικ αλβαναχαμβρη καὶ Ἀνούβιδι κραΙταιῷ ψιρινθ, τῷ τὰς κλεῖδας ἔχοντι τῶν καθ'

(II.B) Ἅιδου, καὶ δαίμοσι καταχθονίοις θεοῖς[44] ἀώροις τε Ι καὶ ἀώραις, μέλλαξί τε καὶ παρθένοις, ἐνιαυτοὺς Ι ἐξ ἐνιαυτῶν, μῆνας ἐκ μηνῶν, ἡμέρας ἐξ ἡμεΙΙρῶν, ὥρας ἐξ ὡρῶν. ὁρκίζω πάντας δαίμονας Ι τοὺς ἐν τῷ τόπῳ τούτῳ συνπαρασταθῆναι

---

passage represents the latter. The Greek equivalent of *plumbum*, μόλιβος/μόλυβδος, can mean "lead tablet" (Wünsch 105b.1, 106b.1, 107a.4 [see above p. 4 n. 18]; Aud. 189a.3 [text uncertain]) but not, to my knowledge, "lead doll." — The 365 knots, one for each day of the year, indicate that the binding force of the love spell, sympathetically represented by the knots, is to be constant and permanent (similarly *PGM* VII 452ff., but not necessarily erotic). The idea is reinforced by the following Αβραcαξ, κατάσχες, especially since the numerical value of the letters of Αβραcαξ is 365 (see *PGM* XIII 156, 466; Hopfner, *OZ* I § 705 [p. 431]; Dornseiff, *Alphabet* 105 [and cf. 42f.]; further on Αβραcαξ below pp. 77f. 365 is an important number in magic, corresponding not only to the number of days of the year but also to the deities who preside over them and (in Gnostic speculation) to the number of heavens and aeons. It thus signifies the concept of totality in various contexts (cf., e.g., the cursing of the "365 members and sinews" of certain athletes in W_{12} 15f. with Wortmann's n., p. 109). In general, for tying magical knots as a rite of erotic binding, see Verg. *Ec.* 8.77f.: *necte tribus nodis ternos, Amarylli, colores; necte, Amarylli, modo et "Veneris" dic "vincula necto,"* on which cf. Abt, *Apol.* 74-76.

41 Gravestones would often indicate that the dead was an ἄωρος; see *SB* I 309, 313, 339, and the numerous other references and discussion in Lattimore, *Epitaphs* 184-87 (§ 47); cf. B. Boyaval, *ZPE* 23 (1976) 225-30 (esp. charts on 226-27). Those who die violently (βίαιοι) are a special case of ἄωροι; cf. below pp. 48f.

42 For flowers as an offering for the dead, cf. Aesch. *Pers.* 618 and Ovid *Fasti* II 539. On the latter, see R. Wünsch, *Rh. Mus.* 56 (1901) 403.

43 That the *logos* is in the first person and refers to the client throughout seems to indicate that it is the client, not the *magus*, who writes and recites the logos and performs the above *praxis* (in the *praxis* cf. the first person line 327f. above). Such an arrangement, however, would have been impossible in many cases, given the large number of *agrammatoi* in Greco-Egyptian society. The complex issue of the precise roles of *magus* and client in the execution of a spell cannot be explored in detail here. It seems that at times responsibilities were shared, as in Dido's ceremony (see above p. 8).

44 καὶ δαίμοσι καταχθονίοις θεοῖς, ms.; θεοῖς καὶ δαίμοσι καταχθονίοις, Preisendanz; see below p. 47.

(II.C 1) τῷ δαί|μονι τούτῳ· καὶ ἀνέγειρέ μοι cαυτόν, ὅcτιc ποτ᾽ εἶ |
εἴτε ἄρρην εἴτε θῆλυc, καὶ ὕπαγε εἰc πάντα τόπον | καὶ εἰc
πᾶν ἄμφοδον καὶ εἰc πᾶcαν οἰκίαν καὶ ἄξον || καὶ κατάδη-
cον· ἄξον τὴν δεῖνα, ἣν ⟨ἔτεκεν ἡ⟩[45] δεῖνα, ἧc ἔχειc τὴν οὐ-
|cίαν, φιλοῦcάν με τὸν δεῖνα, ὃν ἔτεκεν ἡ δεῖνα· μὴ βινη|θήτω,
μὴ πυγιcθήτω μηδὲ πρὸc ἡδονὴν ποιή|[c]ῃ μετ᾽ ἄλλου ἀνδρόc, εἰ
μὴ μετ᾽ ἐμοῦ μόνου, τοῦ δεῖνα· | ἵνα[46] μὴ δυνηθῇ ἡ δεῖνα μήτε
πεῖν μήτε φαγεῖν, μὴ || cτέργειν, μὴ καρτερεῖν, μὴ εὐcταθῆcαι,
(II.C 2) μὴ ὕπνου | [τ]υχεῖν ἡ δεῖνα ἐκτὸc ἐμοῦ, τοῦ δεῖνα, ὅτι cε ἐξορ-
κίζω κατὰ | τοῦ ὀνόματοc τοῦ φοβεροῦ καὶ τρομεροῦ, οὗ ἡ γῆ
ἀκούcα|[c]α τοῦ ὀνόματοc ἀνοιγήcεται, οὗ οἱ δαίμονεc | ἀκού-
cαντεc τοῦ ὀνόματοc ἔνφοβοι[47] φοβηθήcονται, || οὗ οἱ ποταμοὶ
καὶ ⟨ ⟩[48] αἱ πέτραι ἀκούcαντεc τὸ ὄνομα | ῥήccονται. ὁρκί-
ζω cε, νεκύδαιμον, εἴτε ἄρρηc | εἴτε θῆλυc, κατὰ τοῦ βαρ-
βαριθα χενμβρα βα|ρουχαμβρα καὶ κατὰ τοῦ Αβρατ Αβραcαξ
| cεcενγεν βαρφαραγγηc καὶ κατὰ τοῦ αωια || μαρι ἐνδόξου
καὶ κατὰ τοῦ μαρμα⟨ρ⟩εωθ | μαρμαραυωθ μαρμαραωθ μα-
(II.C 3) ρεχθανα | αμαρζα· μαριβεωθ· μή μου παρακούcηc, | νεκύδαι-
μον, τῶν ἐντολῶν καὶ τῶν ὀνομάτων, | ἀλλ᾽ ἔγειρον μόνον cε-
αυτὸν ἀπὸ τῆc ἐχούcηc || cε ἀναπαύcεωc, ὅcτιc ποτὲ εἶ, εἴτε
ἄρρηc εἴτε θῆ|λυc, καὶ ὕπαγε εἰc πάντα τόπον, εἰc πᾶν ἄμφ-
οδον, | εἰc πᾶcαν οἰκίαν καὶ ἔνεγκόν μοι τὴν δεῖνα, καὶ κα-
|τάcχεc αὐτῆc τὴν βρῶcιν καὶ τὴν πόcιν, καὶ | μὴ ἐάcῃc τὴν
δεῖνα ἄλλου ἀνδρὸc πεῖραν λαβεῖν || πρὸc ἡδονήν, μηδὲ ἰδίου
ἀνδρόc, εἰ μὴ ἐμοῦ | μόνου, τοῦ δεῖνα, ἀλλ᾽ ἕλκε τὴν δεῖνα
τῶν τριχῶν, τῶν | cπλάγχνων, τῆc ψυχῆc[49] πρὸc ἐμέ, τὸν δεῖ-

---

[45] <ἔτεκεν ἡ> Haslam. The omission occurred through haplography (ἣν...ἡ).

[46] ἵνα seems imperatival here (Mandilaras §§ 585-589 [esp. 589]; Turner, *Syntax* 94f.; BDR § 387.3a); I thus place a heavier stop before it than Preisendanz's comma. The corresponding ἵνα in C could be either imperatival or final. The word is lacking at this point in the other parallels, which have either the negatived imperative or prohibitive subjunctive (see below p. 59).

[47] ἐνφόβου ms.

[48] For the omitted material, see below p. 69 and critical apparatus below p. 116 n. on line 21.

[49] Preisendanz here cites *Byzantinisch-neugriechische Jahrbücher* 1 (1920) 170f., where R. Ganszyniec argues that in some magical texts (he considers the present passage "unklar") ψυχή means αἰδοῖα, especially the female organ (cf. φύcιc). I find only one of his examples convincing: γράφε εἰc πιττάκιον ἱερατικὸν τὰ ὀνόματα καὶ τοὺc χαρακτῆραc--- καὶ ἐπίθεc ἐπὶ τὴν ψυχὴν αὐτῆc καὶ ἐπερώτα· καὶ

να, πάλ|ϲῃ ὥρᾳ τοῦ αἰῶνοϲ, νυκτὸϲ καὶ ἡμέραϲ, μέ|χρι οὗ ἔλθῃ πρὸϲ ἐμέ, τὸν δεῖνα, καὶ ἀχώριϲτόϲ || μου μείνῃ ἡ δεῖνα. ποίηϲον, κατάδηϲον εἰϲ τὸν | ἅπαντα χρόνον τῆϲ ζωῆϲ μου καὶ ϲυναναγ|καϲον τὴν δεῖνα ὑπουργὸν εἶναί μοι, τῷ δεῖνα, καὶ μὴ | ἀποϲκιρτάτω ἀπ' ἐμοῦ ὥραν μίαν τοῦ αἰῶνοϲ. ἐάν μοι τοῦ- (II.C 4) το τελέϲῃϲ, ἀναπαύϲω ϲε ταχέωϲ· || ἐγὼ γάρ εἰμι Βαρβαρ Αδωναι, ὁ τὰ ἄϲτρα κρύ|βων, ὁ λαμπροφεγγὴϲ οὐρανοῦ κρατῶν, | ὁ κύριοϲ κόϲμου αθθουϊν ϊαθουϊν ϲελ|βιουωθ· Αωθ ϲαρβαθιουθ ιαθθιεραθ | Αδωναι ϊα ρουρα βια βι βιοθη αθωθ || Ϲαβαωθ ηα νιαφα αμαραχθι· ϲαταμα· | ζαυαθθειη ϲερφω ϊαλαδα ϊαλη |ϲβηϲι· ιαθθα· μαραδθα· αχιλθθεε | χοωω οη ηαχω· κανϲαοϲα· αλκμουρι· | θυρ· θαωοϲ· ϲιεχη· εἰμι Θωθ οϲωμαι· (II.C 5) || ἄξον, κατάδηϲον τὴν δεῖνα φιλοῦϲαν, ἐρῶ|ϲαν, τὸν δεῖνα πο- (II.C 6) θοῦϲαν (κοινόν),[50] ὅτι ὁρκίζω ϲε, | νεκύδαιμον, κατὰ τοῦ φοβεροῦ, μεγάλου | ϊαεω βαφρενεμουν οθι λαρικριφια | ευεαϊ φιρκιραλιθον υομεν ερ φαβωεαι,[51] || ἵνα μοι ἄξῃϲ τὴν δεῖνα καὶ κεφαλὴν κεφαλῇ | κολλήϲῃ καὶ χείλεα χείλεϲι ϲυνάψῃ καὶ γαϲτέ|ρα γαϲτρὶ κολλήϲῃ καὶ μηρὸν μηρῷ πε|λάϲῃ καὶ τὸ μέλαν[52] τῷ μέλανι ϲυναρμό|ϲῃ καὶ τὰ ἀφροδιϲιακὰ ἑαυτῆϲ ἐκτελέϲῃ[53] || ἡ δεῖνα μετ' ἐμοῦ, τοῦ δεῖνα, εἰϲ τὸν | ἅπαντα χρόνον τοῦ αἰῶνοϲ.

πάντα ϲοι ἐξομολογήϲει (*PGM* VII 412ff.; from a spell to induce talking in sleep). I would add *PGM* IV 1522ff.: μὴ εἰϲέλθῃϲ αὐτῆϲ διὰ τῶν ὀμμάτων, μὴ διὰ τῶν πλευρῶν, μὴ διὰ τῶν ὀνύχων, μηδὲ διὰ τοῦ ὀμφαλοῦ μηδὲ διὰ τῶν μελῶν, ἀλλὰ διὰ τῆϲ ψυχῆϲ, καὶ ἔμμεινον αὐτῆϲ ἐν τῇ καρδίᾳ καὶ καῦϲον αὐτῆϲ τὰ ϲπλάγχνα --- ἕωϲ ἔλθῃ πρὸϲ ἐμέ, κτλ. (Preisendanz translates ψυχῆϲ "Scham"). See now also *PGM Eng.* p. 339 s.v. Soul.

[50] κοινόν and κοινά ("etc.") became technical terms indicating that the *magus* could proceed with the formula as he wished, or as was "commonly" known; cf., e.g., *PGM* IV 829; VII 358; s.v. κοινόϲ in *PGM* vol. 3 and LSJ (III 4).

[51] For the *ιαεω-logos* palindrome (ιαεω = Yahweh) see below on § A pp. 105ff.

[52] Cf. κολλῶϲα καὶ τὸ μέλαν αὐτῆϲ τῷ ἐμῷ μέλανι ἡδυτάτῳ, *PGM* XVIIa 23; cf. also *P. Münch.* II 28, fr. 5.2 with F. Maltomini's n. *ad loc.*; Ar. *Vesp.* 1374; Henderson, *Muse* 142-43 (§§ 163, 163a).

[53] τὰ ἀφροδιϲιακὰ ἑαυτῆϲ ἐκτελέϲῃ probably means "satisfy her sexual desires" rather than "carry out her sex acts," as *PGM Eng.* renders (similarly Preisendanz's German). Cf. εἰ ἐκτελέϲαιμεν τὸν ἔρωτα (Pl. *Smp.* 193c); αὐτῷ τὴν ἐπιθυμίαν τελέϲαι (Ach. Tat. II 13.3); also Hdt. I 32.6; NT Gal. 5.16; W_1 22 (see above pp. 52 and 59). Cf., however, Hom. *Od.* XI 246, αὐτὰρ ἐπεί ῥ' ἐτέλεϲϲε θεὸϲ φιλοτήϲια ἔργα, where the meaning of ἐτέλεϲϲε is obviously "finished."

(III) εἶτα γράψον εἰς ἕτερον μέρος | τοῦ πλατύματος τὴν καρδί-αν[54] καὶ τοὺς χα|ρακτῆρας, ὡς ὑπόκειται·

ιαεωβαφρενεμουνοθιλαρικριφιαευεαιφιρκιραλιθονυομενερφαβωεαι
αεωβαφρενεμουνοθιλαρικριφιαευεαιφιρκιραλιθονυομενερφαβωεα
εωβαφρενεμουνοθιλαρικριφιαευεαιφιρκιραλιθονυομενερφαβωε
ωβαφρενεμουνοθιλαρικριφιαευεαιφιρκιραλιθονυομενερφαβω
βαφρενεμουνοθιλαρικριφιαευεαιφιρκιραλιθονυομενερφαβ
αφρενεμουνοθιλαρικριφιαευεαιφιρκιραλιθονυομενερφα
φρενεμουνοθιλαρικριφιαευεαιφιρκιραλιθονυομενερφ

[[ι α ε ω β α φ ρ ε ν ε μ ο υ ν ο θ ι λ α ρ ι κ ρ ι φ ι α ε υ ε α ι φ ι ρ κ ι]]

(χαρακτῆρες)

αω
εα
ιω
υο
ιο
οε
ιωαε
εοηι
υαου
ιαωϊ
αηαη
ηϊοϊ
ωϊυα
αωοε
υϊωη
εοαωα
υαυα
ιοηιιη
ιαωι
αοαο
υυοι

ιιι
οεω
οϊεε
οεϋϊ
οευυ
ιαυυ
υυαα
οιιι
υαεε
εωαυ
οουϊ
ηηεα
ααϊα
ιιιω
εεαω
ηηαω
ηϊηε
οαηϊ
ηϊυϊ
ηηοϊ
υααι
ηιια
ααωω

(χαρακτῆρες)

Translation:

(I.A 1) A marvelous love spell that binds. Take wax (or clay) from a potter's wheel and mold two figurines, a male and a female. Make the male as an armed Ares, holding in his left hand a sword, striking

[54] i.e., heart-shaped magical word. See below pp. 19 and 105.

her in the right clavicular region. Make her with her arms behind
her back and kneeling, and attach the substance to her head or neck.
(I.A 2) Write on the figurine of the woman to be drawn: upon her head
(mw + Iao); upon her right ear (mw); upon her left (mw); on her face
(mw + Amoun); on her right eye (mw); on the other (mw); and on
her right collar-bone (mw); on her right arm (mw); on the other
(mw); on her hands (mw); on the breast write the name of the one
to be drawn and her mother's name; on the heart (mw + Thoth); and
under the abdomen (mw); on the vagina (mw); on the buttocks (mw);
(I.A 3) on the sole of the right foot (mw); of the other (mw). And take 13
bronze needles and stick one in the brain while saying, "I pierce
your brain, NN"; and stick two in the ears and two in the eyes and
one in the mouth and two in the abdomen and one in the hands and
two in the vagina and two in the soles of the feet, saying each time,
"I pierce such and such part of NN, that she may think of no one ex-
(I.B 1) cept me NN only." And take a lead plate and write and recite the
(I.B 2) same incantation and bind the tablet to the figurines with thread
from a loom making 365 knots, saying, as you know, "Abrasax, re-
(I.B 3) strain," and at sunset place it by a grave of one who suffered a
premature or violent death, placing beside it also flowers of the sea-
son. The incantation which is written and recited is:

(II.A) "I deposit with you this binding spell, gods of the underworld,
Yesemigadon and Koure Persephone Ereschigal and Adonis, who is
(mw), (and) Hermes-Thoth of the underworld (mw) and mighty A-
(II.B) noubis (mw), who holds the keys to the (gates) of Hades, and (with
you,) chthonic spirits, gods and goddesses who suffered an untimely
death, lads and maidens, year after year, month after month, day af-
ter day, hour after hour. I adjure all spirits who are in this place to
(II.C 1) help this spirit. And rouse yourself for me, whoever you are, wheth-
er male or female, and go into every place and into every quarter
and into every house, and bring and bind; bring NN, whom NN bore,
whose substance you have, loving me, NN, whom NN bore. Let her
not submit to vaginal nor anal intercourse nor do anything with an-
other man for pleasure, except with me, NN, only; NN should be able
neither to drink, nor eat, nor show affection, nor have strength or

(II.C 2) health, nor get sleep apart from me, NN. Because I adjure you by
the fearful and dreadful name of him at the hearing of whose name
the earth will open, at the hearing of whose name the demons will
greatly fear, at the hearing of whose name the rivers and the rocks
are cleft. I adjure you, *nekydaimon*, whether male or female, by the
name (mw), and by (mw) Abrasax (mw), and by the glorious (mw),
(II.C 3) and by (mw). Do not disobey, *nekydaimon*, the commands and the
names, but just rouse yourself from the rest which holds you, who-
ever you are, whether male or female, and go into every place, into
every quarter, into every house, and bring me NN and keep her
from eating and drinking, and do not allow NN to experience another
man for pleasure, not even her own husband, except me, NN, only;
but drag NN by the hair, by the bowels, by the vagina, to me,
NN, at every moment of her life night and day, until she comes to
me, NN, and she, NN, abides inseparable from me. Do this, bind
her for the entire period of my life and compel NN to be subject to
me, NN, and may she not rebel from me for a single moment of her
(II.C 4) life. If you accomplish this for me, I will quickly give you rest. For
I am *Barbaradonai*, who conceals the stars, the bright ruler of heaven,
(II.C 5) the lord of the cosmos (mw + I am Thoth, 7 lines). Bring, bind NN
(II.C 6) loving, adoring, longing for NN etc., because I adjure you, *nekydai-
mon*, by the fearful, great *Iaeo* (mw) that you bring NN to me, and
that NN join head to head, and bind lips to lips, and join belly to
belly, and bring thigh to thigh, and fit the black with the black, and
satisfy her sexual desires with me, NN, for all her life."

(III) Then write on another part* of the tablet the heart and the signs as below: (mw for 24 lines).

Synopsis

I. *Praxis* (296-335)

A. The effigies (296-328)

1. Making and positioning of 2 effigies (296-303)
2. Writing magical formulae on female effigy (304-21)
3. Piercing female effigy with needles (321-28)

B. The tablet (328-35)

1. Writing *logos* on tablet and reciting (328-30)

2. Binding tablet to effigies (330-32)

3. Depositing tablet beside grave (332-34)

II. *Logos* (335-406)

A. Deposition with the underworld gods (335-42)

B. Deposition with and adjuration of the δαίμονες (342-47)[55]

C. Conjuration of the νεκυδαίμων (347-406)

1. First command to bind the beloved (347-56)

2. First threat: "the fearful name" (356-67)

3. Second command (367-84)

4. Second threat: *Barbaradonai* (385-94)

5. Third command (395-96)

6. Final adjuration: *ιαεω-logos* (396-406)

III. Continuation of *praxis* (406-33)[56]

A. *ιαεω-logos Schwindeform*

B. χαρακτῆρες

The chart on p. 17 (Fig. 1) and the following remarks (both keyed to the synopsis) compare the tablets with the full version of P as regards general structure and content. They are not meant to suggest textual relationships nor to provide detailed comparisons, for which see the commentary and textual appendix.

Although the tablets as such preserve only the *logos*, they betray evidence of what their handbooks must have prescribed for the *praxis* (I). For example, only L, as far as we know, was associated with a kneeling effigy (A 1) pierced with 13

[55] M.W. Haslam proposes a different division of A and B to reflect what he considers to be two separate groups of δαίμονες belonging to different parts of the magical process: A. Deposition with underworld gods and spirits (335-45); B. Adjuration of local spirits (to assist *nekydaimon*; 345-47). The suggestion is attractive, but I do not think that there is a rigid distinction between the chthonic spirits and local spirits. In fact the ἄωροι, who are the δαίμονες καταχθόνιοι with whom the spell is deposited, are also without doubt among οἱ ἐν τῷ τόπῳ τούτῳ; cf. in the *praxis* (line 334) where the operator is to leave the tablet by the grave of an ἄωρος (on the ἄωροι, see below pp. 48f.).

[56] The lines which follow (434-66) contain a hexametric prayer to Helios which is probably meant to be part of this spell. Its position, however, in the process is difficult to determine and it has no relevance for M or the other tablets.

Fig.1

Table of Correspondences Between P and Five Tablets (to p. 16)

P	C	L	W_1	W_2	M
I.A 1		–			
I.A 2					
I.A 3		+			
I.B 1	+	+	+	+	+
I.B 2					
I.B 3	+	+	+	+	+
			*	*	*
II.A	+	+	+	–	+
II.B	+	+	+	–	+
II.C 1	+	+	+	–	+
					*
II.C 2	+	+	+	–	+
II.C 3	+	+	–	+	–
			*		*
II.C 4					+
II.C 5					
II.C 6					
III.A			–		+
III.B					+
					*

+ closely corresponds to P – differs significantly from P

* incorporates material not in P

needles (A 3) similar to that described in P.[57] Unlike the latter, only a female figure is involved and without magical words inscribed on it. It was excavated

[57] According to Edgar (p. 43) no figurines were excavated with C. The wax images described recently by D.R. Jordan (*ZPE* 72 [1988] 247) as belonging to the tablet must have been attached to it later by museum personnel. Edgar does say, however, that the two pairs of holes in the tablet were probably designed for attachment of effigies, which did not survive.

with the rolled-up tablet in a clay vase. Whether the two objects were bound together as prescribed in P 330-31 (B 2) is uncertain (see Kambitsis 215 and n. 2). The internal evidence of all the tablets points to their being placed beside a grave as in P 332-33 (B 3). The references to "all the spirits in this place" (C 6; W_1 15; L 5f.; M 5f.) and "this spirit" (C 6; W_1 16; W_2 11; L 6) or *nekydaimon* (M 6) refer respectively to all the ghosts of the cemetery and the specific ghost by whose grave the tablet is placed.

With respect to the *logos*, tablets C and L, as far as they go (II. A, B, C 1-3), follow the scheme of P most closely. The two Wortmann texts and M are more idiosyncratic. W_1 begins with a five-line introduction consisting of the *ιαεω-logos* and other magic words. It continues (6-38) with the deposition with the gods (II.A), the deposition with and adjuration of the δαίμονες (B), the first command to the *nekydaimon* and the first threat (C 1-2), similar to P 335-67. After only the introduction to the second command (C 3), μή μου παρακούςῃς νεκυδέμων, ὅςτις ποτ' οὖν [εἶ, κ]αὶ ἔγειρέ μοι ςεαυτόν (38-39), W_1 proceeds with adjurations of and by Artemis-Hekate (39-83), which occur neither in P nor the other tablets.

After a four-line introduction, W_2 continues with the deposition with the gods and deposition with and adjuration of the δαίμονες (II.A-B), abbreviated by the absence of magical names and in other respects (5-11). Line 12 begins the address to the *nekydaimon* with the first command (C 1), which is interrupted by a shortened version of the beginning of the first threat (C 2), ἐξορκίζω ςε γὰρ κατὰ τοῦ ἁγίου ὀνόματος, οὗ φρίςςι τὰ ὄρη καὶ τρέμι τὰ δεμόνια (14-16). The first command then continues (17-32; different from P in brevity and otherwise) and is followed by the rest of the first threat with magical names somewhat different from those of the other texts (32-48). W_2 ends with the second command (48-72), which is basically consistent with the order and structure of P (C 3).

The *logos* of M (§§ J and K) is introduced by the magical palindrome αβεραμεν etc. It proceeds (§ J 2-10) with the deposition with the gods (II.A), deposition with and adjuration of the δαίμονες (B), and the first command to the *nekydaimon* (C 1) similar to P. After this point there is an additional section (10-14), most of which is not found in the other five texts. Next follows the first threat (14-19), closely corresponding to P (C 2), and the second command (C 3). The first half of the latter (19-22) is similar in structure to P 367-72; the second half (22-26) repeats parts of M 8-14. § J is concluded by a combination of letters and magical symbols (26-28). § K, after some introductory magical formulae (29-30), repeats § J 19-26 with various additions and omissions (30-40). Then follows the second threat (ἐγώ εἰμι βαρβαδωναι + magical words and names), slightly more abbreviated and with a few variations from P 385-94 (C 4). Although none of the tablets contains P's third command and final adjuration (C 5 and 6), there are phrases similar to parts of the former in M and L (cf. below pp. 62f. on ἔλθῃ --- ἐρῶϲα).

Following the *logos* the continuation of the *praxis* (III) begins, εἶτα γράψον εἰϲ ἕτερον μέροϲ τοῦ πλατύματοϲ τὴν καρδίαν καὶ τοὺϲ χαρακτῆραϲ ὡϲ ὑπόκειται (P 406). καρδίαν refers to the heart-shaped diminishing *logos* (*Schwindeform/Schwindeschema*) which is formed by dropping the first and last letter of the ιαεω-palindrome with each repetition. This, with the vertical rows of letters and magical symbols (χαρακτῆρεϲ), is to be written in "another part" of the plate. Of the five tablets, only M preserves these formulae (§§ A, B, G, H, J 26-28)[58] and adds others (§§ C, D, E, F). W_1 also has the ιαεω-palindrome, not heart-shaped, but begun on the first line and continued (with other magical names) in the third. As to the reason for this strange position, perhaps, as Wortmann (p. 68) suggests, the *magus* had completely filled his tablet, but because he did not wish to disobey the instructions of his handbook by omitting this powerful name, he wrote it in the only space available to him, before and after the first line.

In conclusion, C and L, although differing considerably in particulars, most closely resemble each other in structure, containing the depositions with the gods and *daimones* and the first command and threat and the second command to the *nekydaimon*, all very similar to P. The two Wortmann texts, written by the same hand but much varied in content and structure, may be a case in point of how magical handbooks specify optional wording for the same spell (see above pp. 6f.); these differences may, however, simply represent liberties taken by the

---

[58] In P the rows of letters and χαρακτῆρεϲ flank the heart-shaped *Schwindeform* (see above p. 13); in M the rows of letters occupy basically the same position, but the χαρακτῆρεϲ, which are quite different from those in P, follow the main part of the *logos* (§ J 26-28; see below pp. 22 and 28). For the exact form of the χαρακτῆρεϲ in P, cf. the *editio princeps* by C. Wessely, *Griechische Zauberpapyrus von Paris und London* (Denkschrift. Wien. Ak. 36, 1888) p. 55.

magician himself to suit his or his client's purpose. The new Michigan tablet, the only one of the five containing the ἐγώ εἰμι formula (II.C 4) and the *Schwindeform* and rows of vowels prescribed in the continuation of P's *praxis* (III), offers the most complete parallel to the full spell of P, despite its considerable differences from the latter at various points. In the commentary, which follows the text and translation, I will treat the sections of M in the order in which they parallel P, beginning with § J (majority of *logos*), then § K, finally §§ A-H. The text and translation of §§ J and K are keyed to the synopsis (above pp. 15f.).

II. TEXT OF *P. MICH.* 757

Inv. no. 6925 | 29.5 x 20 cm. | 3rd/4th cent. A.D.

Egypt (exact site unknown)

Figure 2 (p. 22) illustrates the arrangement of §§ A-K on the tablet.

§ **A**

ιαεωβαφρενεμουνοθιλαρικριφιαευεαιφιρκιραλιθονυομενερφαβωεαι
αεωβαφρενεμουνοθιλαρικριφιαευεαιφιρκιραλιθονυομενερφαβωεα
εωβαφρενεμουνοθιλαρικριφιαευεαιφιρκιραλιθονυομενερφαβωε
ωβαφρενεμουνοθιλαρικριφιαευεαιφιρκιραλιθονυομενερφαβω
βαφρενεμουνοθιλαρικριφιαευεαιφιρκιραλιθονυομενερφαβ
αφρενεμουνοθιλαρικριφιαευεαιφιρκιραλιθονυομενερφα
φρενεμουνοθιλαρικριφιαευεαιφιρκιραλιθονυομενερφ
ρενεμουνοθιλαρικριφιαευεαιφιρκιραλιθονυομενερ
ενεμουνοθιλαρικριφιαευεαιφιρκιραλιθονυομενε
νεμουνοθιλαρικριφιαευεαιφιρκιραλιθονυομεν
εμουνοθιλαρικριφιαευεαιφιρκιραλιθονυομε
μουνοθιλαρικριφιαευεαιφιρκιραλιθονυομ
ουνοθιλαρικριφιαευεαιφιρκιραλιθονυο
υνοθιλαρικριφιαευεαιφιρκιραλιθονυ
νοθιλαρικριφιαευεαιφιρκιραλιθον
οθιλαρικριφιαευεαιφιρκιραλιθο
θιλαρικριφιαευεαιφιρκιραλιθ
ιλαρικριφιαευεαιφιρκιραλι
λαρικριφιαευεαιφιρκιραλ
αρικριφιαευεαιφιρκιρα
ρικριφιαευεαιφιρκιρ
ικριφιαευεαιφιρκι
κριφιαευεαιφιρκ
ριφιαευεαιφιρ
ιφιαευεαιφι
φιαευεαιφ
ιαευεαι
αευεα
ευε
υ

Fig. 2: *P. Mich.* 757
Arrangement of Text on Tablet

A

ιαεωβαφρενεμουνοθιλαρικριφιαευεαιφιρκιραλιθονυομενερφαβωεαι
αεωβαφρενεμουνοθιλαρικριφιαευεαιφιρκιραλιθονυομενερφαβωεα
εωβαφρενεμουνοθιλαρικριφιαευεαιφιρκιραλιθονυομενερφαβωε
ωβαφρενεμουνοθιλαρικριφιαευεαιφιρκιραλιθονυομενερφαβω
βαφρενεμουνοθιλαρικριφιαευεαιφιρκιραλιθονυομενερφαβ
αφρενεμουνοθιλαρικριφιαευεαιφιρκιραλιθονυομενερφα
φρενεμουνοθιλαρικριφιαευεαιφιρκιραλιθονυομενερφ
ρενεμουνοθιλαρικριφιαευεαιφιρκιραλιθονυομενερ
ενεμουνοθιλαρικριφιαευεαιφιρκιραλιθονυομενε
νεμουνοθιλαρικριφιαευεαιφιρκιραλιθονυομεν
εμουνοθιλαρικριφιαευεαιφιρκιραλιθονυομε
μουνοθιλαρικριφιαευεαιφιρκιραλιθονυομ
ουνοθιλαρικριφιαευεαιφιρκιραλιθονυο
υνοθιλαρικριφιαευεαιφιρκιραλιθονυ
νοθιλαρικριφιαευεαιφιρκιραλιθον
οθιλαρικριφιαευεαιφιρκιραλιθο
θιλαρικριφιαευεαιφιρκιραλιθ
ιλαρικριφιαευεαιφιρκιραλι
λαρικριφιαευεαιφιρκιραλ
αρικριφιαευεαιφιρκιρα
ρικριφιαευεαιφιρκιρ
ικριφιαευεαιφιρκι
κριφιαευεαιφιρκ
ριφιαευεαιφιρ
ιφιαευεαιφι
φιαευεαιφ
ιαευεαι
αευεα
ευε
υ

B

αω
εα
ιω
υο
ιο
εο
ιωαε
εοηι
υαου
ιωαι
αηαη
ηιου
ωιυα
αωοε
υ̣ι̣ω̣η̣
ε̣ο̣α̣ωα
υαυαιο
υοηιη
ιαουα
ιαωι
ιαοαο
υυοι
ιυιι

C

αβλαναθαναλβα
αβλαναθαναλβ
αβλαναθαναλ
αβλαναθανα
αβλαναθαν
αβλαναθα
αβλαναθ
αβλανα
αβλαν
αβλα
αβλ
αβ
α

D

αεηιουω
εηιου
ηι
ι

E

ακραμμαχαμαρει
κραμμαχαμαρει
ραμμαχαμαρει
αμμαχαμαρει
μμαχαμαρει
μαχαμαρει
αχαμαρει
χαμαρει
αμαρει
μαρει
αρει
ρει
ει
ι

F

ωυοιηεα
υοιηε
οιη
ι

G

ρυο
θι
αε
αε
υα
υυ
αι
υα
εω
οο
ηη
αα
ιι
εε
ηη
ηι
ωα
ηι
ηη
ηε
ηι
αα

H

εω
εο
ιι
οο
υυ
αα
ιι
εε
αυ
υι
εα
ια
ιω
αω
ιε
ηι
υι
ου
υα
ιο
ια
ωω

K

αεο ωαηωαιυαυεωιαεωμαρζα
μαριβεωθμημουπαρακουσηστωνεντολων
νεκυδεμωνοστισποτιαλλεγειρεμοισεαυτον
καιυπαγεεισπαντοπονεισπαναμφοδον
εισπασανοικιανκαιαξονκοπριανηνετε
κεμητηρταησισησεχιστασtριχασελουρι
ωνιωετεκεμητηρονοματικοπριπυρου
μενηνκαομενηντηκομενηντηνψυχην
τοπνευματηνγυνεκιανφυσινφιλουσαν
ερωσανερωτιθιωελουριωναονετεκε
μητηρονοματικοπριαμεχριθανατουηδη
ηδηταχυταχυεγωειμιβαρβαδωναιαι
βαρβαδωναιοταασtρακρυβωνοτονου
ρανονκρατεωνοτονκοσμοναληθευων
ιατθεουνιατρεουνσαλβιουθαωθ
αωθσαβαθιουθιατ'θεραθαδωναιαι
ισαρσυριαβιβιβεβιβιουθνατθω
σαβαωθαιαναφααμουραχθησαταμα
ζευσαθερεσφιλαυω

J

αβεραμενθωουλερθεξαναξεθρελυοωθνεμαρεβα
παρατιθημιυμιντονκαταδεσμοντουτονθεοισκαταχθονιοισπλουτωνιτεκαικορηυεσεμμειγαδωνκαικουρηπερσεφονη
ερεσχειγαλκαιαδωνιζιτωκαιβαρβαριθακαιερμηκαταχθονιωθωουωθφωκενσεψευεαρεκταθουμισονκταιχκαιανουβιδι
κρατεωψηριφθατωτασκλιδασεχοντιτωνκαταδουσκαιδεμοσιχθονιοισθεοισαωροιστεκαιαωρεσμελλαξιτεκαιπαρθενοισενιαυ
τουσεξενιαυτωνμηνασεξμηνωνημερασεξημερωννυκτασεξνυκτωνωρασεξωρωνεξορκιζωσεπαντασtουσδαι
μονασtουσεντωτοπωτουτωσυνπαρασtαθηνετωνεκυδαιμονιοστισποτεειητεαρσησειτεθηλιακαιυπαγεεισπαντοπον
εισπαναμφοδονεισπασανοικιανκαικαταδησονκοπριανηνετεκεμητηρταησισησεχιστασtριχαστησκεφαλησαιλουριωνι
ωετεκεμητηρονοματικοπριαοπωσμηβινηθημεδεπυγισθημητεηδονηνποιησηετερωνεανισκωηαλλωανδρι
ειμημονωαιλουριωνιωετεκεμητηρονοματικοπριααλλαμητεδυνηθημητεφαγινμητεπινμητευπνουτυχινδιαπαν
τοσμητεευσταθινηισυχαζιντηψυχητεσφρεσιεπιζητουσαελουριωναονετεκεμητηρκοπριαεωσουεκπηδησηεκπηδη
σηεκπαντοστοπουκαιπασησοικιασκοπριανηνετεκεμητηρονοματιταησισησεχιστασtριχασπυρουμενηκαιερθηπροσελουριωνα
ονετεκεμητηρονοματικοπριαφιλουσαερωσαεξολησψυχησεξολουπνευματοσφιλτροισακαταπαυστοισκαιαδιαλιπτοισ
καιπαραμονιμοισερωτικοισελουριωναονετεκεμητηρονοματικοπριαερωτιθιωαποτησσημερονημερασαποτησαρτι
ωρασεπιτονλοιποντησζωησατησκοπριαχρονονοτισεεξορκιζωνεκυδαιμωνκατατουονοματοστουφοβερουκαιτρο
μερουουηγητοονομαακουσασαανυγησετεουοιδαιμονεστοονομαακουσαντεσεμφοβοιτρεμουσινουοιποταμοικαιε
θαλασσετοονομαακουσαντεσταρασσοντεουεπετρετοονομαακουσαντεσρησσωντεκατατουβαρβαριθαμβαρβαριθααμ
χελομβραβαρουχαμβρααδωναιουκαικατατουαμβραθαβρασαξσεσενγενβαρφαραγγησκαικατατουιαωσαβαωθιαεω
πακενψωθπακενβραωθσαβαρβατιαωθσαβαρβατιανησαβαρβαφαιμαριενδοξουμαρμαραωθκαικατατουουσερβεν
τηθκαικατατουουεερπατηκαικατατουμαρμαραυωθμαρμαραχθαμαρμαραχθααамαρδαμαριβεωθμημουπαρακουσηστων
εντολωννεκυδαιμωνοστισποτιειτεαρρησειτεθηλιααλεγειρεμοισεαυτονκαιυπαγεεισπαντοπονεισπαναμφοδον
εισπασανοικιανκαικαταδησονκοπριανηνετεκεμητηρταησισησεχιστασtριχαστησκεφαλησαιλουριωνιωετεκε
μητηρονοματικοπριαοπωσμηβινηθημηδεπυγισθημητεηδονηνποιησηαλλωνεανισκωηετερωανδριαλ
λαμητεδυνηθημητεφαγινμητεπινμητευπνουτυχινμητεησυχαζιντηψυχηητηδιανοιαεπιζητουσαδιαπαντοσημε
ρεσκενυκτοσελουριωναονετεκεμητηρονοματικοπριαφιλουσαερωσαεξολησκαρδιασεξολουπνευματοσωστηνεαυ
τησψυχηνκοπριαησεχιστασtριχασφιλουσαερωτιθιωμεχριθανατουαιλουριωναονετεκεμητηρονονοματικοπριαηδη
ηδηταχυταχυ [illegible]
[illegible]
αωεμυωαειοωαωαω̣ωαεωαουωο̣ααααααααεωαεαεωιαωιαωαειω .... ε̣α̣

§ B

α ω
εα
ιω
υο
ιο
εο
ιωαε
εοηι
υαου
ιοωι
αηαη
ηιου
ωιυα
αωοε
υ̣ι̣ω̣η̣
εο̣α̣ωα
υαυαιο
υοηιη
ιαουα
ιαωι
ιαοαο
υυοι
ιιυιι

§ G

ριιο
θι
αε
οε
υα
υυ
οι
υα
εω
οο
ηη
αα
ιι
εε
ηη
ηι
ωα
ηι
ηη
ηε
ηι
αα

§ H

εω
εο
ιι
οο
υυ
αα
ιι
εε
αυ
υι
εα
ια
ιω
αω
ιε
ηι
υι
ου
υα
ιο
ια
ωω

§ C

αβλαναθαναλβα
αβλαναθαναλβ
αβλαναθαναλ
αβλαναθανα
αβλαναθαν
αβλαναθα
αβλαναθ
αβλανα
αβλαν
αβλα
αβλ
αβ
α

§ E

ακραμμαχαμαρει
κραμμαχαμαρει
ραμμαχαμαρει
αμμαχαμαρει
μμαχαμαρει
μαχαμαρει
αχαμαρει
χαμαρει
αμαρει
μαρει
αρει
ρει
ει
ι

§ D

αεηιουω
εηιου
ηι
ι

§ F

ωυοιηεα
υοιηε
οιη
ι

Diplomatic Transcription

§ J

1 αβεραμενθωουλερθεξαναξεθρελυοωθνεμαρεβα
II.A παρατιθημι υμιν τον καταδεσμον τουτον θεοις καταχθονιοις
πλουτωνι τε και κορη υεσεμμειγαδων και κουρη περσε-
φονη
ερεσχειγαλ και αδωνιζι τω και βαρβαριθα και ερμη κατα-
χθονιω θωουωθ φωκενσεψευ εαρεκταθου μισονκταιχ και
ανουβιδι
II.B 4 κρατεω ψηριφθα τω τας κλιδας εχοντι των κατ αδους και
δεμοσι χθονιοις θεοις αωροις τε και αωρες μελλαξι τε και
παρθενοις ενιαυ-
τους εξ ενιαυτων μηνας εξ μηνων ημερας εξ ημερων νυκτας
εξ νυκτων ωρας εξ ωρων εξωρκιζω σε παντας τους δαι-
μονας τους εν τω τοπω τουτω συνπαρασταθηνε τω νεκυδαι-
II.C 1 μονι οστις ποτε ει ητε αρσης ειτε θηλια και υπαγε εις παν
τοπον
εις παν αμφοδον εις πασαν οικιαν και καταδησον κοπριαν ην
ετεκε μητηρ ταησις ης εχις τας τριχας της κεφαλης αιλου-
ριωνι
8 ω ετεκε μητηρ ονοματι κοπρια οπως μη βινηθη μεδε πυγισθη
μητε ηδονην ποιηση ετερω νεανισκω η αλλω ανδρι
ει μη μονω αιλουριωνι ω ετεκε μητηρ ονοματι κοπρια αλλα
μητε δυνηθη μητε φαγιν μητε πιν μητε υπνου τυχιν δια
παν-
τος μητε ευσταθιν η ισυχαζιν τη ψυχη η τες φρεσι επιζητουσα
ελουριωνα ον ετεκε μητηρ κοπρια εως ου εκπηδηση εκπη-
δη-
ση εκ παντος τοπου και πασης οικιας κοπρια ην ετεκε μητηρ
ονοματι ταησις ης εχις τας τριχας πυρουμενη και ερθη προς
ελουριωνα
12 ον ετεκε μητηρ ονοματι κοπρια φιλουσα ερωσα εξ ολης ψυχης
εξ ολου πνευματος φιλτροις ακαταπαυστοις και αδιαλιπ-
τοις

Edited Text

§ J

αβεραμενθωουλερθεξαναξεθρελυοωθνεμαρεβα
II.A παρατίθημι ὑμῖν τὸν κατάδεσμον τοῦτον θεοῖς καταχθονίοις
Πλούτωνί τε καὶ Κόρῃ υεσεμμειγαδων καὶ Κούρῃ Περσε-
φόνῃ
Ερεσχειγαλ καὶ Ἀδώνιδι τῷ καὶ βαρβαριθα καὶ Ἑρμῇ κα-
ταχθονίῳ Θωουωθ φωκενσεψευ εαρεκταθου μισονκταιχ
καὶ Ἀνούβιδι
κραταιῷ ψηριφθα, τῷ τὰς κλεῖδας ἔχοντι τῶν καθ' Ἅιδους,
II.B καὶ δαίμοσι χθονίοις θεοῖς ἀώροις τε καὶ ἀώραις, μέλλαξί
τε καὶ παρθένοις, ἐνιαυ-
τοὺς ἐξ ἐνιαυτῶν, μῆνας ἐκ μηνῶν, ἡμέρας ἐξ ἡμερῶν, νύκ-
τας ἐκ νυκτῶν, ὥρας ἐξ ὡρῶν. ἐξορκίζω σε πάντας τοὺς
δαί-
μονας τοὺς ἐν τῷ τόπῳ τούτῳ συμπαρασταθῆναι τῷ νεκυδαί-
II.C 1 μονι· ⟨ἔγειρέ μοι σεαυτόν, νεκυδαίμων,⟩ ὅστις ποτὲ εἶ εἴτε
ἄρσην εἴτε θήλεια, καὶ ὕπαγε εἰς πᾶν τόπον,
εἰς πᾶν ἄμφοδον, εἰς πᾶσαν οἰκίαν, καὶ κατάδησον Κοπρίαν,
ἣν ἔτεκε μήτηρ Ταῆσις, ἧς ἔχεις τὰς τρίχας τῆς κεφαλῆς,
Αἰλουρίωνι,
ᾧ ἔτεκε μήτηρ ὀνόματι Κοπρία, ὅπως μὴ βινηθῇ μηδὲ πυγισθῇ
μήτε ἡδονὴν ποιήσῃ ἑτέρῳ νεανίσκῳ ἢ ἄλλῳ ἀνδρὶ
εἰ μὴ μόνῳ Αἰλουρίωνι, ᾧ ἔτεκε μήτηρ ὀνόματι Κοπρία, ἀλλὰ
μηδὲ δυνηθῇ μήτε φαγεῖν μήτε πιεῖν μήτε ὕπνου τυχεῖν διὰ
παν-
τὸς μήτε εὐσταθεῖν ἢ ἡσυχάζειν τῇ ψυχῇ ἢ ταῖς φρεσὶ ἐπι-
ζητοῦσα Αἰλουρίωνα, ὃν ἔτεκε μήτηρ Κοπρία, ἕως οὗ ἐκ-
πηδήσῃ {ἐκπηδή-
σῃ} ἐκ παντὸς τόπου καὶ πάσης οἰκίας Κοπρία, ἣν ἔτεκε μή-
τηρ ὀνόματι Ταῆσις, ἧς ἔχεις τὰς τρίχας, πυρουμένη καὶ
ἔλθῃ πρὸς Αἰλουρίωνα,
ὃν ἔτεκε μήτηρ ὀνόματι Κοπρία, φιλοῦσα ἐρῶσα ἐξ ὅλης ψυχῆς,
ἐξ ὅλου πνεύματος, φίλτροις ἀκαταπαύστοις καὶ ἀδια-
λείπτοις

και παραμονιμοις ερωτικοις ελουριωνα ον ετεκε μητηρ ονο-
ματι κοπρια ερωτι θιω απο της σημερον ημερας απο της
αρτι
II.C 2 ωρας επι τον λοιπον της ζωης ατης κοπρια χρονον οτι σε εξ-
ορκιζω νεκυδαιμων κατα του ονοματος του φοβερου και
τρο-
μερου ου η γη το ονομα ακουσασα ανυγησετε ου οι δαιμονες το
ονομα ακουσαντες εμφοβοι τρεμουσιν ου οι ποταμοι και ε
θαλασσε το ονομα ακουσαντες ταρασσοντε ου ε πετρε το ονο-
μα ακουσαντες ρησσωντε κατα του βαρβαριθαμ βαρβαρι-
θααμ
χελομβρα βαρουχαμβρα αδωναιου και κατα του αμβραθ α-
βρασαξ σεσενγεν βαρφαραγγης και κατα του ιαω σαβα-
ωθ ιαεω
πακενψωθ πακενβραωθ σαβαρβατιαωθ σαβαρβατιανη σα-
βαρβαφαι μαρι ενδοξου μαρμαραωθ και κατα του ουσερ-
βεν-
τηθ και κατα του ουεερπατη και κατα του μαρμαραυωθ μαρ-
II.C 3 μαραχθα μαρμαραχθαα αμαρδα μαριβεωθ μη μου παρα-
κουσης των
εντολων νεκυδαιμων οστις ποτ ι ειτε αρρης ειτε θηλια αλ ε-
γειρε μοι σεαυτον και υπαγε εις παν τοπον εις παν αμ-
φοδον
εις πασαν οικιαν και καταδησον κοπριαν ην ετεκε μητηρ
ταησις ης εχις τας τριχας της κεφαλης αιλουριωνι ω ετε-
κε
μητηρ ονοματι κοπρια οπως μη βινηθη μηδε πυγισθη μητε ηδο-
νην ποιηση αλλω νεανισκω η ετερω ανδρι αλ-
λα μητε δυνηθη μητε φαγιν μητε πιν μητε υπνου τυχιν μητε
ησυχαζιν τη ψυχη η τη διανοια επιζητουσα δια παντος
ημε-
ρες κε νυκτος ελουριωνα ον ετεκε μητηρ ονοματι κοπρια φι-
λουσα ερωσα εξ ολης καρδιας εξ ολου πνευματος ως την
εαυ-

13 καὶ παραμονίμοις ἐρωτικοῖς, Αἰλουρίωνα, ὃν ἔτεκε μήτηρ ὀνόματι Κοπρία ἔρωτι θείῳ ἀπὸ τῆς σήμερον ἡμέρας, ἀπὸ τῆς ἄρτι

II.C 2 ὥρας ἐπὶ τὸν λοιπὸν τῆς ζωῆς αὐτῆς Κοπρία⟨ς⟩ χρόνον. ὅτι σε ἐξορκίζω, νεκυδαίμων, κατὰ τοῦ ὀνόματος τοῦ φοβεροῦ καὶ τρο-

μεροῦ, οὗ ἡ γῆ τὸ ὄνομα ἀκούσασα ἀνοιγήσεται, οὗ οἱ δαίμονες τὸ ὄνομα ἀκούσαντες ἔμφοβοι τρέμουσιν, οὗ οἱ ποταμοὶ καὶ αἱ

16 θάλασσαι τὸ ὄνομα ἀκούσαντες ταράσσονται, οὗ αἱ πέτραι τὸ ὄνομα ἀκούσαντες ῥήσσονται, κατὰ τοῦ βαρβαριθαμ βαρβαριθααμ

χελομβρα βαρουχαμβρα Ἀδωναίου καὶ κατὰ τοῦ αμβραθ Αβρασαξ σεσενγεν βαρφαραγγης καὶ κατὰ τοῦ Ιαω Σαβαωθ Ιαεω

πακενψωθ πακενβραωθ σαβαρβατιαωθ σαβαρβατιανη σαβαρβαφαι μαρι ἐνδόξου μαρμαραωθ καὶ κατὰ τοῦ ουσερβεν-

τηθ καὶ κατὰ τοῦ ου⟨σ⟩ερπατη καὶ κατὰ τοῦ μαρμαραυωθ

II.C 3 μαρμαραχθα μαρμαραχθαα αμαρδα μαριβεωθ μή μου παρακούσῃς τῶν

20 ἐντολῶν, νεκυδαίμων, ὅστις ποτ' εἶ εἴτε ἄρρην εἴτε θήλεια, ἀλλ' ἔγειρέ μοι σεαυτὸν καὶ ὕπαγε εἰς πᾶν τόπον, εἰς πᾶν ἄμφοδον,

εἰς πᾶσαν οἰκίαν, καὶ κατάδησον Κοπρίαν, ἣν ἔτεκε μήτηρ Ταῆσις, ἧς ἔχεις τὰς τρίχας τῆς κεφαλῆς, Αἰλουρίωνι, ᾧ ἔτεκε

μήτηρ ὀνόματι Κοπρία, ὅπως μὴ βινηθῇ μηδὲ πυγισθῇ μήτε ἡδονὴν ποιήσῃ ἄλλῳ νεανίσκῳ ἢ ἑτέρῳ ἀνδρί, ἀλ-

λὰ μηδὲ δυνηθῇ μήτε φαγεῖν μήτε πιεῖν μήτε ὕπνου τυχεῖν μήτε ἡσυχάζειν τῇ ψυχῇ ἢ τῇ διανοίᾳ ἐπιζητοῦσα διὰ παντὸς ἡμέ-

24 ρας καὶ νυκτὸς Αἰλουρίωνα, ὃν ἔτεκε μήτηρ ὀνόματι Κοπρία, φιλοῦσα ἐρῶσα ἐξ ὅλης καρδίας ἐξ ὅλου πνεύματος ὡς τὴν ἑαυ-

25 της ψυχη⟦c⟧ν κοπρια ης εχιc τας τριχας φιλουcα ερωτι θιω
μεχρι θανατου αιλουριωνα ον ετεκε μητηρ ονονοματι κο-
πρια ηδη

ηδη ταχυ ταχυ[1] 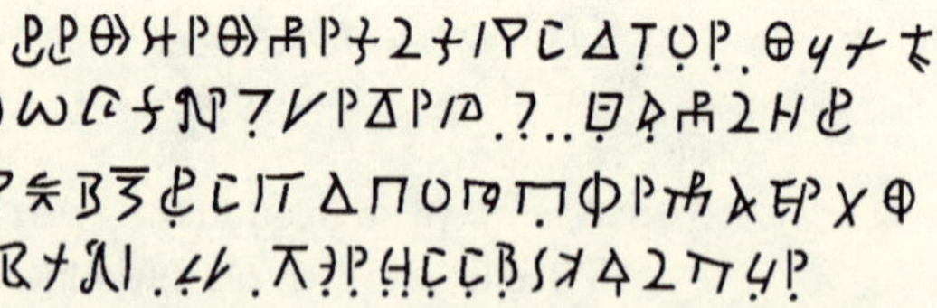

28 αωεμυωαειοωαωαωωαεωαουωοααααααεωαεαεωιαωι
αωαειω ....ε̣α

§ K

29 αεο ..ωαηωαιυαυεωιαεωμαρζα
μαριβεωθ μη μου παρακουcης των εντολων
νεκυδεμων οcτις ποτ ι αλλ εγειρε μοι cεαυτον
32 και υπαγε εις παν τοπον εις παν αμφοδον
εις παcαν οικιαν και αξον κοπριαν ην ετε-
κε μητηρ ταηcιc ης εχιc τας τριχας ελουρι-
ωνι ω ετεκε μητηρ ονοματι κοπρι πυρου-
36 μενην καομενην τηκομενην την ψυχην
το πνευμα την γυνεκιαν φυcιν φιλουcαν
ερωcαν ερωτι θιω ελουριωνα ον ετεκε
μητηρ ονοματι κοπρια μεχρι θανατου ηδη
II.C 4 40 ηδη ταχυ ταχυ εγω ειμι βαρβαδωναιαι
βαρβαδωναι ο τα αcτρα κρυβων ο τον ου-
ρανον κρατεων ο τον κοcμον αληθευων
ιατθεουν ιατρεουν cαλβιουθ αωθ
44 αωθ cαβαθιουθ ιατ᾽θεραθ αδωναιαι
ιcαρ cυρια βιβιβε βιβιουθ νατθω

[1] In the following drawings of the magical letters and signs the dots beneath letters and empty spaces retain their usual papyrological meaning and indicate uncertain readings and unreadable traces. They are not part of the drawing.

25 τῆc ψυχὴν Κοπρία, ἧc ἔχειc τὰc τρίχαc, φιλοῦcα ἔρωτι θείῳ
μέχρι θανάτου Αἰλουρίωνα, ὃν ἔτεκε μήτηρ ὀνόματι Κο-
πρία· ἤδη
ἤδη ταχὺ ταχύ (26-28 γράμματα καὶ χαρακτῆρεc).[2]

§ K

29 αεο ̣ ̣ ̣ωαηωαιυαυεωιαεωμαρζα
μαριβεωθ. μή μου παρακούcῃc τῶν ἐντολῶν,
νεκυδαίμων, ὅcτιc ποτ' εἶ, ἀλλ' ἔγειρέ μοι cεαυτὸν
32 καὶ ὕπαγε εἰc πᾶν τόπον εἰc πᾶν ἄμφοδον
εἰc πᾶcαν οἰκίαν καὶ ἄξον Κοπρίαν, ἣν ἔτε-
κε μήτηρ Ταῆcιc, ἧc ἔχειc τὰc τρίχαc, Αἰλουρι-
ῶνι, ᾧ ἔτεκε μήτηρ ὀνόματι Κοπρία, πυρου-
36 μένην καιομένην τηκομένην τὴν ψυχὴν
τὸ πνεῦμα τὴν γυναικείαν φύcιν, φιλοῦcαν
ἐρῶcαν ἔρωτι θείῳ Αἰλουρίωνα, ὃν ἔτεκε
μήτηρ ὀνόματι Κοπρία, μέχρι θανάτου· ἤδη
II.C 4 40 ἤδη ταχὺ ταχύ. ἐγώ εἰμι βαρβαδωναιαι
βαρβαδωναι ὁ τὰ ἄcτρα κρύβων, ὁ τὸν οὐ-
ρανὸν κρατέων, ὁ τὸν κόcμον ἀληθεύων·
ιατθεουν ιατρεουν cαλβιουθ Αωθ
44 Αωθ cαβαθιουθ ιατ'θεραθ Αδωναιαι
ιcαρ cυρια βιβιβε βιβιουθ νατθω

[2] Beginning approximately 22 cm. into line 27, a deep stroke extends, slanting upward, to the right edge of the tablet between lines 23 and 24. Another lighter stroke begins at the bottom left edge of the tablet beneath line 28, slopes upward, intersecting the line, and runs above it, ending just after the 18th cm. The original function of these lines may have been to indicate where a larger lead sheet was to be cut for this tablet.

46 ϲαβαωθ αιαναφα αμουραχθη ϲαταμα
ζευϲ αθερεϲ̣φιλαυω

Translation: § J

1 *aberamenthooulerthexanaxethreluoothnemareba*
II.A I deposit with you this binding spell, gods of the underworld, Pluto
and Kore *yesemmeigadon* and Koure Persephone Ereschigal and A-
donis, who is also *barbaritha*, and underworld Hermes-Thoth *phoken-*
4 *sepseu earektathou misonktaich* and mighty Anubis *pseriphtha*, who
II.B holds the keys to the (gates) of Hades, and (with you,) chthonic spir-
its, gods and goddesses who suffered an untimely death, boys and
maidens, year after year, month after month, day after day, night af-
ter night, hour after hour. I adjure you, all spirits in this place, to
II.C 1 assist the *nekydaimon*. (Rouse yourself for me, *nekydaimon*,) who-
ever you are, whether male or female, and go into every place, into
every quarter, into every house, and bind Kopria, whom her mother
8 Taesis bore, the hair of whose head you have, for Ailourion, whom
his mother named Kopria bore, that she may not submit to vaginal
nor anal intercourse, nor gratify another youth or another man ex-
cept Ailourion only, whom his mother named Kopria bore, and may
she not even be able to eat nor drink nor ever get sleep nor enjoy
good health nor have peace in her soul or mind for her desire of Ai-
lourion, whom his mother Kopria bore, until Kopria, whom her
mother Taesis bore, whose hair you have, spring up from every
place and every house, burning with passion, and come to Ailouri-
12 on, whom his mother named Kopria bore, loving, adoring Ailouri-
on, whom his mother named Kopria bore, with all her soul, with
all her spirit, with unceasing and unremitting and constant loving
affection, with a divine love, from this very day, from the present
II.C 2 hour, for the rest of her, Kopria's, life. For I adjure you, *nekydai-*
mon, by the fearful and dreadful name of him at the hearing of
whose name the earth will open, at the hearing of whose name the
spirits tremble with fear, at the hearing of whose name the rivers
16 and seas are tossed, at the hearing of whose name the rocks are cleft,

46 Ϲαβαωθ αιαναφα αμουραχθη ϲαταμα
Ζεὺϲ αθερεϲ̣φιλαυω.

by the name *barbaritham barbarithaam chelombra barouchambra* Adonai and by the name *ambrath* Abrasax *sesengen barpharanges* and by the name Iao Sabaoth Iaeo *pakenpsoth pakenbraoth sabarbatiaoth sabarbatiane sabarbaphai mari* glorious *marmaraoth* and by the name *Ouserbenteth* and by the name *Ouserpate* and by the name *marmarau-*
II.C 3 *oth marmarachtha marmarachthaa amarda maribeoth.* Do not dis-
20 obey my commands, *nekydaimon*, whoever you are, whether male or female, but rouse yourself for me and go into every place, into every quarter, into every house, and bind Kopria, whom her mother Taesis bore, the hair of whose head you have, for Ailourion, whom his mother named Kopria bore, that she may not submit to vaginal nor anal intercourse, nor gratify another youth or another man; and may she not even be able to eat nor drink nor get sleep nor be at
24 peace in her soul or mind because of her constant longing, day and night, for Ailourion, whom his mother named Kopria bore, loving, adoring him as her own life, with all her heart, with all her spirit, Kopria, whose hair you have, loving Ailourion, whom his mother named Kopria bore, with a divine love until death. Now now quickly quickly! (26-28 letters and magical symbols).

§ K

29 *aeo ̣ ̣ ̣ oaeoaiuaueoiaeomarza*
maribeoth. Do not disobey my commands, *nekydaimon*, whoever
32 you are, but rouse yourself for me and go into every place, into every quarter, into every house and bring Kopria, whom her mother Taesis bore, whose hair you have, to Ailourion, whom his mother
36 named Kopria bore, burning, blazing, melting away in her soul, her spirit, her feminine part, loving, adoring with a divine love until
40 death Ailourion, whom his mother named Kopria bore. Now now

II.C 4 quickly quickly! I am *Barbadonaiai Barbadonai* who conceals the stars, who preserves heaven, who establishes the cosmos in truth.
44 *iattheoun iatreoun salbiouth aoth aoth sabathiouth iat'therath* Adonaiai *isar suria bibibe bibiouth nattho* Sabaoth *aianapha amourachthe satama* Zeus *atheresphilauo.*

III. COMMENTARY

Section J[1]

1 αβεραμεν --- νεμαρεβα: This palindrome, as Preisendanz (*Wien. Stud.* 41 [1919] 12) notes, is frequently associated with Typhon-Seth and/or magical epithets often connected with him (esp. ιω ερβηθ ιω πακερβηθ etc.); cf. *PGM* III 67f., 117f.; XIV 24; XXXVI 7f., 10-14; LVIII 36; *P. Laur.* IV 148. 14-16 with F. Maltomini's n. *ad loc.* (p. 50); abbrev. αβεραμενθωου λό(γος), *PGM* IV 181, 3272 (cf. below on ιαεω-palindrome p. 105). The formula does not, however, refer to this deity in our text, nor in *PGM* LIX 6 (listed with three other palindromes, the four being οἱ καλοὶ θεοὶ καὶ ἔνδοξοι); *PGM* V 178f. (Hermes); two amulets mentioned by Bonner 203 (Harpocrates). The fact that in *PGM* I 294 it occurs in an invocation to Apollo (Horus), the enemy of Seth, is perhaps not as surprising as Bonner (*loc. cit.*) thinks, since in various strands of Egyptian theology the two gods were reconciled and syncretised (R.W. Daniel, *ZPE* 50 [1983] 151f.; H. Te Velde, *Seth God of Confusion* [Leiden 1967] 63-73; J.G. Griffiths, *The Conflict of Horus and Seth* [Liverpool 1960] 12, 35-37, 148); cf. also *PGM* II 125f., where the palindrome is preceded by Sethian ιω ιω ερβηθ in 115 and followed by an Apollo invocation in 132ff.

The syncretism of both Yahweh and Jesus with Typhon-Seth (Daniel, *loc. cit.*; R. Wünsch, *Sethianische Verfluchungstafeln aus Rom* [Leipzig 1898] 108-113, 116) is probably what accounts for Αβεραμενθω as a name for Jesus in *Pistis Sophia* (IV 136, 139, 140, Schmidt/MacDermott pp. 354 [with n. 1], 360, 367; cf. Eitrem on *P. Oslo* I 1 [= *PGM* XXXVI], 5ff.; Maltomini *loc. cit.*; W. Fauth, *Oriens Christianus* 57 [1973] 106-120*). Conversely, for Seth as Satan, see below on cαταμα (p. 104).

---

[1] The commentary is arranged as it corresponds to P (see above p. 20).

2-4: Deposition with the Underworld Gods

M [2] παρατίθημι ὑμῖν τὸν κατάδεϲμον τοῦτον θεοῖϲ καταχθονίοιϲ, Πλούτωνί τε καὶ Κόρῃ υεϲεμμειγαδων καὶ Κούρῃ Περϲεφόνῃ | Ερεϲχειγαλ καὶ Ἀδώνιδι τῷ καὶ βαρβαριθα καὶ Ἑρμῇ καταχθονίῳ Θωουωθ φωκενϲεψευ εαρεκταθου μιϲονκταιχ καὶ Ἀνούβιδι |[4] κραταιῷ ψηριφθα, τῷ τὰϲ κλεῖδαϲ ἔχοντι τῶν καθ' Ἅ̣δουϲ.

P [335] παρακατατίθεμαι | ὑμῖν τοῦτον τὸν κατάδεϲμον θεοῖϲ χθονίοιϲ | υεϲεμιγαδων καὶ Κούρῃ Περϲεφόνῃ Ερεϲχιγαλ | καὶ Ἀδώνιδι τῷ βαρβαριθα, Ἑρμῇ καταχθονίῳ | Θωουθ φωκενταζεψευ αερχθαθου μι|[340]ϲονκταικ αλβαναχαμβρη καὶ Ἀνούβιδι κρα|ταιῷ ψιρινθ, τῷ τὰϲ κλεῖδαϲ ἔχοντι τῶν καθ' Ἅ̣|δου.

C [1] παρακατα{θ}τίθομαι ὑμεῖν θεοῖϲ καταχθον[ίοιϲ] καὶ θεαῖϲ καταχθονίαιϲ, Πλούτωνι | υεϲμιγαδωθ καὶ Κ̣ο̣ύ̣ρ̣ῃ̣ Περϲεφόνῃ Εροϲχιγαλ καὶ Ἀδώνιδι τῷ καὶ βαρβαριθα καὶ Ἑρμῇ | καταχθονίῳ Θοουθ καὶ Ἀνούβιδι κραταιῷ ψηριφθα, τῷ τὰϲ κλεῖδαϲ ἔχοντι τῶν καθ' Ἅ̣δ̣[ου].

W₁ [6] παρακατατίθημι ὑμῖν τοῦτον τὸν κατάδεζμον θεοῖϲ κα|ταχθονίοιϲ καὶ Πλούτωνι υεϲϲεμιγαδων ορθω Βαυ|[8]βω, Κόρῃ Περϲεφονίῃ Ερεϲχιγαλ καὶ Ἀδώνιδι τῷ βαρβα|ριωνηθ καὶ Ἑρμίᾳ καταχθονίῳ Θωουθ φωκενταζ̣ε̣|ψευ καὶ Ἀνούβιδι καρτερῷ ψηριχθα κανχενε[...]θ τῷ | τὰϲ κλῖδαϲ ἔχοντι τῶν καθ' Ἅ̣δουϲ πυλῶν.

W₂ [5] παρ[α]καταθίθημι ὑμῖν τὸν κατά|δεϲζμον τοῦτον θεοῖϲ κατα|χθονίοιϲ Πλούτωνι καὶ Κόρῃ |[8] καὶ Περϲεφόνῃ.

L [1] παρακατατίθεμαι ὑμῖν τοῦτον τὸν κατάδεϲμον θεοῖϲ καταχθονίοιϲ, Πλούτωνι καὶ Κόρῃ Φερϲεφόνῃ | Ερεϲχιγαλ καὶ Ἀδώνιδι τῷ καὶ βαρβαριθα καὶ Ἑρμῇ καταχθονίῳ Θωουθ φωκενϲεψευ ερεκ̣ταθου μιϲον|κταικ καὶ Ἀνούβιδι κραταιῷ ψηριφθα τῷ τὰϲ κλεῖδαϲ ἔχοντι τῶν κατ̣ὰ Ἅ̣δ̣ουϲ.

The chthonic deities are invoked by their normal Greek or Egyptian names followed by magical names and *logoi*; cf. esp. Aud. 38.2ff., 6ff., 15ff., 32ff.: Ἑρμῇ χθόνιε αρχεδαμα φωχενcεψευc αρερταθου μιcονκαικτ καὶ Πλούτων υεcεμμιγαδων μααρχαμα καὶ Κόρη Ερεcχιγαλ ζαβαρβαθουχ καὶ Φερcεφόνη ζαυδαχθουμαρ. Such obscure combinations of vowels and consonants appear constantly in magical papyri, tablets, and gems. Both popular and literary sources designate them as βάρβαρα/βαρβαρικὰ ὀνόματα; e.g., *PGM* VIII 20f. οἶδά cου καὶ τὰ βαρβαρικὰ ὀνόματα· φαρναθαρ βαραχηλ χθα; cf. βαρβάροιc τε καὶ ξενίζουcι τὴν ἀκοὴν ὀνόμαcι (Heliod. *Aeth.* VI 14.23f. Colonna = VI 14.4 Rattenbury-Lumb); βαρβαρικά τινα καὶ ἄcημα ὀνόματα καὶ πολυcύλλαβα (Lucian *Nec.* 9; cf. *D. Meretr.* 4.5). Cf. also φωνὰc βαρβαρικάc (Xen. Eph. I 5.7); βάρβαρα μέλη (Eur. *Iph. Taur.* 1337-38); *barbaro carmine* ([Quint.] *Decl. Maior.* X 2 p. 190,25 Lehnert); *externa verba atque ineffabilia* (Pliny *NH* XXVIII 20); cf. Dodds, *Greeks and Irrat.* 204f. n. 95.

βαρβαρικά refers to the non-Greek (often Semitic/Egyptian) nature of these words; the magical papyri occasionally specify the languages to which they supposedly belong: ἐπικαλοῦμαί cε κατὰ μὲν Αἰγυπτίουc· Φνω εαι Ιαβωκ, κατὰ δ' Ἰουδαίουc· Ἀδωναῖε Cαβαωθ, κατὰ Ἕλληναc· ὁ πάντων μόναρχοc βαcιλεύc (*PGM* XII 263f.); ἐγώ εἰμι ὁ ἐπικαλούμενόc cε Cυριcτὶ θεὸν μέγαν ζααλαηριφφου. καὶ cὺ μὴ παρακούcῃc τῆc φωνῆc, Ἑβραϊcτί· αβλαναθαναλβα αβραcιλωα (V 472f.). Such statements, however, are not always to be taken seriously; e.g., Hopfner (*OZ* I § 708) notes that in *PGM* V 114f., the name Osiris combined with his Egyptian epithet *Unnofer* (Οcορονvωφριc) is interpreted as Hebrew: τοῦτό ἐcτιν cοῦ τὸ ὄνομα τὸ ἀληθινὸν τὸ παραδιδόμενον τοῖc προφήταιc Ἰcτραήλ. Nevertheless, belief in the power and efficacy of the magical names profited considerably from the aura of antiquity and sacredness associated with the Semitic languages. In addressing the question διὰ τί --- τὰ βάρβαρα (*sc.* ὀνόματα) πρὸ τῶν ἑκάcτῳ οἰκείων προτιθῶμεν, Iamblichus answers, διότι γὰρ τῶν ἱερῶν ἐθνῶν, ὥcπερ Αἰγυπτίων τε καὶ Ἀccυρίων, οἱ θεοὶ τὴν ὅλην διάλεκτον ἱεροπρεπῆ κατέδειξαν, --- καὶ διότι πρῶτοc καὶ παλαιόc ἐcτιν ὁ τοιοῦτοc τρόποc τῆc φωνῆc, καὶ μάλιcτα ἐπειδὴ οἱ μαθόντεc τὰ πρῶτα ὀνόματα περὶ τῶν θεῶν, --- παραδεδώκαcιν ἡμῖν (*de Myst.* VII 4, Parthy 256, 3-13 [p. 192f. Des Places]). With his last reason cf. Hdt. II 50.1: cχεδὸν δὲ καὶ πάντων τὰ οὐνόματα τῶν θεῶν ἐξ Αἰγύπτου ἐλήλυθε ἐc τὴν Ἑλλάδα. διότι μὲν γὰρ ἐκ τῶν βαρβάρων ἥκει, πυνθανόμενοc οὕτω εὑρίcκω ἐόν· δοκέω δ' ὦν μάλιcτα ἀπ' Αἰγύπτου ἀπῖχθαι.

Since the *nomina barbara* were the most ancient, it is not surprising that they were also regarded as the gods' "true" or "authentic" names (Τυφῶν μέγιcτε, ἄκουcόν μου --- λέγω γάρ cου τὰ ἀληθινὰ ὀνόματα ιωερβηθ ιωπακερβηθ, *PGM* IV 277f.; cf. V 114f.; VIII 41, 43; XIII 621f.; XXXIIa 24f.) and as those whose power was irresistible (ἐπικαλοῦμαί cε τοῖc ἁγίοιc cου ὀνόμαcιν --- ὧν οὐ δύνῃ [παρα]κοῦcαι, *PGM* VII 690f.; cf. Hopfner, OZ I § 688). Thus, Iamblichus warns against attempts to translate them: κἂν εἰ οἷόν τε αὐτὰ μεθερμηνεύειν, ἀλλὰ τήν γε δύναμιν οὐκέτι φυλάττει τὴν αὐτήν (*de Myst.* VII 5 Parthey 257, 13-14 = p. 193 Des Places); cf. *Oracula Chaldaica* fr. 150 Des Places: ὀνόματα βάρβαρα μήποτ' ἀλλάξῃc. For skeptical reaction against the foreign names, see Plutarch *Mor.* (*de Sup.*) 166b; Porphyry *Epist. ad Anebonem* 33 Parthy (p. XL, 11ff. in his ed. of *de Myst.* = p. 22 Sodano); Hopfner, OZ I §§ 716ff.

On the βαρβαρικὰ ὀνόματα in general, see Kopp III pp. 110-28 (§§ 106 -23); Abt, *Apol.* pp. 226-31; Kropp III pp. 116-122 (§§ 195-200); and esp. Hopfner, OZ I §§ 706-31. In addition to the present passage, magical names occur in § J 1 (cf. above p. 33), 16-19 (below pp. 76ff.), § K 40-47 (below pp. 92ff.), and §§ A, C, and E (below pp. 105ff.).

2 **παρατίθημι:** The active occurs elsewhere in magical papyri, but not in this technical sense of depositing a spell. It may be a mistake for one of the forms more commonly used with this meaning, either the middle of this verb (Aud. 29.25f., τὴν παραθήκην ὑμῖν παρατίθομε [i.e., -ομαι]; cf. 22.39; 26. 27f.; 27.23; 30.31; 31.25; 32.27; 35.26) or παρακατατίθεμαι/ομαι (P, C, L, *PGM* VII 449) or παρακατατίθημι (W_1 and W_2; cf. the various versions of the formula κατάδηcον τοὺc ἵππουc ὧν τὰ ὀνόματά cοι παρακατατίθημι/παρακατατέθηκα in Aud. 234.30ff.; 237.3f., 21f.; 238.6f.; 239.4f., 18f.; 240. 4f., 20f.). In the case of the above cited Aud. 29.25f. *et al.*, Audollent (index p. 474 and intro. lvii) incorrectly restores the first pl. παρατίθομεν of an uncontracted thematic active παρατίθω (on the analogy of 22.39); the contexts and sense require -μαι (cf. Harrauer, *Meliouchos* 59 n. 62). In light of the active forms of παρακατατίθημι in the Wortmann and Audollent texts, it may not be necessary to assume παρατίθημι incorrect.

παρατίθεcθαι and (to a lesser extent) παρακατατίθεcθαι mean "deposit" in various commercial and legal contexts: πρὸ τούτου παρεθέμην cοι [...] χρυcίου νομιcμάτια δόκιμα (*BGU* III 941.8f.); ἠνάγκαcεν τὴν δι' ἐναντίας παρακατάθεc[θα]ι τὰ δύο τάλ[α]ντα παρὰ κοινῷ μεcείτῃ Κολλούθῳ (*P. Stras.* I 41.14). See Preisigke, *Wörterbuch* s.vv.; *idem*, *Fachwörter* s.v. παρατίθημι; K. Kaster, *Die zivilrechtliche Verwahrung des gräko-ägyptischen Obligationenrechts im Lichte der Papyri* (Nürnberg 1962), *passim*, esp. evidence collected on pp. 86ff.; W. Otto, *Priester und Tempel im hellenistischen Ägypten* [Leipzig and Berlin 1905] I 319f. on *P. Grenf.* I 14). Cf. esp. the above cited Aud. 29.25f. *et al.*, where the curse tablet is itself called a παραθήκη, the thought being, as in our text, that the invoked deities and *daimones* are the guarantors of the spell and responsible for its execution (cf. Harrauer, *Meliouchos* 58f.).

Πλούτωνί τε καὶ Κόρῃ υεcεμμειγαδων: E. Kuhnert (*Rh. Mus.* 49 [1894] 49 n. 11) and F. Legge (*PSBA* 22 [1900] 121f.) have pointed out the connection of *yesemmeigadon* with Pluto in Aud. 38 (Wessely, *Ephesia Grammata* 244): Πλούτων υεcεμμιγαδων μααρχαμα καὶ Κόρη Ερεcχιγαλ (3, 7f., 17f., 33f.); similarly in C 1f. (Πλούτωνι υεcεμιγαδωθ) and W_1 7 (Πλούτωνι υεccεμιγαδων ορθω Βαυβω). Pluto, however, is lacking in P 336f. (θεοῖc χθονίοιc υεcεμιγαδων) and *yesem.* in W_2 and L. M's Κόρῃ υεcεμμειγαδων suggests a female deity, as do parts of the common magical *logos* where *yesem.* occurs most frequently: υεccεμμιγαδων ορθω Βαυβω νοηρε cοιρε cοιρη cανκανθαρα Ερεcχιγαλ cανκιcτη δωδεκακιcτη ἀκρουροβόρε κοδηρε (*PGM* II 32ff.; cf. V 424ff.; VII 680ff.; XIII 923ff.; W_1 46ff. [in Artemis-Hekate adjuration]; Aud. 295.1ff.; *DMP* VII 25; J.M.R. Cormack, *HTR* 44 [1951] 26, col. IV 3ff. and nn. pp. 31ff.; the first three words occur in W_1 7 cited above). The following elements indicate a particular connection with Hekate and her circle:

a) ορθω: possibly a variation of Artemis' name 'Ορθία or 'Ορθωcία (see Höfer in Roscher III 1.1210ff. s.v.; Cormack, *op. cit.* 32). For Artemis' identification with Hekate/Selene, see, e.g., Theoc. 2.33; *PGM* IV 2523, 2720f., 2816; W_1 39ff. with Wortmann's nn. (pp. 75ff.); cf. F. Maltomini's n. on *P. Münch.* II 28, fr. 13.1-2.

b) Βαυβω: This name, originally associated with Demeter's myth and cult (F. Wehrli, *ARW* 31 [1934] 79ff.; N.J. Richardson, *The Homeric Hymn to Demeter* [Oxford 1974] 80ff.; 215f.), came to represent Hekate (h. to Hekate 59, 13.2 Heitsch [*PGM* IV 2715]; *PGM* IV 2958 [ms. Βαιβω]; VII 886 [Hekate/Selene]; inscription from Paros cited and discussed by O. Kern, *MDAI*, Ath. Abt. 16 [1891] 6-7 with n. 2). For Βαυβω in general, see T. Hopfner, *AO* 13 [1942] 183; Rohde *Psyche* II 408 (Eng. 591); F. Graf, *Eleusis und die orphische Dichtung Athens in vorhellenistischer Zeit* (RGVV 33, Berlin/New York 1974) 168ff.; Schultz in Roscher I 1.752f. s.v. Βαυβω; Kern in *RE* III 150f. s.v.; Fauth in *Kleine Pauly* I 843ff. s.v.

c) νοηρε: probably for Coptic ΝΟΥΡЄ, "vulture" (Crum 228B), a bird which was thought to be only of the female sex and was thus sacred to a number of goddesses, including Hekate-Selene (see R.W. Daniel, *ZPE* 19 [1975] 261 on P. Köln inv. no. 5512.7).

d) Ερεϲχιγαλ: Babylonian goddess equated with Hekate-Persephone; cf. below p. 40 on Κούρῃ Περϲεφόνῃ Ερεϲχιγαλ.

e) ἀκρουροβόρε (*sc.* δράκων): "serpent swallowing the end of its tail"; cf. the more common οὐροβόροϲ. The diagram of a serpent forming a circle by biting its tail occurs in magical papyri (*PGM* VII col. xvii, vol. 2 Taf. I 4; P. Berol. 21165 [ed. Wm. Brashear, *ZPE* 17, 1975, 28]) and especially in amulets (Bonner 250; Delatte/Derchain index p. 364). As a symbol of eternity, resurrection, and the underworld, the image is mainly connected with Helios-Osiris (i.e., Pluto; cf., e.g., Dittenberger, *Syll.* 996.20f. cited below p. 39), but on a secondary level may also be associated with the moon and thus Hekate, as is the case in the following invocation: Κόρη --- Ἑκάτη ἀκρουροβόρη Cελήνη (Aud. 41a.6). On οὐροβόροϲ, see Delatte/Derchain p. 48 with lit. cited in nn. 2 and 3; M.P. Nilsson, *Geschichte d. griechischen Rel.* II (München[2] 1961) 499 n. 7, 502f.; F. Maltomini, *SCO* 29 (1979) 92; L. Koenen, *ICS* 1 (1976) 135 with n. 32.

In addition, Kore, usually connected with Persephone (see below p. 40), is associated also with Hekate, sometimes called Persian (Nausik. fr. 2 Meineke [vol. IV 575] = fr. 2 Kock [vol. II 295]; A.R. IV 1020; Nonnos *Dion.* XIII 401;

Porphyry, *De Philosophia ex Oraculis haurienda* II 167 p. 151c Wolff; *Orph. h.* 1.9 Quandt; h. to Hekate 59, 13.4 and 22 Heitsch = *PGM* IV 2719, 2746; *PGM* XII 6 [on which see T. Hopfner, *AO* 13, 1942, 169]; W_1 60-61; ἀγάλματα Πλούτωνος Ἡλίου καὶ Κούρης Cελήνης in Dittenberger, *Syll.* III 996.20-21 and cf. F.J. Dölger, *Sol Salutis* [Münster, Westf., 1925] 347 with nn. 1 and 4; Aud. 41a.6 [cited above]; Κούρα τριώνυμος in Aud. 22.41, 23.1, 24.24, etc. [index p. 462; cf. Wortmann p. 79 note h]).

It is therefore possible to interpret υεcεμμειγαδων in our text as an epithet of Kore Hekate, but it may also function with Pluto, since no other magical name occurs with him. The different versions of M and the parallels probably reflect a chthonic invocation which originally began with the great king and queen of the dead, Pluto with the magical name *yesem.* and Persephone preceded by the common Kore and followed by her Babylonian counterpart Ereschigal (so C; adopted in the hypothetical archetype below p. 114). Problems developed, however, over *yesem.*, which was also felt to be connected with Artemis-Hekate-Selene. This perception may have generated the τε καὶ Κόρη expansion in our text and the ορθω Βαυβω addition in W_1; it may also explain the omissions of Πλούτωνι in P and *yesem.* in L. Since W_2 in this section omits most *nomina barbara,* it cannot provide reliable evidence on this point. One may note, however, that its reading Πλούτωνι καὶ Κόρῃ καὶ Περcιφόνῃ envisions, like M, a chthonic trinity rather than dyad; so also in Aud. 38, Πλούτων --- καὶ Κόρη --- καὶ Φερcεφόνη (fuller citation above pp. 34f.).

Our difficulties with υεcεμμειγαδων are compounded by the lack of any adequate etymology. J.M.R. Cormack (*HTR* 44, 1951, 32 [citing Eisler]) suggests Hebrew *hu'a* (used in glosses for *id est*) + *semo* ("his name") + a corruption of *gadol* ("great") thus, "i.e., his name is great." The element *-meigadon* has also been connected with *adon* (אדון) "Lord," or with the name Μιχάδων, one of the twenty-four elders (Rev. 4.4 *et al.*) mentioned in a Byzantine charm (A. Vassiliev, *Anecdota Graeco-Byzantina* [Moscow 1893] 342; see *PGM* vol. 3 p. 232), or with Ἁρ Μαγεδών, Mt. Magedon of Rev. 16.16, the site of the final conflict between Christ and the demonic powers (cf. Baudissin, "Adonis" 444f. n. 2; Drexler in Roscher II 2.2647 s.v. *Meliuchos*; F. Legge, *PSBA* 22 [1900] 121f.). In connection with the last, υεcε may be associated with the Phosteres [I]ЄCCЄΥC and [IЄCCЄ]ⲀЄKЄΥ[C] of the Gnostic *Apoc. of Adam* (*CG* V 85.19ff. [*NHLib. Eng.* 264]), whose names seem to be variations of the name of Jesus (cf. L. Koenen in *The Rediscovery of Gnosticism* II [Leiden 1981] 751f. with n. 73). The entire name, "Jesus of Magedon," would thus denote Christ as apocalyptic victor. υεcε could also be a play on various spellings of Isis; e.g., Copt. ΗCЄ; Gk. Ec-, -ηcι; (see *Lex. Äg.* III 186f.; Gignac I 242 n. 2). The advantage of this interpretation is that the underworld affiliations of Isis (Drexler in Roscher II 1. 462ff. s.v.), her syncretism with Hekate (*ibid.* 468; *P. Oxy.* XI 1380.113; Griffiths, *Isis Book* 152f.), and her occasional epithet Κόρη (*P. Oxy. ibid.*, 72, 105) are very congenial to our context. The problem, however, is that we are left without a suitable explanation of -μειγαδων.

2-3 Κούρη Περcεφόνη Ερεcχιγαλ: in all parallels (with spelling variations) exc. W_2, which has Κόρη καὶ Περcεφόνη. Magical texts associate the Babylonian underworld goddess Ereschigal with Persephone as here (*PGM* VII 984; Drexler in Roscher II 1.1584f. s.v. Ereschigal), but more frequently with Hekate; e.g., *PGM* LXX 4, 5, 9; most likely Κόρη Ερεcχιγαλ in Aud 38 (cited above pp. 34f.; cf. also p. 39). The combination (Ἀκτιῶφι) Ερεcχιγαλ Νεβουτοcουαληθ (Delatte/Derchain 254 bis; Aud. 38.13, 242.42; *DMP* XXIII 16 p. 146; *PGM* IV 1417f., 2484f., 2749f., 2913f.; VII 317f.) is also Hekatean, Νεβουτοcουαληθ being one of her names (K. Preisendanz in *RE* XVI 2158f. s.v.; Delatte/Derchain p. 192 [on # 254 bis] and p. 338 [on # 517]). For Ereschigal in general, cf. Delatte/Derchain p. 192 (on # 254 bis); *DMP* VII 26 and n. (p. 61); Bonner 86, 197. See above p. 38f. for Κόρη as a name for both goddesses. On the Hekate/Persephone/Selene syncretism, see Steuding in Roscher I 2.1898 s.v. Hekate; Bloch *ibid.* II 1.1335 s.v. Kora; D. Wortmann, *ZPE* 2 (1968) 158.

3 Ἀδώνιδι: so spelled in L P W_1 (om. W_2); Λδώνιζι M. Confusion of A and Λ is a frequent error in manuscripts (examples in Renehan, *Gk. Text. Crit.* 45-47 [§§ 38, 42, 43] 56-59 [§ 49]; West, *Text. Crit.* 27; H.C. Youtie, *TAPA* 83 [1952] 102 [*Scriptiunculae* I 236]) and magical amulets (Bonner 13). The interchange between δ and ζ is late (2nd/3rd cent. on, cf. Gignac I 75f.; no examples in Ptolemaic pap. given by Mayser/Schmoll) and especially rare in Attic (Threatte 549f.). With Ἀδώνιζι cf. Cαράπιζι (for Cαράπιδι) *PSI* XIII 1332 (*SB* V 7992),5-6 and 13; Εὐεργέτιζει (for Εὐεργέτιδι) *BGU* I 94.2.

In our standard editions of magical papyri, tablets, and amulets the name Adonis occurs only (besides in P) in the threat against Aphrodite of *PGM* IV 2903:

οὐκ ὄψῃ τὸν Ἄδωνιν ἀνερχόμενον Ἀΐδαο. The operator continues the threat by asserting that he will bind Adonis in Hades. He then commands Aphrodite to bring him his beloved and adjures her by Ερεcχιγαλ Νεβουτοcουαληθ (Hekate-Persephone [see preceding n.]), i.e., the one who indeed has the power either to suppress or allow Adonis' return. Elsewhere in magic, Adonis appears within the same mythic context but with the obscure name Μελιοῦχοc (see H.J. Thissen, *ZPE* 73, 1988, 304, against Ch. Harrauer's recent etymology). In texts discussed by Harrauer, *Meliouchos* 53-63, the god becomes closely identified with Osiris and is seen in connection with Hekate-Persephone (sometimes *Neboutosoualeth*), who reconstitutes his limbs (*PGM* III 45; prob. Aud. 27.19), brings them down to Hades (Aud. 22.32), and brings them up again (*sc.* to Aphrodite; Aud. 38.11f.). In general for the chthonic aspects of Adonis' myth and cult, see Lucian *de Syria Dea* 6-8; Baudissin, "Adonis" 442ff.; W. Burkert, *Structure and History in Greek Mythology and Ritual* (Berkeley 1979) 105-11, esp. 109f.; further bibliography in W. Atallah, *Adonis* (Paris 1966) 332-34. M and its parallels are unique, in that Adonis is not mentioned as a subordinate to the great underworld goddesses in adjurations by them, but is invoked with them as a chthonic deity in his own right and given the lofty but inappropriate *supernomen* βαρβαριθα.

τῷ καὶ βαρβαριθα: same in C and L; καὶ omm. P W_1. To my knowledge, the ὁ καὶ form is not elsewhere connected with deities in magical texts, the normal practice being to append epithets and *nomina barbara* asyndetically (see A.D. Nock, *JEA* 15 [1929] 223 [in an excursus not in *Essays*]). In inscriptions, cf., e.g., Χνοῦβει τῷ καὶ Ἄμμωνι, Cάτει τῇ καὶ Ἥρᾳ, Ἀνούκει τῇ καὶ Ἑcτίᾳ, Πετεμπαμέντει τῷ καὶ Διονύcῳ, κτλ. (Dittenberger, *OGIS* I 130.7ff.; cf. also *ibid.*, index III [vol. 2, pp. 598ff.] s. vv. Ἄμμων, Διόνυcοc, Ἑρμῆc, Ἑcτία; similarly ὃc καί in Vanderlip hymn IV 26 p. 63); in papyri: Cοκνεπτύνεωc τ[ο]ῦ καὶ Κρόνου, *P. Tebt.* II 294.5 (=*W.Chr.* 78). For this and other conventions of attaching second names (variously termed *signa, agnomina, supernomina*), cf. M. Lambertz, *Glotta* 4 (1913) 78-143, 5 (1914) 99-170; Kubitschek in *RE* (ser. 2) II 2448-52 s.v. *signum*; R. Calderini, *Aegyptus* 21 (1941) 221ff., esp. 226-35; more recently, I. Kajanto, *Supernomina* (Commentationes Humanarum Litterarum 40 [1] 1966) 7f.; L.C. and H.C. Youtie and U. and D. Hagedorn, *Das Archiv des Petaus* (Cologne and Opladen 1969) p. 54ff.; P. Thrams, *ZPE* 9 (1972) 140 and n. 5; Horsley, *New Docs.* I 89-96 (§ 55).

Barbaritha is most likely a Hebrew epithet (see below pp. 76f.) which usually occurs in a *logos* containing other Hebrew elements (see below p. 76). Both in and apart from the *logos* it is usually connected with Adonai (אדני "Lord"), one of the many names of the great God of the Jews. The name Adonis is most likely derived from the same Semitic root (cf. Baudissin, "Adonis" 423-42 [esp. 429]; W. Atalla, *op. cit.* 303ff., 335; W. Burkert, *op. cit.* 105f. with 192 n. 3 [n. 4 for opposing views]). It is probably for no reason other than the similarity of the two names that *barbaritha*, properly belonging to Adonai, is here applied to Adonis.

Ἑρμῇ καταχθονίῳ Θωουωθ: This spelling of Thoth (cf. Θωουθ P W_1 L; Θοουθ C) reflects a tendency in magical texts to make divine names palindromic (ου counted as one sound); cf. esp. Θωθουθωθ in W_4 25 with Wortmann's n. p. 99. For various spellings of the month name Θωυθ, see Gignac I 95, 186. This Egyptian god was equated with Hermes, e.g., in his principal underworld role as ψυχοπομπός (P. Boylan, *Thoth the Hermes of Egypt* [Oxford 1922] 140f.; A. Rusch, *RE* [ser. 2] VI 1.367, 383ff. s.v. Thoth; Bonnet 812A s.v. Thoth; cf. also below on Anubis), and as the inventor and giver of spoken and written language (*PGM* V 402, 407; VII 669f.; XVIIb 2, 4; Plato *Phdr.* 274c-d and *Phlb.* 18b-d; L. Kakošy, *Acta Archaeologica Academiae Scientiarum Hungaricae* 15, 1963, 124 and nn. 3, 7, 8; J. Černý, *JEA* 34 [1948] 121f.). The latter aspect is closely associated with the status of Hermes-Thoth as a god of magic, since among his linguistic accomplishments is the creation of magical language and magical books (δεῦρό μοι --- ἐπεί cου λέγω τὰ ὀνόματα, ἃ ἔγραψεν ἐν Ἡλιουπόλει ὁ τριcμέγιcτος Ἑρμῆc ἱερογλυφικοῖc γράμμαcι, *PGM* IV 883ff.; cf. XIII 14ff.; XXIVa 2f.; Hopfner, OZ I § 707; Bonnet 808-09 s.v. Thoth; cf. also the general discussion of *voces magicae* above pp. 34ff.). In general, for Hermes-Thoth as a god of magic and his role in magical texts, cf. Hom. *Od.* X 281-306 (Hermes gives Odysseus the magical plant μῶλυ to counteract Circe's spell; see H. Rahner, *Griechische Mythen in christlicher Deutung* [Zürich 1957] 169ff. [Eng., *Greek Myths and Christian Mystery*, London 1963, 190ff.]); Borghouts *AEMT* # 5 (p. 2), # 91 (p. 65); J.G. Griffiths, *ZPE* 26 (1977) 287; N.O. Brown, *Hermes the Thief* (New York 1969) 11-21 (and index s.vv. "magic" and "Hermes as magician"); T. Hopfner, *AO* 3 (1931) 129-31.

φωκενcεψευ εαρεκταθου μιcονκταιχ: om. C; φωκενταζεψευ only, W_1 9f.; φωκενcεψευ ερεκταθου μιcονκταικ L 2f.; φωκενταζεψευ αερχθαθου μιcονκταικ αλβαναχαμβρη P 339f. M and L prove that the last two words of P should be so printed rather than Preisendanz's μιcονκται καλβαναχαμβρη. Since Preisendanz did not have this evidence, the articles in *PGM* vol. 3 s.vv. καλβ αναχ αμβρη (p. 259B), αλβαναχαμβρη (p. 245A), and cαλβαναχαμβρη (p. 269B) reflect this misreading. For αλβαναχαμβρη, cf. *PGM* XII 471 and below on αβλαναθαναλβα (p. 108f.).

The *φωκενcεψ-logos* is applied to Hermes-Thoth also in *PGM* LXVII 11-12 (on which see L. Koenen, *ZPE* 8 [1971] 205) and Aud. 38.2, 6f., 16, 33 (cited above p. 34f.). Karl Fr. Schmidt (*GGA* 193 [1931] 452) explains φωκενγεψ (spelling in *PGM* III 513) from the Egyptian *p3-ẖkr-n- ḫpš*, "der mit dem Schwert Geschmückte." The sword in question here is more specifically the scimitar (*ḫpš*), which one of the gods presents to the reigning Pharaoh as a symbol of victory and royal power (Rosetta Stone line 39 Grk. [= 23 Demot., R6 Hierogl.]; A.H. Gardiner, *Egyptian Grammar* [Oxford 1957] 584; W. Wolf, *Die Bewaffnung des altägyptischen Heeres* [Leipzig 1926] 66-68). Due to its sickle shape, it may be connected with the crescent moon, which is the knife (*dš*) used by the moon god Thoth to behead the wicked (Bonnet 807B; H. Kees, *ZÄS* 60 [1925] 2ff.; for the lunar associations of Hermes-Thoth, see *PGM* V 400f.; VIII 46; Plutarch *Is. et Os.* 12 [355d] and 41 [367d] with Griffith's comments *ad locc.* [pp. 293f.; 458]; Rusch in *RE* [ser. 2] VI 1.354ff. s.v. Thoth; Roeder in Roscher V 845f. s.v. Thoth; as noted above, the element αλβανα [Heb. "moon"; cf. below p. 109] is connected with this *logos* in P). On the Greek side, Hermes uses the scimitar to decapitate Argos (Ovid *Met.* I 717f. and cf. Lucan IX 662ff.; cf. also a gem noted by Höfer in Roscher II 1.275).

The scimitar or sickle (ἅρπη) is also connected with other deities, e.g., Seth (Massart, *Leid. Mag. Pap.* Recto II 2f. [p. 52] and Recto X 13f. [p. 81]); Zeus ([Apollod.] *Bibliotheca* I 6.3; *PGM* IV 3116); Kronos (*PGM* IV 3093; Hesiod *Theog.* 175 and M.L. West's n. *ad loc.* [p. 217f.], where he argues that the ἅρπη is the normal weapon in Greek myth for dismembering monsters and is not the scimitar but the agricultural sickle; cf. M.P. Nilsson, *Annual of the British School at Athens* 46, 1951, 122ff. [*Opuscula Selecta* III 215ff.]). In connection with the first two, see *PGM* III 78f. (left) where the *φωκενcεψ-logos* occurs with common magical epithets of Seth; in *ibid.* 513f., 545f. it is associated with Helios (i.e., Zeus; see, e.g., *PGM* V 4).

3-4 Ἀνούβιδι κραταιῷ: thus also parallels (καρτερῷ W_1 10). The Egyptian god Anubis is associated with Thoth in his underworld roles as ψυχοπομπός and judge of the dead (cf. above on Ἑρμῇ καταχθονίῳ Θωουωθ; B. Altenmüller in *Lex. Äg.* I 328 s.v. Anubis; S. Morenz, *RG* 516; cf. also the representations of Anubis on linen discussed by Morenz in *Staatliche Museen zu Berlin, Forschungen und Berichte* I [1957] 52-70, Abb. 1, 8, 9 [*RG* 231-47 Abb. 3, 9, 10]). For Anubis in magical texts, see Hopfner, *AO* 3 (1931) 129; *ibid.* 7 (1935) 97ff.; Delatte/Derchain pp. 89-103; Bonner index p. 327 s.v.

4 ψηριφθα: so spelled in C 3, L 3; ψηριχθα W_1 10; ψιρινθ P 341. In this *nomen barbarum* of Anubis, the elements ρι φθα probably represent Re Ptah. ρι also occurs in the combinations ωρι *PGM* I 133 ("Gross ist Re," Schmidt *GGA* 193 [1931] 443) and cουωρι I 135 ("Gross leuchtend ist Re" *ibid.* 444); Ρα and Φρη are preferred spellings in *PGM* (cf. φρι XIXa 4; *PGM Eng.* p. 338 s.v. Ra). Ptah was a creator god (see below on § K 42 pp. 98f.) and patron of all crafts (thus equivalent to Hephaistos; cf. *PGM* IV 1584f. with Hopfner's comment in *AO* 3, 1931, 327 with nn. 15 and 16; Höfer in Roscher III 2.2470f. s.v. Ptah). Later Egyptian theology (i.e., Middle/New Kingdom) closely associated Re and Ptah, and Amon-Re-Ptah were an important triad (cf. Leiden h. to Amon, cited by E. Hornung, *Conceptions of God in Ancient Egypt* [Ithaca 1982] 219; H. te Velde in *Lex. Äg.* IV 1178 s.v. Ptah; cf. also M. Holmberg, *The God Ptah* [Lund 1946] 150-54). In *PGM* Ptah usually occurs with Re: Φθα Ρα Φθα ιη Φθα (XII 155); Ἥλιε Τιτάν, [ἐλθὲ καὶ] Ιαα καὶ Φθα καὶ Φρη (XXIII 5-6); Οcορνωφρι Εμ Φρη Φρη Φθα (V 353); Φρηυ Φθα (VII 362); Αρcενοφρη ηυ Φθα ηωλι (i.e., ἡλίῳ, II 118; cf. *PGM* vol. 3 p. 232 s.v. Φθα. K.Fr. Schmidt's interpretation of the first word is *wršj-nfr-R'*, "the good watcher Re" [*GGA* 196, 1934, 173]; for others see H.J. Thiessen, *ZPE* 73, 1988, 305).

It is difficult to account for ψη-. It may represent Shai (Ψοϊ in *PGM*; equivalent to Greek Ἀγαθοδαίμων), the Egyptian god of destiny, sometimes associated with Re (*PGM* IV 1643; XXXVIII 16; "Son of Re" in Coptic invocation, III 680; cf. φηρ ψοι IV 2411 [= φρη ψοϊ? See *PGM* vol. 3 p. 233 s.v. ψοϊ]; see also J. Quaegebeur, *Le Dieu Égyptien Shaï* [Leuven 1975] 76-80, 100f.; Bonnet 671f. s.v. Schai; T. Hopfner, *AO* 3 [1931] 149ff. With our word cf. esp. χαριφθα, *PGM* IV 3013 [Preisendanz divides χαρι φθα]; χα, i.e., Shai?). On the other hand, ψηρι is very similar to Copt. ϢΗΡЄ/ ϢΗΡΙ, "son" (Crum 584f.), but I find no evidence for Anubis as a son of Ptah. In some accounts, however, he is son of Re (Bonnet 42B s.v. Anubis; Budge, *Gods* II 261), and if we take ψη as ϢЄ, a frequent abbreviation for ϢΗΡЄ in Coptic magical texts (cf. Kropp I index p. 111), we have "son of Re-Ptah."

τῷ τὰϲ κλεῖδαϲ ἔχοντι τῶν καθ' ᾍδουϲ: ᾍδου P 341-342; ᾍδουϲ W_1 10f., L 3 (for the sigma, see Mayser/Schmoll I 1.183); ᾍδ[C 3. After τῶν καθ' ᾍδουϲ, *sc.* πυλῶν, which is explicit in W_1 11 (cf. Wortmann p. 70f.). This relatively rare use of κατά c. gen. denotes position at or in rather than motion downward; e.g., Diod. Sic. V 79.2: δικαϲτὴν αὐτὸν ἀποδεδεῖχθαι καθ' ᾍδου, "He (Rhadamanthys) has been appointed judge in Hades." Cf. *idem* I 92.5; IV 26.1; κατὰ νηδύοϲ, "in the womb" (of the *Argo*), A.R. IV 1328, 1354, 1373; κατὰ νώτου, "at the rear," Thuc. IV 32.4, 33.1, 36.2 (see KG 1.476).

For Anubis with keys, see *PGM* IV 1466f. (κλειδοῦχέ τε Ἄνουβι φύλαξ); Delatte/Derchain 122; Wortmann p. 70 n. (f); Morenz, *Äg. Rel.* 262 with n. 79, Eng. 247f. with n. 8 (article cited in this n. also appears in *RG* 510ff.); J. Jeremias in *TDNT* III 745f. s.v. κλείϲ; *PGM Eng.* p. 332 s.v. Anubis. Similarly, Christ says, ἔχω τὰϲ κλεῖϲ τοῦ θανάτου καὶ τοῦ ᾍδου, NT Rev. 1.18; cf. 9.1, 20.1, Bauer s.v. ᾍδηϲ.

4-6: Deposition with and Adjuration of the δαίμονεϲ

M 4 καὶ δαίμοϲι χθονίοιϲ θεοῖϲ ἀώροιϲ τε καὶ ἀώραιϲ, μέλλαξί τε καὶ παρθένοιϲ, ἐνιαυ|τοὺϲ ἐξ ἐνιαυτῶν, μῆναϲ ἐκ μηνῶν, ἡμέραϲ ἐξ ἡμερῶν, νύκταϲ ἐκ νυκτῶν, ὥραϲ ἐξ ὡρῶν. ἐξορκίζω ϲε πάνταϲ τοὺϲ δαί|μοναϲ τοὺϲ ἐν τῷ τόπῳ τούτῳ ϲυμπαραϲταθῆναι τῷ νεκυδαίμονι·

P 342 καὶ δαίμοϲι καταχθονίοιϲ θεοῖϲ ἀώροιϲ τε | καὶ ἀώραιϲ, μέλλαξί τε καὶ παρθένοιϲ, ἐνιαυτοὺϲ |344 ἐξ ἐνιαυτῶν, μῆναϲ ἐκ μηνῶν, ἡμέραϲ ἐξ ἡμε|ρῶν, ὥραϲ ἐξ ὡρῶν. ὁρκίζω πάνταϲ δαίμοναϲ | τοὺϲ ἐν τῷ τόπῳ τούτῳ ϲυνπαραϲταθῆναι τῷ δαί|μονι τούτῳ.

C [4] καὶ δαίμοϲι καταχθονίοιϲ ἀώροιϲ τε καὶ ἀώραιϲ, μέλλαξί τε καὶ παρθένοιϲ, ἐννιαυτοὺϲ [ἐξ ἐν]|νιαυτῶν, μῆναϲ ἐκ μηνῶν, ἡμέραϲ ἐξ ἡμερῶν, νύκταϲ ἐγ νυκτῶν, ὥραϲ ἐξ ὡρῶν. ὁρκ[ίζω] | πάνταϲ τοὺϲ δαίμοναϲ τοὺϲ ἐν τῷ τόπῳ τούτῳ, συνπαράϲτατε τῷ δαίμονι τούτῳ.

W₁ [11] κα[ὶ δεμ]οϲ[ι κα]|[12]ταχθονίοιϲ θεοῖϲ τε καὶ ἀώροιϲ, μέλλαξί τε [και παρ]|θένοιϲ, ἐνιαυϲίουϲ ἐξξ ἐνιαυτῶν, μήνεϲ ἐκ μ[ηνῶν, ἡ]|μέραιϲ ἐξξ ἡμερῶν, νύκτε{κτε}⟨ϲ⟩ ἐκ νυκτῶν, ὥρεϲιν [ἐξ]ξ ὡρ[ῶ]ν. | [ὁρ]κίζω πάνταϲ τοὺϲ δέμοναϲ τοὺϲ ἐν τῷ τόπῳ τ[ού]τῳ ϲυμ|[16][{ϲυμ}?]παραϲταθῆναι τῷ δέμονι τούτῳ.

W₂ [8] καὶ δέμονεϲ κα|[9]ταχθονίοιϲ νεκροῖϲ τε καὶ ἀώ|ροιϲ, παρθένοιϲ καὶ μέλλαξιν, ϲυν|παραϲταθῆναι τῷ δέμονι τούτῳ.

L [3] καὶ δαίμοϲι κατα|[4]χθονίοιϲ θεοῖϲ ἀώροιϲ τε καὶ ἀώραιϲ, μέλλαξι καὶ παρθένοιϲ, ἐνιαυτοῖϲ ἐξ ἐνιαυτῶν, μήναϲι | ἐκ μηνῶν, ἡμέραιϲ ἐκ ἡμερῶν, ὥραϲι ⟨ἐξ⟩ ὡρῶν, νύκτεϲ ἐκ νυκτῶν. ὁρκίζω πάνταϲ τοὺϲ δαί|μοναϲ τοὺϲ ἐν τῷ τόπῳ τούτῳ ϲυνπαραϲτῆναι τῷ δαίμονι τούτῳ Ἀντινόῳ.

The word δαίμων covered so broad a spectrum of meaning that Aeschylus (*Pers.* 620) could use it for "spirit of the dead" (i.e., of Darius) and, a few lines later (628), "gods" (Ge, Hermes). The former, which is the sense in our text, appears as early as Hesiod *Op.* 122 (cf. West *ad loc.*) and is especially frequent in Lucian; e.g., *Philops.* 17, 29; *Peregr.* 27, etc. (in general, see Foerster in *TDNT* II 6ff. and Andres in *RE* Supp. III 275ff.; for δαίμων meaning "god" see below pp. 47f.). The more specific νεκυδαίμων is late and apparently confined to magic (Preisendanz in *RE* XVI 2240f. s.v. *nekydaimon*). Two points are especially important both for what follows and what has preceded. First, Greek thought distinguished between the spirits of the blessed and wretched dead, describing the former as μάκαρεϲ, μακάριται, etc. (e.g., of Alcestis, αὕτα ποτὲ προὔθαν' ἀνδρόϲ, νῦν δ' ἐϲτὶ μάκαιρα δαίμων, Eur. *Alc.* 1002f.; cf. Aesch. *Pers.* 633; Xen. *Ages.* 11.8; Theoc. 2.70 with K.J. Dover's n. [*Theocritus*, Basingstoke and London 1971, p. 105]; see Rohde, *Psyche* I p. 308 n. 1 [Eng. p. 246 n. 10]). Such stand in contrast to the ἄταφοι, βιοθάνατοι, and in our text ἄωροι, "the premature dead" (see below pp. 48f.). Second, the δαίμονεϲ were viewed as the subjects and attendants of the great underworld gods (ὁ αὐτὸς δὲ τῷ Πλούτωνι ὁ θεός [*sc.* Cάραπις], καὶ διὰ τοῦτο μάλιστα δαιμόνων ἄρχων, Porphyry, *De philosophia ex oraculis haurienda* II p. 147c Wolff), esp. Hekate (Ἑκάτην --- ψυχαῖς νεκύων μέτα βακχεύουσαν, *Orph. h.* 1.1f. Quandt; Ἑκάτη --- φάσματ' ἔχουσα --- σε καλῶ σὺν ἀποφθιμένοισιν ἀώροις, *PGM* IV 2727ff.; cf. Porphyry, *op. cit.* p. 150b Wolff). Thus our spell, having first addressed the gods, proceeds to the lower rung of the chthonic hierarchy (cf. *PGM* IV 1443ff.; Aud. 22.35ff.; *et al.*). One should also note that while it is the underworld deities who are first invoked, it is the *nekydaimon*, assisted by the *daimones*, who accomplishes the spell. We see here reflected the principle stated by Plato (*Symp.* 202e), and further developed in Stoic and later Platonic theology, that the *daimones* as minor divinities function as mediators between the gods and men (see Foerster in *TDNT* II 3ff.).

4 **καὶ δαίμοσι χθονίοις θεοῖς ἀώροις τε καὶ ἀώραις**: thus also P (exc. καταχθονίοις) and L. The other readings may reflect theological difficulties posed by θεοῖς (see below), which C and W_2 omit. Wortmann (p. 69) proposes the following emendations for his tablets: κ[αὶ τοῖς] κ[α]ταχθονίοις θεοῖς τε καὶ ⟨δαίμοσι⟩, ἀώροις ⟨τε καὶ ἀώραις⟩ (W_1 11f.); καὶ δαίμοσι καταχθονίοις νεκροῖς, ⟨ἀώραις⟩ τε καὶ ἀώροις (W_2 8f.). With respect to the former, however, I choose to read with Koenen κα[ὶ δέμ]ọς[ι κα]ταχθονίοις θεοῖς ⟨ἀώροις⟩ τε καὶ ἀώρ⟨α⟩ις.

δαίμοσι χθονίοις is normal word order for such anarthrous phrases (BDR § 474.1, see nn. to this section and Schwyzer 2.181 for exceptions); similarly, δαίμων καταχθόνιε (*PGM* I 253).* In apposition to these words are θεοῖς ἀώροις τε καὶ ἀώραις, "gods and goddesses who suffered a premature death" (for the polarism, see below p. 53). It seems inconsistent that our spell (with P, L, and perhaps W_1) clearly distinguishes between the great chthonic gods and the lesser δαίμονες χθόνιοι, but yet designates the latter also as θεοί (thus Preisendanz's acceptance of Weinreich's emendation of P: θεοῖς καὶ δαίμοσι καταχθονίοις, ἀώροις τε καὶ ἀώραις; cf. A.D. Nock, *JEA* 15 [1929] 233 and n. 3 [in an excursus not in *Essays*]; Kambitsis p. 220). Two points, however, must be considered. First, there is a long history of interchangeability between θεός and δαίμων; e.g., δαίμων is equivalent to θεός in Homer (*Il.* I 222; VI 115; XXIII 595; *Od.* III 166 [Zeus]), *h. Hom.* IV 343 (Hermes), Aesch. *Pers.* 628 (χθόνιοι δαίμονες, i.e., the great underworld gods), Theoc. 2.28 (Hekate), esp. in the *Orphic hymns* (Quandt Πρὸς Μουσαῖον 12; 17.8; 32.13; 34.5; further examples in Hopfner, OZ I § 166). In general, see A.D. Nock, *HTR* 23 (1930) 260ff. with n. 39 (*Essays* I 260f. with n. 39); Hopfner, OZ I §§ 11-12. Second, in various strands of religious thought the spirits of the blessed dead acquire divine status and constitute a secondary class of deities; cf. Lat. *Di Manes* (Steuding in Roscher II 2. 2316f.); Egyptian *3ḫw* (Griffiths, *Is. et Os.* p. 383f.; A. Erman, H. Grapow, *Wörterbuch der äg. Sprache* I 15f.).

The real difficulty is that the *daimones* which are here called gods are not those of the blessed dead (see above p. 46) but of the ἄωροι, "the premature dead," i.e., those who die before fulfilling their allotted fate. The qualification of the ἄωροι in our text with μέλλαξί τε καὶ παρθένοις, "boys and maidens," emphasizes that the group especially included those who die unmarried and/or without children, a fact which we already know from ancient grave inscriptions (e.g., κλαύσατ' ἄωρον ἐμὴν ἡλικίαν ἄγαμον, *SB* III 6706.16; παρθένος ἄωρος, *SB* I 2028; ἄορε ἄτεκνε, *SB* I 2642, III 6170 and 6231, IV 7296; cf. the curse formulae in Hom. *Il.* III 40 and *Od.* XVII 476). With this concept of the ἄωροι as a special chthonic class, cf. the more general topos, common to both literature and epitaphs, of early death as especially pathetic (e.g., Soph. *Ant.* 810-16; further material in Lattimore, *Epitaphs* 184-99, §§ 48-52).

Like the unburied (ἄταφοι) and those who die violently (βίαιοι/βιοθάνατοι), the ἄωροι cannot enter Hades, but must remain in a state of restless waiting and wandering until their destined time is fulfilled, a fact which makes them especially valuable for the purposes of magic, because of both their availability and hostility (Rohde, *Psyche* II 411ff., 424f. [Eng. 593ff., 603f.]; J.H. Waszink, *Tertulliani de anima* [Amsterdam 1947] pp. 564-86, on *de An.* chh. 56-57 [and cf. A.D. Nock's review in *Vigiliae Christianae* 4, 1950, 129ff. = *Essays* II 712ff.]; *idem*, *RAC* II 391ff. s.v. *Biothanati*; Norden, *Aen. VI* pp. 10-16, 41-43; R.W. Daniel, *ZPE* 19 [1975] 255f. and cited lit.). These categories of wretched spirits are sometimes grouped together, as in Aud. 29.19f.: ὁρκίζω ὑμᾶς, δέμονας πολυάνδριοι κὲ βιοθάνατοι κὲ ἄωροι κὲ ἄποροι τάφης (cf. 22.30f.; 25.4f.; 26.20f.; *et al.*). Lucan merges the concepts of untimely and violent death in a description of one of Erichtho's rites: *viventis animas et adhuc sua membra regentis / infodit busto, fatis debentibus annos / mors invita subit* (VI 529ff.). In Verg.

Aen. IV 620, Dido prays upon Aeneas the fate of both ἄωρος and ἄταφος: *sed cadat ante diem mediaque inhumatus harena.*

The problem of calling these unglorified souls θεοί becomes all the more acute when we take into account the widely accepted Egyptian idea that the spirits of the blessed dead (i.e., those who died having fulfilled their fates) become underworld deities by becoming Osiris. This transformation is sometimes described as occurring when the dead partake of Osiris through drinking water, which represents the Nile (S. Morenz, *Eranos Jahrbuch* 34 [1965] 420f., 428f. [=*RG* 197f., 206f.]; *idem*, *Staatliche Museen zu Berlin, Forschungen und Berichte* 1 [1957] 52ff. [=*RG* 231ff.]; *idem* in *Religions en Égypte hellénistique et romaine* [Colloque de Strasbourg 1967, Paris 1969, 75ff. = *RG* 248ff.]; Bonner 115 and n. 47; Wortmann 94f.; on Osiris as water, see *PGM* XII 234; Hopfner, OZ I §§ 455, 461 [p. 251]). Since the ἄωροι, the spirits which are invoked in our text, are not among the blessed dead, they have not yet become Osiris and so technically have not yet become gods (Wortmann 95; cf. P. J. Sijpesteijn's comment on πανάτιμος [*ZPE* 4, 1969, 190f.], which in the text under discussion seems to mean a spirit "without any honor," i.e., one which has not been glorified and become Osiris). Our spell, however, does not begrudge them the privilege of being called θεοί in anticipation of their future status, perhaps as a further means of persuading them to fulfill the wishes of Ailourion.

4-5 ἐνιαυτοὺς ἐξ ἐνιαυτῶν --- ὡρῶν: om. W_2; νύκτας ἐκ νυκτῶν om. P; L reverses the order of the last two phrases. C and W_1 have the same five elements as M in the same order, but spelling varies widely (see also textual appendix below pp. 114f.); e.g., M has ἐξ instead of ἐκ before μηνῶν and νυκτῶν (cf. ἐξ μέςῃ in *SB* I 4284.18; ἐξ ṿọṭου *P. Oxy.* XIV 1631.26; Gignac I 172f.); C has the common assimilated spelling ἐγ before νυκτῶν (Threatte 583f.; Mayser/Schmoll I 1.200; Gignac I 174); for W_1's ἐξξ, cf. Threatte 555 with n. 1; Gignac I 162. In M, P, and C the first noun of each pair is accusative. W_1 and L have an odd mixture of datives and accusatives; both cases expressed "extent of time" in *koine* (BDR § 201). On the late -ες accusatives in both tablets, cf. Gignac II 46f.

Such phrases are elsewhere singular; e.g., ἡμέραν ἐξ ἡμέρας (Eur. *Rhes.* 445; Henioch 5.13 Kassel-Austin [*PCG* V]); NT 2Pet. 2.8; LXX Gen. 39.10, Ps. 60.9, 95.2, Is. 58.2, *al.*); ἐνιαυτὸν ἐξ ἐνιαυτοῦ (LXX Lev. 25.53; Deut. 15.

20); μῆνα ἐκ μηνός (LXX Paralip. I 27.1; Num. 28.14); in series: μῆνα ἐκ μηνὸς καὶ σάββατον ἐκ σαββάτου (LXX Is. 66.23); ἡμέραν ἐξ ἡμέρας καὶ μῆνα ἐκ μηνός (LXX Est. 3.7); see M. Johannessohn, *Der Gebrauch der Präpositionen in der Septuaginta* (Berlin 1925) 289f.; Bauer s.v. ἡμέρα 2; and esp. W. Headlam's commentary on Herodas 5.85 (Cambridge 1922, pp. 268ff.). There seems to be a flexibility in Greek between singular and plural in certain time idioms, esp. with respect to νύξ; cf. ἐκ νυκτός (Xen. *Cyr.* I 4.2) and ἐκ νυκτῶν (Eur. *Rhes.* 13, 17) "after nightfall" (R. Renehan, *Greek Lexicographical Notes* [*Hypomnemata* 45, 1975] s.v. νύξ; W. Havers in *Festschrift für Paul Kretschmer* [Wien 1926] 49f.). With the datives in L and W_1, cf. ὥραις ἐξ ὡρᾶν νόμον ἀεὶ τόνδε σέβοντας, "always revering this law for all time" (i.e., time after time), Isyllos 25 (ed. I.U. Powell, *Collectanea Alexandrina*, p. 133); on the grounds of this text, Wilamowitz emends ὥρας ἐξ ὥρας in Plutarch *Lycurg.* 6.2 to ὥραις ἐξ ὡρᾶν (*Isyllos von Epidauros* [Philologische Untersuchungen 9, 1885] 11).

In M the phrases modify παρατίθημι, "I deposit with you ... year after year, etc."; i.e., the effect of the deposition, Kopria's love, should last for all time. Although I find no examples of this wording in other magical texts besides M and parallels, the thought is common: ποίησον αὐτὸν τὸν 'Αμώνειον --- ⟨φιλεῖν⟩ αὐτὸν Σεραπιακόν --- πᾶσαν ὥραν καὶ πᾶσαν ἡμέραν καὶ πᾶσαν νύκτα (*PGM* XXXIIa 16ff.); μὴ ἐάσῃς αὐτὸν λαλήσεν (i.e., -σαι) αὐτῷ μήτε νύκταν (sic!) μήτε ἡμέραν μήτε μίαν ὥραν (*PGM* O 1.9ff.). Cf. also below p. 67 on ἀπὸ τῆς --- χρόνον line 13f.

5-6 ἐξορκίζω σε πάντας τοὺς δαίμονας: om. W_2; ὁρκίζω *cett.* Only our text has σε, resulting in a confusing progression from plu. (δαίμοσι line 4) to sing. (σε) to plu. (δαίμονας). In each instance where strange shifts in number occur in magical texts, we must discern whether they arise from mere carelessness in the use of common formulae or from other causes, such as religious orientation. M displays the former tendency, as is evident by way of comparison with Youtie-Bonner, "Beisan" obv. frag. 1.19f.: ὁρκίζω σε (mw) κύριοι ἄνγελοι φιμώσ[ατε] κὲ ὑπατάξατε κτλ.; cf. also ἀνάστηθι, δαίμων καταχθόνιε, (mw), ὃ ἐὰν ἐπιτάξω ὑμῖν ἐγὼ ὁ δεῖνα, ὅπως ἐπήκοοί μοι γένησθε, *PGM* I 253ff.; ταχέω[ς] ἄξον (mw + Greek formulae) ἄξατε κτλ., P. Köln inv. no. 5512.10ff. (ed. R.W. Daniel, *ZPE* 19 [1975] 258). In these texts the circumstances are different: the initial adjuration/invocation of the *daimon* in the singular is followed by *nomina barbara* and/or *voces magicae* so that by the time he is addressed again, the one has become the many through the multiplying of magical names (cf. *PGM Eng.* p. 44 n. 65 on *PGM* IV 294). In such cases, carelessness may have caused the shift, but it is more likely that we are dealing with syncretistic ideas of a multiplicity of gods viewed as a single deity and *vice versa* (cf. Youtie/Bonner, "Beisan" 59f./625f.; Daniel, *op. cit.* 264; *idem, ZPE* 50 [1983] 153f.). Closer to the situation of M is Aud. 38. 4, where ὁρκίζω cε is applied to several gods for no apparent reason other than negligence.

6 cυνπαραcταθῆναι: thus also P 346, W_1 15f., W_2 10f.; cυνπαραcτῆναι L 6; cυνπαράcτατε (= -cτητε?) C 6. The verb is used elsewhere of divine aid; cf. ἅπαντι δαίμων ἀνδρὶ cυμπαρίcταται εὐθὺc γενομένῳ (Men. fr. 714 K.); τὸν --- cυμπαραcτάντα αὐτῷ μέγιcτον θεόν (Dittenberger, *OGIS* I 194. 18f.; cf. Lampe s.v.).

τῷ νεκυδαίμονι: only M; τῷ δαίμονι τούτῳ *cett.*; both refer to the specific ghost by whose grave the operator places the tablet and whom all the other spirits in the same cemetery (πάνταc τοὺc δαίμοναc τοὺc ἐν τῷ τόπῳ τούτῳ) are commanded to assist in drawing his beloved to him. On the word νεκυδαίμων, see above p. 46.

6-10: First Command to the νεκυδαίμων

M 6 ⟨ἔγειρέ μοι cεαυτόν, νεκυδαίμων,⟩ ὅcτιc ποτὲ εἶ εἴτε ἄρcην εἴτε θήλεια, καὶ ὕπαγε ειc πᾶν τόπον, | ειc πᾶν ἄμφοδον, ειc πᾶcαν οἰκίαν, καὶ κατάδηcον Κοπρίαν, ἣν ἔτεκε μήτηρ Ταῆcιc, ἧc ἔχειc τὰc τρίχαc τῆc κεφαλῆc, Αἰλουρίωνι, |8 ᾧ ἔτεκε μήτηρ ὀνόματι Κοπρία, ὅπωc μὴ βινηθῇ μηδὲ πυγιcθῇ μήτε ἡδονὴν ποιήcῃ ἑτέρῳ νεανίcκῳ ἢ ἄλλῳ ἀνδρὶ | εἰ μὴ μόνῳ Αἰλουρίωνι, ᾧ ἔτεκε μήτηρ ὀνόματι Κοπρία, ἀλλὰ μηδὲ δυνηθῇ μήτε φαγεῖν μήτε πιεῖν μήτε ὕπνου τυχεῖν διὰ παν|τὸc μήτε εὐcταθεῖν ἢ ἡcυχάζειν τῇ ψυχῇ ἢ ταῖc φρεcὶ ἐπιζητοῦcα Αἰλουρίωνα, ὃν ἔτεκε μήτηρ Κοπρία·

P 347 καὶ ἀνέγειρέ μοι cαυτόν, ὅcτιc ποτ' εἶ |348 εἴτε ἄρρην εἴτε θῆλυc, καὶ ὕπαγε ειc πάντα τόπον | καὶ ειc πᾶν ἄμφοδον καὶ ειc πᾶcαν οἰκίαν καὶ ἄξον | καὶ κατάδηcον· ἄξον τὴν δεῖνα· ἣν ⟨ἔτεκεν ἡ⟩ δεῖνα, ἧc ἔχειc τὴν οὐ|cίαν, φιλοῦcάν με τὸν δεῖνα, ὃν ἔτεκεν ἡ δεῖνα· μὴ βινη|[352]θήτω, μὴ πυγισθήτω μηδὲ πρὸς ἡδονὴν ποιή|[σ]ῃ μετ' ἄλλου ἀνδρός, εἰ μὴ μετ' ἐμοῦ μόνου, τοῦ δεῖνα· | ἵνα μὴ δυνηθῇ ἡ δεῖνα μήτε πεῖν μήτε φαγεῖν, μὴ | στέργειν, μὴ καρτερεῖν, μὴ εὐσταθῆσαι, μὴ ὕπνου |[356] [τ]υχεῖν ἡ δεῖνα ἐκτὸς ἐμοῦ, τοῦ δεῖνα·

C [6] διέγι|ρέ μοι σεαυτόν, νέκυς δαίμων, ὅστις ποτὲ εἶ, εἴτε ἄρσης εἴτε θήλια, καὶ ὕπαγε {ισ}ἰς πάντα τόπον καὶ |[8] εἰς πᾶν ἄμφοδον καὶ εἰς πᾶσαν οἰκίαν καὶ κατάδησον Ἡρωνοῦν, ἣν ἔτεκεν Πτολεμαΐς, ἐμοὶ Ποσι|δωνίῳ, ὃν ἔτεκεν Θσενουβάσθις, ὅπως μὴ βεινηθῇ, μὴ πυγισθῇ, μὴ λεικάσῃ, μηδὲν πρὸς | ἡδονὴν ποιήσῃ ἄλλῳ ἀνδρὶ εἰ μὴ ἐμοὶ μόνῳ Ποσιδωνίῳ, ἵνα μὴ δύνηται Ἡρωνοῦς μὴ | φαγεῖν, μὴ πεῖν, μὴ στέργειν, μὴ καρτερεῖν, μὴ εὐσταθεῖν, μὴ ὕπνου τυγχάνειν ἐκτὸς ἐμοῦ |[12] Ποσιδωνίου·

W₁ [16] ἔγειρέ μοι σεαυτὸν | [ἀπὸ τ]ῆ[ς] ἐχούσης σε ἀναπαύσεως καὶ ὕπαγε εἰς πᾶν | [τό]πον καὶ εἰς πᾶν ἄμφοδον ⟦ε̣⟧ καὶ εἰς πᾶσαν οἰκίαν | [καὶ π]ᾶν καπηλῖον καὶ ἄξον, κατάδησον Ματρῶναν, |[20] [ἣν ἔτ]εκεν Ταγένη{ς}, ἧς ἔχις τὴν ουσίας (i.e., -αν)—ἑ τρίχες τῆς | [κεφ]α̣λῆς αὐτῆς—ταύτην, ὅπως μὴ βινηθῇ, μὴ πυγισθῇ, μη | [λαι]κάσ̣ῃ̣ μ̣ή̣τ̣ε̣ ἀφρο⟨δι⟩σιακὸν ἐπιτελέσῃ μεθ' ἑτέρου, μὴ | [ἄλ]λῳ ἀντρὶ συνέλθις (i.e., -θῃ) εἰ μὴ Θεοδώρῳ, ὃν ἔτεκεν Τεχῶσις, |[24] [ἀλλ]ὰ μ̣ὴ̣ [δυ]ν̣ηθήτω πώποτε Ματρῶνα χωρὶς Θεοδώρο`υ´ | [μὴ καρτε]ρῖν, μὴ εὐσταθῖν, μηδὲ ὕπνου τυχεῖς (i.e., -εῖν) νυκτὸς | [ἢ ἡμέρας Ματ]ρῶνα, ἣν ἔτεκεν Ταγένη, οὗ ἰσιν ἑ τρίχες | [τῆς κεφαλῆς] αὐτῆς, χωρὶς Θεοδώρου, ὃν ἔτεκε Τεχῶσις·

W₂ [12] ὅστις ποτὲ εἶ, `Κ̣αμ̣ῆ⟦ ̣ ⟧ς´ νεκυδαίμων, ἔγει|ρέ μοι σεαυτὸν ἀπὸ τῆς ἐχούσης | σε ἀναπαύσεως. --- |[17] οἴπαγε εἰς ⟦ου⟧ πᾶν τόπον καὶ εἰς `π´ᾶν | ἄμφοδον καὶ εἰς πᾶσαν οἰκίαν | καὶ εἰς πᾶν καπηλῖον καὶ κατά|[20]δησον Ματρῶναν, ἣν ἔτεκεν | Ταγένη, ἧς ἔχις τὰς τρίχες τῆς κεφα|λῆς αὐτῆς, ἐπὶ φιλίᾳ Θεοδώρου, | ὃν ἔτεκεν Τεχῶσις. ποίησον τὴν |[24] Ματρῶναν ὑποταγῆναι Θεοδώρῳ, | μὴ δ̣αμῇ ἐκτὸς Θεοδώρω μη{δεν}|δὲ ὕπνου τυγχάνῃ Ματρῶνα | νυκτὸς καὶ ἡμέραις, ἕως ἔλθῃ |[28] Ματρῶνα πάσῃ ὥρᾳ πρὸς Θε|όδωρον φιλοῦσα αὐτόν.[2]

---

[2] For the interruption of the first command in lines 14-16 cf. above p. 18. For μὴ δ̣αμῇ, 25f. see ZPE 83 (1990) 235-36.*

L [6] διέργειραί μοι cε|αυτὸν καὶ ὕπαγε εἰc πᾶν τόπον, εἰc πᾶν ἄμφοδον, εἰc πᾶcαν οἰκείαν καὶ κατάδηcον Πτολε|[8]μαΐδα, ἣν ἔτεκεν Ἀϊᾶc, τὴν θυγατέρα Ὡριγένουc, ὅπωc μὴ βινηθῇ, μὴ πυγιcθῇ, μη|δὲν πρὸc ἡδονὴν ποιήcῃ ἑταίρῳ ἀνδρὶ εἰ μὴ ἐμοὶ μόνῳ τῷ Cαραπάμμωνι, ὃν ἔτε|κεν Ἀρέα, καὶ μὴ ἀφῇc αὐτὴν φαγεῖν, μὴ πεῖν, μὴ cτέγειν μήτε ἐξελθεῖν μήτε | ὕπνου τυχεῖν ἐκτὸc ἐμοῦ τοῦ Cαραπάμμωνοc, οὗ ἔτεκεν Ἀρέα.*

For the repetition of much of this material in the second command, see below pp. 85f. The entire passage, as well as the preceding (lines 4-6; cf. above pp. 45ff.), achieves intensity through various stylistic devices, esp. polar expression (i.e., the exhaustion of a concept by the juxtaposition of two contrasting words or ideas, such as male/female, young/old, day/night, etc.; cf. esp. E. Kemmer, *Die polare Ausdrucksweise in der griechischen Literatur* [Beiträge zur historischen Syntax der griechischen Sprache 15, ed. M. Schanz] Würzburg 1903; also KG 2. 587f. [Anm. 2]; J.B. Hofmann, *Glotta* 15 [1927] 45ff.; H. Zilliacus, *Zur Abundanz der spätgriechischen Gebrauchssprache* [Commentationes Humanarum Litterarum 41.2, 1968] pp. 32ff.; G.E.R. Lloyd, *Polarity and Analogy* [Cambridge 1966] 90ff.; M.L. West, *Hesiod Works and Days* [Oxford 1978] p. 197 [on line 175]). E.g., θεοῖc ἀώροιc τε καὶ ἀώραιc (line 4; cf. ὀμνύω ὑμῖν θεοὺc πάνταc καὶ πάcαc, Xen. *An.* VI 1.31; εὔχεcθε τοῖc θεοῖcι τοῖc Ὀλυμπίοιc καὶ ταῖc Ὀλυμπίαιcι, Ar. *Thes.* 331f.; see also Kemmer, *op. cit.* p. 146; Höfer in Roscher III 1.1551ff. s.v. *pantes theoi*); μέλλαξί τε καὶ παρθένοιc (4; cf. κόρῳ καὶ κόρῃ, Plato *Legg.* 785a); εἴτε ἄρcηc εἴτε θήλεια (6; cf. περὶ τελευτήcανταc δή, εἴτε τιc ἄρρην εἴτε τιc θῆλυc ᾖ, *ibid.* 958d and cf. below pp. 54f.); ἡμέραc ἐξ ἡμερῶν, νύκταc ἐξ νυκτῶν (5, cf. νύκτεc τε καὶ ἤματα, Hom. *Od.* XI 183; νύκτεc ἡμέραι τε, Eur. *Iph. Aul.* 398); ὅπωc μὴ βινηθῇ μηδὲ πυγιcθῇ (8); μήτε φαγεῖν μήτε πιεῖν (9; for polarism with various verbs, see Kemmer, *op. cit.* 209ff.). It is not surprising that many of the above parallels occur either in legal or religious contexts, since there were similar tendencies in both toward meticulousness and emphasis, as also in magic (cf. below. p. 56 on Κοπρίαν --- Ταῆcιc; Zilliacus, *op. cit.* p. 33).

6-7 ὅcτιc --- Κοπρίαν: Although this section makes sense as it stands (καὶ ὕπαγε --- καὶ κατάδηcον), the parallels, esp. C 6f., make probable the following haplography: --- νεκυδαίμονι. ⟨ἔγειρέ μοι cεαυτὸν νεκυδαίμων⟩

ὅστις ποτὲ εἶ κτλ. (cf. νεκυδαίμων ὅστις in line 20 and parallel sections of C and W_1 [below pp. 83f.]).

6 ὅστις ποτὲ εἶ εἴτε ἄρσην εἴτε θήλεια: addressed to the *nekydaimon*, the identity of its corpse being unknown (as in P 347f., C 7; om. W_1). In L 6 (above p. 46) the name of the dead (Ἀντίνοος) is known and applied to his spirit (see Kambitsis 216f.; Rohde *Psyche* II 425 [Eng. 604]). According to Daniel - Maltomini, in W_2 12 the scribe added the name Καμῆ⟦ν̣⟧ς after ὅστις ποτὲ εἶ (*Suppl. Mag.* p. 209). Similar phrases occur in Greek and Latin prayers when the petitioner, wishing to avoid calling the gods by inappropriate names, resorts to generalities and to mentioning several options. In general, cf. ὦ γῆς ὄχημα κἀπὶ γῆς ἔχων ἕδραν | ὅστις ποτ' εἶ σύ, δυστόπαστος εἰδέναι | Ζεύς, εἴτ' ἀνάγκη φύσεος εἴτε νοῦς βροτῶν | προσηυξάμην σε, Eur. *Tro.* 884ff.; *in Capitolio fuit clipeus consecratus, cui inscriptum erat "genio urbis Romae, sive mas sive femina." et pontifices ita precabantur: "Iuppiter optime maxime, sive quo alio nomine te appellari volueris"; nam et ipse* (Verg. *Aen.* IV 576) *ait: "sequimur te, sancte deorum, quisquis es."* Servius *ad Aen.* II 351 (Thilo-Hagen I 277; Harvard II 416); cf. esp. Lucius' prayer to Isis (Apul. *Met.* XI 2 on which see Griffiths, cited below p. 55): *regina caeli, sive tu Ceres --- seu tu caelestis Venus --- seu Phoebi soror --- seu --- Proserpina --- quoquo nomine, quoquo ritu, quaqua facie te fas est invocare: tu meis iam nunc extremis aerumnis subsiste*; with the last text cf. Anchises' greeting of Aphrodite in *h. Hom.* V 92ff.

More specifically, for ὅστις ποτ' (οὖν) εἶ (and related phrases), usually applied to *daimones* in magical texts, cf. *PGM* IV 1240, 1244; V 334f.; Aud. 234.1; 235.1; 237-240 (first line); 242.1; 249a col. 1, 1; first line of most of Aud.'s Cyprus tablets (22, 25-26, 28-35); applied to gods: Hom. *Od.* V 445; Aesch. *Ag.* 160 (with E. Fraenkel's commentary *ad loc.* [vol. II pp. 99f.]); Plato *Cra.* 400e (further Platonic parallels in J. Burnet's commentary on *Phaedo* [Oxford 1911], p. 111 [n. on 100d 6]); Catul. 34.21f.; Livy I 2.6; Ovid *Met.* I 32. εἴτε --- εἴτε, similarly, of *daimones* in magic: ὁρκίζω σε πᾶν πνεῦμα δαιμόνιον --- εἴτε ἐπίγειον εἴτε ὑπόγειον ἢ καταχθόνιον (*PGM* IV 3037ff.); βιοθάνατοι εἴτε ξένοι ἴτε ἐντόπιοι ἴ[τε ἄωροι ἴτε ἄποροι τάφης] (Aud. 25.4-6); applied to gods: A.R. IV 1411ff., 1597ff.; Hor. *Carm. Saec.* 15f.; hymn to Attis, 44.2.1f. Wolbergs: εἴτε Κρόνου γένος εἴτε Διὸς μάκαρ | εἴτε Ῥέας μεγάλας, χαῖρε. For distinguishing male and female, cf. πᾶν ἀκάθαρτον πνεῦμα ἄρσεν καὶ θῆλυ in the amulet of Cod. Paris. 1316, 318^{v} ss. (R. Reitzenstein, *Poim.* 298); Aud. 198.4-5; 25.2 (cf. also above p. 53 on polar expression).

For other examples, interpretations, and literature on such predications as the above, see esp. Norden, *Ag. Th.* 144-47; Griffiths, *Isis Book* 119ff. (on Apul. *Met.* XI 2 cited above); see also Kagarow 41; Kopp III § 114 (pp. 120ff.); H. Usener, *Götternamen* (Frankfurt/Main 1948) 336 with n. 11; C. Ausfeld, *De Graecorum precationibus quaestiones* in *Jahrbücher für classische Philologie*, Supp. 28 (1903) 517f.; H.S. Versnell in *Faith, Hope, and Worship* (ed. Versnell), Leiden 1981, 14-16.

ἄρcην: tab. ἄρcηc, as also in C; ἄρρην P; cf. ἄρρηc M 20 and P 361, 370. For ἄρcηc cf. also *P. Oxy.* III 465.147; Jeremiah 30.6 Symmachus (see *Origenis Hexapla*, ed. F. Field [Oxford 1895] II p. 653 with n. 12; cf. also J.F. Schleusner, *Novus Thesaurus Philologico-criticus* [Glasgow^{2} 1822], s.v. ἄρcηc). The final -c spellings of both stems may reflect an interchange of final -c and -ν, which tended to be silent letters (Gignac I 131f.; e.g., in W_1 οὐcίαc for ουcίαν 20; τυχείc for τυχεῖν 25; examples also in 23, 54, and 70).

6f. ὕπαγε εἰc πᾶν τόπον --- κατάδηcον Κοπρίαν: identical to L 7, where also the phrases are asyndetic. C 7f. differs only in the addition of καί's (καί's also in W_1 17f., W_2 17ff., P 348ff.; for πᾶν/πάντα τόπον, see next note). W_1 and W_2 add εἰc πᾶν καπηλῖον to the sequence (see above p. 7). ἄξον (καὶ) precedes κατάδηcον in P 349f. and W_1 19. These two words are joined elsewhere (e.g., P 395; *PGM* XXXII 14; ἄξαι καὶ καταδῆcαι *ibid.* 4f.); see also in our text § K 33, where ἄξον replaces κατάδηcον in a reiteration of these formulae.

For the thought cf. ἔγειρε cεαυτήν, Ζμύρνα, καὶ ὕπαγε εἰc πᾶν τόπον καὶ ἐκζήτηcον τὴν δεῖνα καὶ ἄνοιγον αὐτῆc τὴν δεξιὰν πλευρὰν καὶ εἴcελθε ὡc βροντή --- ἕωc --- ἔλθῃ πρὸc ἐμέ (*PGM* XXXVI 353ff.). The structure of these "binding" spells closely resembles that of certain "loosing" spells, the difference being a heavenly rather than an earthly sphere of operation in the latter: χώρει, κύριε, εἰc τὸν ἴδιον κόcμον καὶ εἰc τοὺc ἰδίουc θρόνουc, εἰc τὰc ἰδίαc ἀψῖδαc καὶ διατήρηcόν με καὶ τὸν παῖδα τοῦτον ἀπημάντουc (*PGM* V 41ff.); cf. II 181f.; IV 920ff., 3122f.; see also J.H. Niggemeyer, *Beschwörungsformeln aus dem "Buch der Geheimnisse"* (Judaistische Texte und Studien III [New York 1975]) 97f.

πᾶν τόπον: thus W_1 17f., W_2 17, L 7; πάντα P 348, C 7. For πᾶν as the accusative sing masc./fem., see Gignac II 134 with n. 2; Mayser I 2.32; in the LXX πᾶν πόνον (Paralip. II 6.28); πᾶν λόγον (*ibid.* 19.11); see R. Helbing, *Grammatik der Septuaginta* (Göttingen 1907) 51.

ἄμφοδον: "Street" is the more restricted sense; more often, "quarter," "ward," "block of houses surrounded by streets." See C.D. Buck, S.J. Case, *Classical Philology* 17 (1922) 116 n. 1; s.v. in Bauer; Preisigke, *Wörterbuch* III Abs. 22; *idem*, *Fachwörter*. Thus, the three phrases represent a narrowing circumference ("place --- block --- house") as the *nekydaimon* "closes in" on Kopria. For a similar rhetorical effect, cf. Cicero's triad *Italia* --- *urbes* --- *tecta* (*In Cat.* I 11.29).

7 Κοπρίαν ἣν ἔτεκε μήτηρ Ταῆϲιϲ: Only M has μήτηρ. Cf. P 315f. (*praxis*; above p. 9), where the instructions specify to write on the effigy τὸ ὄνομα τῆϲ ἀγομένηϲ μητρόθεν. Such is the common practice in Greco-Egyptian magic, probably because the mother was the indisputable parent (L 6, however, gives both parents' names [see Kambitsis *ad loc.* and F. Maltomini, *Aegyptus* 59, 1979, 282]). On τὸ μητρόθεν ὄνομα in general, cf. F. Maltomini, *loc. cit.*; D.R. Jordan, *Philologus* 120 (1976) 128ff., esp. 130 n. 8; R. Wünsch, *Antike Fluchtafeln*, p. 9 (on # 2, line 3). The practice is indicative of the meticulous, legalistic nature of ancient prayer language in general and of magic in particular. Spells, like contracts, had to be precise, in order to avoid both predictable and unpredictable misunderstandings between the parties involved (in our case, between Ailourion and the *nekydaimon*); cf. below p. 57 on ὅπωϲ μὴ --- μηδὲ etc. and R.W. Daniel, *ZPE* 50 (1983) 147 with n. 2.

ἧϲ ἔχειϲ τὰϲ τρίχαϲ τῆϲ κεφαλῆϲ: most similar to W_2 21f.: ἧϲ ἔχιϲ τὰϲ τρίχεϲ τῆϲ κεφαλῆϲ αὐτῆϲ; for P and W_1 see above p. 7; omm. C and L. The hair functions as the οὐϲία, the "element" or "property" of the beloved which allows the invoked spirits to identify her (in Eur. *Hipp.* 514 it is called ϲημεῖον, "token"). Cf. Lucian *D. Meretr.* 4.4f. (the different possibilities are enumerated, ἱμάτια ἢ κρηπῖδαϲ ἢ ὀλίγαϲ τῶν τριχῶν ἤ τι τῶν τοιούτων); Apul. *Met.* III 16 (hair); Theoc. 2.53 (clothing). See also above p. 9 n. 38; F. Maltomini on *P. Münch.* II 28, fr. 10; B. Kötting in *RAC* 13,179f. s.v. Haar; Wortmann 68-69 n. (c); Abt, *Apol.* 181f.; Hopfner, OZ I §§ 669-77; *idem, RE* XIV 332f. s.v. *mageia.*

8-9 ὅπως μὴ βινηθῇ μηδὲ πυγισθῇ μήτε ἡδονὴν ποιήσῃ --- Αἰλουρίωνι: For μήτε following μηδέ, see Denniston 510 and KG 2.289, who cite, among others, Pl. *Chrm.* 171c: οὐ δῆτα. οὐδέ γε ἄλλος οὐδεὶς --- οὔτε δὴ ὁ σώφρων. M's reading may be a simple case of the indiscriminate use of negatives which sometimes occurs in tablets (and in manuscripts); e.g., Aud. 234. 18ff. (curse on race horses): ἵνα μὴ δυνασθῶσιν --- μήτε τρέχειν μήτε περιπατεῖν μήτε νεικῆσαι μηδὲ ἐξελθεῖν τοὺς πυλῶνας τῶν ἱππαφίων μήτε προβαίνειν τὴν ἀρίαν μήτε τὸν σπάτιον μηδὲ κυκλεῦσαι τοὺς καμπτῆρας. Almost identical formulae occur several times in the family of tablets to which 234 belongs with varying patterns of negatives: μὴ - μηδὲ - μηδὲ - μηδὲ - μηδὲ - μήτε - μήτε (Aud. 237.12ff.); μὴ - μήτε - μήτε - μήτε - μηδὲ - μηδὲ - μηδὲ (240.10ff.); μή - μήτε (6 times) 236.9ff. Parallels: μὴ - μὴ - μηδὲ (P 351f.); μὴ - μὴ - μηδὲν (L 8f.); μὴ - μὴ - μὴ - μηδὲν (C 9f.); μὴ - μὴ - μὴ - μήτε - μὴ (W_1 21f.). W_1 is difficult, since the beginning of line 22 is damaged; I prefer Daniel-Maltomini's reading μὴ | [λαι]κάσῃ μήτε (21f.) to the readings of the earlier editors.* W_2 23f. replaces the entire section with ποίησον τὴν Ματρῶναν ὑποταγῆναι Θεοδώρῳ.

As in magic, we find also in legal and commercial writing a tendency to multiply prohibitions, so as to leave no doubt as to the situations covered by the language; e.g., receipts: καὶ μηθὲν [ἐγ]καλεῖν --- μηδ' ἐπελεύσεσ{ασ}θα[ι] Θερμούθ[ι]ον μηδ' ἄλλον ὑπὲρ αὐτῆς τῷ Δι[ο]σκοῦτι μηδὲ τοὺς παρ' αὐτοῦ μήτ(ε) περὶ τούτων μηδὲ περὶ μηδενὸς ἁπλῶς μέχρι τῆς ἐνεστώσης ἡμέρας, *P. Mich.* III 194.20ff. Cf. *P. Soter.* 7.18ff.; H.-A. Rupprecht, *Studien zur Quittung im Recht der graeco-ägyptischen Papyri* (Münch. Beitr. 57 [1971]) 16f. Our text is especially reminiscent of the style of marriage contracts, where the forbidden activities are specifically sexual: καὶ μὴ ἐξέστω Φιλίσκῳ γυναῖκα ἄλλην ἐπ[α]γ[α]γεσθαι ἀλλὰ 'Απολλωνίαν μηδὲ παλλακὴν μηδὲ π[αιδ]ικὸν ἔχειν μηδ[ὲ τεκνο]ποιεῖσθαι ἐξ ἄλλης γυναικὸς --- κατὰ τὰ αὐτὰ δὲ μηδὲ 'Απολλωνίᾳ ἐξέστω ἀπόκοιτον μη[δὲ] ἀφήμερον γίνεσθαι ἀπὸ τῆς Φιλίσκου οἰκίας --- μηδ' ἄλλῳ ἀνδρ[ὶ] συνεῖναι (*P. Tebt.* I 104.18-20, 27-29; cf. *BGU* IV 1100.20ff., 31ff.; *ibid.* 1051.18ff., 28ff.; *ibid.* 1098.31ff.; *P. Eleph.* 1.8f.; *P. Oxy.* III 497.3ff.). Conversely, in divorce agreements it is stated positively that the woman is now allowed συνοικεῖν ἑτέρῳ ἀνδρί (*P. Dur.* 31. 9ff.; *P. Mil. Vogl.* III 185.19f.; cf. E.M. Yamauchi, *Mandaic Incantation Texts*

[New Haven 1967] 64 for the relationship between Jewish legal divorce formulae and Mandaic spells).

8 ὅπως μὴ βινηθῇ μηδὲ πυγιϲθῇ: thus L (exc. μὴ inst. μηδὲ); om. W_2; μὴ βινηθήτω μὴ πυγιϲθήτω P; C and perhaps W_1 (see above p. 57) add to the sequence μὴ λαικάϲῃ (λεικάϲῃ C) (cf. lines 4f. of a Geneva lead tablet: μήτε βινηθῆναι μήτε πυγιϲθῆναι μήτε ληκάζειν [V. Martin, *Genava* 6, 1928, 56ff. = *Suppl. Mag.* I 38]). The forms of βινεῖν are spelled with the root βιν- in all the parallels except C, which has βεινηθῇ. In a paper presented at the 1983 APA Convention, Prof. J.F. Gannon concluded that βειν- is the original spelling, since it most satisfactorily explains βεν- of the early Attic graffitti (cf. Threatte 138) and predominates in the literary papyri (e.g., *P. Oxy.* I 11 col. i, 1 = Adesp. Com. fr. 254 Austin; *P. Oxy.* III 413 verso col. ii, 108 (Wiemken p. 82); *P. Oxy.* XVIII 2174 fr. 16 col. ii, 16 = Hippon. fr. 84 West [normalized to βιν-]; *al.*). βιν- gradually supplanted βειν- because of the common ι/ει interchange (Gignac I 189f.) and the association of the word with κινεῖν and perhaps also, by way of an ancient etymology (Schol. Ar. *Ran.* 740), with βίοϲ (see W. Süss, *Aristophanes Frösche mit Scholien* [Bonn 1911] = *Kleine Texte* 66, p. 51).

βινεῖν is passive when a woman is the subject (Henderson, *Muse* 152, § 207). I find the passive of the rare πυγίζειν only in our text (+ parallels) and in the above-cited Geneva tablet (cf. *pedicari* Mart. VI 56.6). For heterosexual anal intercourse, see K.J. Dover, *Greek Homosexuality* (London 1978) 99-101 and 188; J. Boardman, *Athenian Red Figure Vases. The Archaic Period* (London 1975) fig. 219.

μήτε ἡδονὴν ποιήϲῃ ἑτέρῳ νεανίϲκῳ ἢ ἄλλῳ ἀνδρί: a generalization to include any other possible sexual gratification not covered by the former two terms. ἡδονὴν ποιεῖν τινι, "cause someone pleasure" (*voluptate aliquem afficere*, Stephanus s.v. ἡδονή), occurs elsewhere in nonsexual contexts; e.g., μὴ τοῖϲ ἐχθροῖϲ ἡδονὴν ποιῶϲι, Demos. 19.298; cf. *ibid* 299; Aesch. *Supp.* 1008f. Similar to M are C 9f. and L 8f.: μηδὲν πρὸϲ ἡδονὴν ποιήϲῃ ἄλλῳ (ἑταίρῳ L) ἀνδρί, "May she do nothing for another man's pleasure." Cf. the idiom πρὸϲ ἡδονήν τι λέγειν, "to say something for (another's) pleasure," i.e., "flatter." (Thuc. II 65.8; Dittenberger, *Syll.* III [p. 396] 1268.19 [right] with n.). P 352f., however, may focus more on the woman's fulfillment: μηδὲ πρὸϲ ἡδονὴν ποιήϲῃ μετ' ἄλλου ἀνδρόϲ, "May she do nothing for pleasure with another man"; so also W_1 22: μήτε ἀφρο⟨δι⟩ϲιακὸν ἐπιτελέϲῃ μεθ' ἑτέρου (see P 404, above p. 12 and n. 53).

ἑτέρῳ νεανίϲκῳ ἢ ἄλλῳ ἀνδρί: first 3 wds. not in parallels (cf. preceding n.). No distinction between ἑτέρῳ and ἄλλῳ is intended here (Turner, *Syntax* 197; Mayser II 2.88f.; A.T. Robertson, *A Gram. of the Greek NT* [Nashville 1934] 746ff.); cf. line 22, where the order of the two is reversed.

9 ᾧ --- Κοπρία: see above p. 56 on line 7 Κοπρίαν --- Ταῆϲιϲ.

9-10 ἀλλὰ μηδὲ (tab. μήτε) **δυνηθῇ μήτε φαγεῖν --- φρεϲί:** In a continued series, ἀλλά is often progressive ("further," "again") rather than adversative, and as such is often followed by adverbial οὐδέ/μηδέ (thus, "and not even"; cf. Alcm. 1.71 Page; Lys. 10.10; esp. *P. Tebt.* I 27.38; Denniston 21f.; Mayser II 3.118 δ) but not to my knowledge by οὔτε/μήτε (for confusion between μήτε and μηδέ, see above p. 57).

The parallels vary with respect to beginning formula (ἵνα μὴ δυνηθῇ ἡ δεῖνα, P 354; ἵνα μὴ δύνηται Ἡρωνοῦϲ, C 10; [αλλ]ὰ μ[ὴ δυ]ν̣ηθήτω πώποτε, W_1 24; καὶ μὴ ἀφῇϲ αὐτήν, L 10; om. W_2), the arrangement of the subsequent negatives (μήτε - μήτε - μὴ - μὴ - μὴ - μὴ, P 354f.; μὴ 6 times, C 10f.; [μὴ] -μὴ - μηδὲ, W_1 25; μὴ - μηδὲ, W_2 25; μὴ - μὴ - μήτε - μήτε, L 10), and the things prohibited (P and C have the same six elements: φαγεῖν - πεῖν [π. φ. P] - ϲτέργειν - καρτερεῖν - εὐϲταθεῖν [εὐϲταθῆναι P] - ὕπνου τυχεῖν [τυγχάνειν C]; W_1 has only the last three, W_2 the last two [subjunctives rather than infinitives], both add νυκτὸϲ καὶ [or ἢ] ἡμέραϲ; L adds ἐξελθεῖν after ϲτέργειν and om. καρτερεῖν and εὐϲταθεῖν; M om. ϲτέργειν and καρτερεῖν and adds at the end of the sequence ἢ ἡϲυχάζειν τῇ ψυχῇ ἢ ταῖϲ φρεϲί). Only M and W_2 continue with some form of ἕωϲ κτλ., which usually follows formulae of this type (see below).

This set of prohibitions extends the demand of the former group (i.e., that Kopria have no other lover) to the point that she not even be able to enjoy basic health and necessities until she unite with Ailourion (ἕωϲ οὗ --- ἔλθῃ πρὸϲ Αἰλουρίωνα κτλ. below lines 10bf., p. 61). Cf. καὶ μὴ δυνηθῇ μήτε πιεῖν μήτε φαγεῖν ἄχρι οὗ ἔλθῃ πρὸϲ ἐμέ (*PGM* LXI 17f.); ἆξον ἐμοὶ τῷ δεῖνα τὴν δεῖνα --- πεινῶϲαν, διψῶϲαν, ὕπνου μὴ τυγχάνουϲαν, φιλοῦϲαν ἐμὲ

--- ἕωϲ ἂν ἔλθῃ (XXXVI 110ff.; similarly, *ibid.* 147ff., 356ff.; IV 1425ff., 1515ff., ἕωϲ κτλ. not until 1531; W_4 6f., 45ff. [cited below pp. 61f.]; P. Köln inv. no. 5514.8ff., ed. R.W. Daniel, *ZPE* 19 [1975] 251 with n. p. 254).

Wasting away through sleeplessness and not eating or drinking are all symptoms of love-sickness. Cf. esp. Longus *Daph. et Chl.* II 7.4, where Philetas relates his past suffering over his love for Amaryllis: οὔτε τροφῆϲ ἐμεμνήμην οὔτε ποτὸν προϲεφερόμην οὔτε ὕπνου ᾐρούμην; similarly elsewhere in the romances: *ibid.* II 8.2; Ach. Tat. I 5.3; 6.1-2; 9.1; Heliod. *Aeth.* IV 7.32-40 Colonna [IV 7.7 Rattenbury/Lumb]. Cf. also Eur. *Hipp.* 135ff.; Galen, *In Hipp. Progn. comment.* I 4.18 [Corpus Medicorum Graecorum V 9.2 p. 206f.]; *idem, Prog.* VI 2ff. [Corpus Medicorum Graecorum V 8.1 p. 100ff.]; for love-sickness in ancient and medieval medicine, cf. H. Crohns, *Archiv für Kulturgeschichte* 3 (1905) 66ff.; see also, with special reference to ancient humoural theory, P. Keyser, *Philologus* 133 (1989) 75ff.

Thus, as A.E. Hanson has suggested to me, the real intention of μήτε φαγεῖν μήτε πιεῖν κτλ. may be that the beloved be infected with this well-known malady. These formulae, however, have applications other than the erotic; e.g., NT Acts 23.12: οἱ Ἰουδαῖοι ἀνεθεμάτιϲαν ἑαυτοὺϲ λέγοντεϲ μήτε φαγεῖν μήτε πιεῖν ἕωϲ οὗ ἀποκτείνωϲιν τὸν Παῦλον. The self-cursing represented here is a variation on that commonly found in oaths, where one condemns oneself to some suffering *if* certain terms *are not* fulfilled (see W. Burkert, *Gk. Religion* [Cambridge, Mass. 1985] 251f.). In the Biblical text, the Jews condemn themselves to abstinence from food and drink *until* certain terms *are* fulfilled. The thought, although not the exact form, is as old as Homer *Il.* XIX 199-214, where Achilleus asserts that until he kills Hektor (cf. πρίν 209 and surrounding context) neither drink nor food (οὐ πόϲιϲ οὐδὲ βρῶϲιϲ 210) will enter his stomach. Cf. also OT 1Sam. 14.24ff., where Saul puts the Israelites under oath not to eat until he has avenged himself on the Philistines. Our formula also finds close parallels in various "judicial prayers" of some *defixiones*. I cite one example, a tablet from Roman Britain (edd. M.W.C. Hassal and R.O.S. Tomlin, *Britannia* 10 [1979] 341f.): *(Cenacus) erogat deum Mercurium ut ne ante sanitatem habeant nis{s}i ⟦nis{s}i⟧ repraese[n]taverint mihi iumentum quod r[a]puerunt* (side A, 6-side B, 5). With *nec --- sanitatem habeant* cf. M's μήτε εὐϲταθεῖν. For an excellent analysis of this tablet and others similar to it, cf. H.S. Versnel's contribution in the forthcoming *Ancient Greek Magic and Religion* (see above p. 5 n. 24).

A full investigation of the "neither eat nor drink until..." prescription and its variants is not feasible here. For the present we may simply say that it was an ancient curse formula employed in different contexts, and that the topos of love-sickness probably facilitated its frequent use in the later Greco-Egyptian erotic magic.*

πιεῖν: tab. πιν, i.e., πεῖν; a common late contraction (BDR §§ 31. 2; 101 # 70; Gignac I 295f.; Preisendanz's n. on P 353).

10 εὐσταθεῖν ἢ ἡσυχάζειν: tab. ευσταθιν η ισυχαζιν; for η > ι see Gignac I 335f.

εὐσταθεῖν --- φρεσί: See below p. 63 on φιλοῦσα ἐρῶσα for intensification through synonyms and pp. 63f. on ἐξ ὅλης ψυχῆς etc. for psychological terms in erotic magic.

ἐπιζητοῦσα Αἰλουρίωνα: instead of ἐκτὸς ἐμοῦ NN, P 356, C 11f., L 11; χωρὶς Θεοδώρου W_1 27.

10-14: Continuation of the First Command

M [10] ἕως οὗ ἐκπηδήσῃ {ἐκπηδή|σῃ} ἐκ παντὸς τόπου καὶ πάσης οἰκίας Κοπρία, ἣν ἔτεκε μήτηρ ὀνόματι Ταῆσις, ἧς ἔχεις τὰς τρίχας, πυρουμένη καὶ ἔλθῃ πρὸς Αἰλουρίωνα, |[12] ὃν ἔτεκε μήτηρ ὀνόματι Κοπρία, φιλοῦσα ἐρῶσα ἐξ ὅλης ψυχῆς, ἐξ ὅλου πνεύματος, φίλτροις ἀκαταπαύστοις καὶ ἀδιαλείπτοις | καὶ παραμονίμοις ἐρωτικοῖς, Αἰλουρίωνα, ὃν ἔτεκε μήτηρ ὀνόματι Κοπρία ἔρωτι θείῳ ἀπὸ τῆς σήμερον ἡμέρας ἀπὸ τῆς ἄρτι | ὥρας ἐπὶ τὸν λοιπὸν τῆς ζωῆς αὐτῆς Κοπρία⟨ς⟩ χρόνον.

All the parallels lack this section except W_2 27ff., which preserves it in very compressed form: ἕως ἔλθῃ Ματρῶνα πάσῃ ὥρᾳ πρὸς Θεόδωρον φιλοῦσα αὐτόν. For similar material in the second command of the parallels, see below pp. 62f. We have seen from the texts cited above (pp. 59f.) that ἕως/ἄχρι κτλ. is often the natural continuation of μὴ δυνηθῇ μήτε φαγεῖν μήτε πιεῖν κτλ. and similar formulae. With the whole cf. esp. W_4 45ff.: καὶ μὴ ἐάσητε αὐτὴν φαγῖν μὴ πῖν μηδὲ ὕπνου τυχῖν ---, ἀλλὰ ποιήϲατε αὐτὴν ἐκπηδῆϲαι ἀπὸ παντὸϲ τόπου καὶ πάϲηϲ οἰκίαϲ --- ἕωϲ ἔλθῃ πρὸϲ ἐμέ, Θέωνα, φιλοῦϲά{ν} με, ἐρῶϲά{ν} με, Θόον (i.e., Θέωνα), ἔρωτα ἀκατάπαυϲτον καὶ φιλίαν μανικήν. Without preceding μήτε φαγεῖν κτλ., cf. *PGM* XIXa 50ff.: ἄξον --- [και]ομένην, πυρουμένην, κέντει ⟨βα⟩ϲανιζομένην τὴν ψυχήν, τὴν καρδίαν τῆϲ Κάρωϲα --- ἄχριϲ ἂν ἐκπηδήϲαϲα [ἔλ]θῃ πρὸϲ Ἀπαλῶϲ --- ἐπὶ ἔρωτι καὶ φιλίᾳ ἐν τῇ ἄρτι ὥρᾳ. Cf. also XXXVI 82; W_4 32f.

10-11 ἐκπηδήϲῃ {ἐκπηδή|ϲῃ}: Magical texts, like prayers, display extensive repetition, but usually within the confines of certain types of words and constructions; e.g., divine names (Aud. 38.14, 151.7ff.), stereotyped phrases such as ἤδη ἤδη ταχὺ ταχύ (see below p. 88), and imperatives (*PGM* IV 1060af.; VII 330) or quasi-imperatives such as ὁρκίζο ὑμᾶϲ --- εἵνα (i.e., ἵνα) κατήϲχητε κατήϲχητε κτλ. (Aud. 169.11ff.). In the absence of any convincing parallel for M's repetition of ἐκπηδήϲῃ, it seems merely dittographic. Such errors often occur at line-end (e.g., W_2 25 above p. 52; W_2 55-56, 56-57 below p. 85), and in this case, as M.W. Haslam points out to me, the mistake was facilitated by the following ἐκ παντόϲ.

11 μήτηρ --- τρίχαϲ: see above p. 56 on line 7.

πυρουμένη: The verb is used of various fervent emotions, e.g., anger (NT 2Cor. 11.29; Philo *Vit. Mos.* II 280); grief (LXX 3Mac. 4.2); pious devotion (Philo *Leg. Al.* I 84; *Spec. Leg.* III 126); and, as in our text, erotic arousal: Ἔρωϲ, ϲὺ δ' εὐθέωϲ με πύρωϲον (*Anacreontea* 11.14f.); κρεῖττον γάρ ἐϲτιν γαμῆϲαι ἢ πυροῦϲθαι (NT 1Cor. 7.9). In magic, active: *PGM* XIXa 50; O 2. 27f.; LXI 23; passive: XIXa 50; XXXVI 111, 128f., 195, 200 (cf. also below pp. 63f. on ἐξ ὅληϲ ψυχῆϲ κτλ. and p. 90 on § K 35f.; s.v. in Bauer and *TDNT* VI 948ff.). For the general topos of *eros* as a consuming fire, the *locus classicus* is A.R. III 286-98, on which see M. Campbell, *Studies in the Third Book of Apollonius Rhodius' Argonautica* (Hildesheim 1983) 27f. with nn. p. 104. Cf. also the rich literary material and bibliography collected in A.S. Pease, *Virgil Aeneid IV* (Cambridge, Mass. 1935) p. 86f. (s.v. *igni*). For the various images in Aristophanes, see Henderson, *Muse* 177f.

11-12 ἔλθῃ --- ἐρῶϲα: Four of the parallels contain similar material in the "second command" (part of which occurs in our text at 19ff.; see above pp.

18f. and below pp. 83f., 85): μέχρι οὗ ἔλθῃ Ἡρωνοῦς πρὸς ἐμὲ Ποσιδώνιον (C 24); ἕως ἔλθῃ πρὸς ἐμὲ τὸν Σαραπάμμωνα ὃν ἔτεκεν Ἀρέα --- φιλοῦσάν με, ἐρῶσάν μου (L 21, 27); μέχρι οὗ ἔλθῃ πρὸς ἐμὲ τὸν δεῖνα (P 378f.); ἕως ἔλθῃ πρὸς Θεόδωρον (W_2 65f.); similarly, in the third command (only in P), κατάδησον τὴν δεῖνα φιλοῦσαν ἐρῶσαν τὸν δεῖνα ποθοῦσαν (P 395f.). Cf. also below on φιλοῦσα ἐρῶσα.

ἔλθῃ: tab. ερθη (λ > ρ mainly fayumic; Gignac I 103ff., esp. 105).

12 φιλοῦσα ἐρῶσα: cf. in M φιλοῦσα ἐρῶσα --- φιλοῦσα below lines 24f., φιλοῦσαν ἐρῶσαν below § K 37f.; cf. also P 395 and L 27 (cited above); φιλοῦσά με ἐρῶσά με (W_4 48). Similarly, ἐρῶντα μαινόμενον βασανιζόμενον ἐπὶ τῇ φιλίᾳ καὶ ἔρωτι καὶ ἐπιθυμίᾳ (Aud. 271.40f.; cf. *ibid.* 6f.,14f., 30f.); ἄχρις ἂν --- [ἔλ]θῃ --- ἐπὶ ἔρωτι καὶ φιλίᾳ (*PGM* XIXa 51f.; cf. VII 888f.; XVI 5f., 14, 22, 30; XIXa 53; W_1 56 with Wortmann's n. p. 77).

Intensification through accumulation of synonyms is also common in documentary (esp. legal and commercial) texts (H. Zilliacus, *Zur Abundanz der spätgriechischen Gebrauchssprache* [Commentationes Humanarum Litterarum 41.2, 1968] 37ff.). E.g., the participial style of the "Gesundheitsklausel" in wills, τάδε διέθετο νοῶν καὶ φρονῶν, "He made this will being of good and sound mind." Cf. (with minor variations) *P. Pet.* 15.11 (= *Cunn. Mem.* VIII p. 45); *SB* I 4637.14, 5294.3; *P. Oxy.* III 494.2; asyndetic and with other elements added: τάδε διέθετο ὑγιαίνων νοῶν φρονῶν (*P. Grenf.* I 21.1); παρεθέμην --- νοῶν φρονῶν ἐρρωμένην ἔχων τὴν διάνοιαν καὶ ἐπ' ἀκριβείας πολλῆς φέρων τὸν λογισμόν (*M. Chr.* 319.10f., p. 370f.); cf. also *P. Lond.* V 1727.17ff.; *P. Cair. Masp.* III 312.11ff. Similarly, also in wills, ἑκόντες καὶ πεπεισμένοι, *P. Lond.* V 1724.12; *ibid.* 1727.22 (Preisigke, *Wörterbuch* II s.v. πείθω 8). For other clusters of synonyms in our text, cf. above line 10, εὐσταθεῖν ἢ ἡσυχάζειν τῇ ψυχῇ ἢ ταῖς φρεσί· below 12f., φίλτροις ἀκαταπαύστοις καὶ ἀδιαλείπτοις καὶ παραμονίμοις ἐρωτικοῖς (and see n. *ad loc.*); below § K 35f., πυρουμένην καιομένην τηκομένην. In tablets, cf. also κατήσχητε καὶ συνδήσητε καὶ καταδήσητε (Aud. 163. 29f.; 169.14ff.; *al.* [Kagarow 35f.]).

ἐξ ὅλης ψυχῆς, ἐξ ὅλου πνεύματος: In line 24 below, καρδίας replaces ψυχῆς; cf. τὴν ψυχὴν τὸ πνεῦμα, § K 36f. "Heart" and/or "soul" are often described as the *loci* which erotic magic affects, e.g., by "burning" (*PGM* VII

472; XXXIIa 3f., 7f.; XXXVI 80f.; O 2.27f.; cf. πυρουμένη(ν) above line 11, below § K 35f.), "melting" (*PGM* XVI 13f., 21; τηκομένην below § K 36), "goading" (*PGM* XIXa 51), or even "making fly through the air" (ἀεροπέτηcον τὴν ψυχὴν καὶ τὴν καρδίαν Λεοντίας, P. Köln inv. no. 5514.6f. in *ZPE* 19 [1975] 251 with R.W. Daniel's comments, pp. 249f. and 254).

The specific wording of this common sentiment in our text resembles phrases in the Jewish *Shema*: ἄκουε, Ιcραηλ --- ἀγαπήcειc κύριον τὸν θεόν cου ἐξ ὅληc τῆc καρδίαc cου καὶ ἐξ ὅληc τῆc ψυχῆc σου καὶ ἐξ ὅληc τῆc δυνάμεώc cου (LXX Deut. 6.4f.); cf. ἐξ ὅληc τῆc καρδίαc cου καὶ ἐξ ὅληc τῆc ψυχῆc cου (Deut. 11.13); ἐξ ὅληc τῆc διανοίαc ὑμῶν καὶ ἐξ ὅληc τῆc ψυχῆc ὑμῶν (Josh. 22.5); ἐξ ὅληc τῆc καρδίαc cου καὶ ἐξ ὅληc τῆc ψυχῆc cου καὶ ἐξ ὅληc τῆc διανοίαc cου κτλ. (NT Mk. 12.30; in Mat. 22.37 and Lk. 10.27 mostly ἐν τῇ ὅλῃ κτλ.; cf. LXX 4Regn. 23.25). Two points on variant readings: first, mss. often omit the articles after ὅληc, as in our text; second, wherever καρδίαc occurs, other mss. read διανοίαc and *vice versa*; thus ἐξ ὅληc τῆc καρδίαc/διανοίαc cου both render בכל־לבבך (see Behm in *TDNT* IV 966 n. 11 s.v. διάνοια). I find no examples of our ἐξ ὅλου πνεύματοc as a variant for this or any of the other phrases, but given the flexibility of the tradition and the interchangeability of Hebrew anthropological terms, it is not surprising (on the latter point see Jacob in *TDNT* IX 629f. with n. 85 s.v. ψυχή; E. Hatch, *Essays in Biblical Greek* [Oxford 1889] 94-109; see also below pp. 90ff. for πνεῦμα/ψυχή). Similar phrases occur in religious documents likely to be influenced by the *Shema* (e.g., LXX 4Mac. 7.18, Wisd. 8.21; 1Clement 33.8). Although secular literature offers a few parallels, they are not in series as in the *Shema* and our text (e.g., ἐξ ὅληc τῆc διανοίαc, Epict. *Gnom.* II 2.13; ἐξ ὅληc ψυχῆc, *ibid.* II 23.42; ὅλῃ τῇ ψυχῇ, Xen. *Mem.* III 11.10; cf. also ἐξ ἅπαντοc τοῦ νοῦ --- φίλοc γενέcθαι, Plato *Grg.* 510b; similarly Hdt. VIII 97.2).

The *Shema* was one of the portions of Holy Scripture which many Jews believed to have magical power. One rabbinical treatise maintains it to be especially useful against fevers (*Jewish Encyclopedia* III 203 s.v. Bibliomancy), and the Talmud vouches for its effectiveness as a night prayer to ward off demons (J. Trachtenberg, *Jewish Magic and Superstition* [New York 1939] p. 156 with n. 5 p. 298). Parts of it occur in magical documents, both Jewish and non-Jewish (Peterson, *EIC ΘEOC* 295 n. 2). Thus, the ἐξ ὅληc/ὅλου phrases, used in our text to express a common topos of erotic magic in a very uncommon (to my knowledge, unique) form, most likely owe their presence in M to the influence of the *Shema* at some point in M's tradition.

12-13 φίλτροις ἀκαταπαύστοις καὶ ἀδιαλείπτοις καὶ παραμονίμοις ἐρωτικοῖς: φίλτρον means "love charm" (*PGM* IV 2227; VII 293, 405, 459, 462, 661; XII 306; XIII 319; LXI 35) or "spell" in general (LSJ s.v. I 2) or, as here, simply "love," "affection" (the dominant sense in Patristic lit., see Lampe s.v.). Cf. φιλῇ με Νῖλος φίλτρον αἰώνιον, "Let Nilos love me with an eternal love," *PGM* XV 21; for the plu. φίλτρα as "love," see *Anth. Graec.* VII 623. Against LSJ s.v. I 3, P.T. Stevens on Eur. *Androm.* 540 (Oxford 1971, p. 161f.) doubts this meaning for the classical period. The rare στέργηθρον has a similar ambiguity of "love"/"love spell" (LSJ s.v.).

With respect to the entire phrase, I offer three options: 1. supply καὶ before ἐρωτικοῖς, making it the last in a series of adjectives modifying φίλτροις (similarly, in a love charm edited by P.J. Sijpesteijn [*ZPE* 24, 1977, 89f.] lines 12f.: ἔρωτι μανικῷ καὶ ἀκατα[πα]ύστῳ ἀφ`θ'ίρτῳ· he translates, "...mit einer manischen und unablässigen *und* unvergänglichen Liebe."); 2. take ἐρωτικοῖς as a substantive (e.g., as often in Plato, normally with art.) modified by παραμονίμοις, thus, "with unceasing and unremitting affection and constant acts of love"; 3. (suggested by M.W. Haslam) take φίλτροις --- ἐρωτικοῖς as a conceptual unit enclosing three adjectives. I prefer the last, because it gives the best sense ("with unceasing and unremitting and constant loving affection") and is well suited to the penchant for groups of three elsewhere in the text (e.g., above lines 6-7, 8; below § K 35f., etc.). This pattern of a noun and adjective "bracketing" three other adjectives also occurs in Cicero *Fam.* V 8.5, where he urges Crassus to write him *de omnibus minimis maximis mediocribus rebus*; similarly, Plaut. *St.* 737: *Mea suavis amabilis amoena Stephanium.* With φίλτρα ἐρωτικά, cf. in philosophic discussion the pairing of φιλία with adjectives such as ἐρωτική, ἑταιρική, and συγγενική to denote the specific kind of love intended (Stählin in *TDNT* IX 149 with n. 27 s.v. φιλία).

ἀκαταπαύστοις καὶ ἀδιαλείπτοις καὶ παραμονίμοις well illustrate intensification through piling up synonymous adjectives (for participles, see above p. 63), often with alliteration through similar prefixes such as *alpha privativum.* So also in business and legal style: τὴν δεσποτίαν --- ἀκέραιον καὶ ἄτρωτον,

P. Oxy. XVI 1890.14; ὁμολογῶ χαρίζεcθαι coὶ χάριτι ἀναφαιρέτῳ καὶ ἀμετανοήτῳ, *P. Grenf.* II 68.4f.; ἀδιαιρέτῳ καὶ ἀμετανοήτῳ καὶ ἀμετα-[τρέπτῳ λογιcμῷ], *SB* I 4669.11 (see H. Zilliacus, *op. cit.* [above p. 63] 47-52). In both legal and magical contexts, the device often reinforces the notions of permanence and/or completeness (in M, of the spell's effect on Kopria). Cf. the banishment formulae and other material discussed by E. Fraenkel on Aesch. *Ag.* 412 (vol. 2 p. 217 with n. 1).—For ἀκατάπαυcτοc see Horsley, *New Docs.* II 46.

13 ἔρωτι θείῳ: cf. below line 25 and § K 38. Like the preceding φίλ-τροιc --- ἐρωτικοῖc, these words depend on φιλοῦcα ἐρῶcα, further compounding the pleonasm so characteristic of this text. Biblical Greek grammarians often attribute to Semitic influence the frequency of the "cognate dative" instead of the cognate accusative in the NT and LXX (e.g., ἐπιθυμίᾳ ἐπεθύμηcα, Lk. 22.15; ἀναθέματι ἀνεθεματίcαμεν, Acts 23.14); but even in these contexts such usage is unusual in the case of nouns with adjectives, as our ἔρωτι θείῳ (e.g., χαρᾷ χαίρει, Jn. 3.29; but ἐχάρηcαν χαρὰν μεγάλην, Mat. 2.10; see Turner, *Syntax* 241f.; BDR § 198.6; C.F.D. Moule, *An Idiom Book of New Testament Greek* [Cambridge 1968] 32, 177f.). Cf. however, ἐξέcτηcαν ἐκcτάcει μεγάλῃ, Mk. 5.42; δόξῃ μεγάλῃ ἐδόξαcαν, 1Mac. 14.29; *P. Grenf.* II 68.4f. cited above. There is also some classical precedent: θάνον οἰκτίcτῳ θανάτῳ, Hom. *Od.* XI 412; βιαίῳ θανάτῳ ἀποθνῄcκειν, Xen. *Hiero* IV 3; *al.* (KG 1.308; Schwyzer 2.166). In magic, cf. φιλοῦcάν με ἔρωτι --- ἔρωτι μανιώδει (W_4 30f.); the accusative construction, however, prevails: φιλήcειc με --- θεῖον ἔρωτα (*PGM* XV 2f.); φιλείτω με ἡ [δεῖνα] τὸν δεῖνα θεῖον [ἔρωτα] (X 7f.); ἐρῶcα ἔρωτα μανιώδη (W_4 7f.); φιλοῦcά με, ἐρῶcά με Θέωνα ἔρωτα ἀκατά-παυcτον καὶ φιλίαν μανικήν (W_4 48f.); cf. *PGM* XV 21 cited above p. 65.

With θεῖον ἔρωτα in *PGM* XV 3 A.D. Nock (*HTR* 27 [1934] 66 [*Essays* I 367f.]) compares Verg. *Aen.* VIII 373, where Venus arouses "divinum amorem" in her husband Volcanus. The sense of θεῖοc in our text is not too far removed from μανιώδηc/μανική of the above-cited W_4 7, 48; both describe a love which is superhuman and totally obsessive (the adjective has a similar force in Xen. *Hell.* VII 2.21, ὡc δὲ τάχιcτα ἐκηρύχθη, θείᾳ τινὶ προθυμίᾳ καὶ οἱ μιcθοφό-ροι ταχὺ ἐξέδραμον). This desire that the beloved have ἔρωc θεῖοc for the lover is expressed elsewhere through the classic Egyptian paradigm: φιλίτω με ἡ δεῖ-να --- ὡc ἐφίληcεν ἡ Ἶcιc τὸν Ὄcιριν (*PGM* XXXVI 288f.; cf. W_3 8). Similarly with respect to Christian *agape*, οἱ ἄνδρες, ἀγαπᾶτε τὰς γυναῖκας, καθὼς καὶ ὁ Χριςτὸς ἠγάπηςεν τὴν ἐκκληςίαν (NT Eph. 5.25).

13-14 ἀπὸ τῆς ςήμερον ἡμέρας --- χρόνον: triad of prep. phrases as above 6f. In 25 and § K 39 below, these are replaced by μέχρι θανάτου. For the thought, cf. εἰς τὸν ἅπαντα χρόνον τοῦ αἰῶνος (P 405f)., and esp. W_1 79f.: φιλοῦςα⟨ν⟩ αὐτὸν νυκτὸς καὶ ἡμέραις (*lege* -ας) πάςᾳ ὥρᾳ τοῦ αἰῶνος αὐτῆς (see also above pp. 49f. on line 4f., ἐνιαυτοὺς ἐξ ἐνιαυτῶν κτλ.).

The wording here resembles pleonastic formulations used in business transactions, esp. sales, of the Roman and Byzantine periods: ὁμολογοῦμεν --- πεπρακέναι ςοι ςήμερον καὶ καταγεγραφέναι ἀπὸ τοῦ νῦν ἐπὶ τὸν ἀεὶ καὶ ἑξῆς ἅπαντα χρόνον τὴν --- οἰκίαν (*P. Lond.* V 1722.8ff.); cf. *BGU* I 153. 14, 282.5, 319.9; *P. Mich.* XIII 659.234f., 662.14f., 664.9f., 665.12f.; *P. Cair. Masp.* I 97.56f.; for further illustration and discussion, see Zilliacus, *op. cit.* (above p. 63) 34f.

14 αὐτῆς Κοπρίας: tab. ἀτῆς Κοπρία (αυ > α Gignac I (226)-227 with n. 1; omission of final ς *ibid.* 124f.). The meticulous style of the documentary papyri also frequently employs both a proper name and forms of αὐτός when either would have sufficed.

14-19: First Threat against the νεκυδαίμων

M [14] ὅτι ςε ἐξορκίζω, νεκυδαίμων, κατὰ τοῦ ὀνόματος τοῦ φοβεροῦ καὶ τρο|μεροῦ, οὗ ἡ γῆ τὸ ὄνομα ἀκούςαςα ἀνοιγήςεται, οὗ οἱ δαίμονες τὸ ὄνομα ἀκούςαντες ἔμφοβοι τρέμουςιν, οὗ οἱ ποταμοὶ καὶ αἱ |[16] θάλαςςαι τὸ ὄνομα ἀκούςαντες ταράςςονται, οὗ αἱ πέτραι τὸ ὄνομα ἀκούςαντες ῥήςςονται, κατὰ τοῦ βαρβαριθαμ βαρβαριθααμ | χελομβρα βαρουχαμβρα Ἀδωναίου καὶ κατὰ τοῦ αμβραθ Αβραςαξ ςεςενγεν βαρφαραγγης καὶ κατὰ τοῦ Ιαω Cαβαωθ ιαεω | πακενψωθ πακενβραωθ ςαβαρβατιαωθ ςαβαρβατιανη ςαβαρβαφαι μαρι ἐνδόξου μαρμαραωθ καὶ κατὰ τοῦ ουςερβεν|τηθ καὶ κατὰ τοῦ ου⟨ς⟩ερπατη καὶ κατὰ τοῦ μαρμαραυωθ μαρμαραχθα μαρμαραχθαα αμαρδα μαριβεωθ.

P [356] ὅτι cε ἐξορκίζω κατὰ | τοῦ ὀνόματος τοῦ φοβεροῦ καὶ τρομεροῦ, οὗ ἡ γῆ ἀκούcα|[c]α τοῦ ὀνόματος ἀνοιγήcεται, οὗ οἱ δαίμονες | ἀκούcαντες τοῦ ὀνόματος ἐνφόβου φοβηθήcονται, |[360] οὗ οἱ ποταμοὶ καὶ αἱ πέτραι ἀκούcαντες τὸ ὄνομα | ῥήccονται. ὁρκίζω cε, νεκύδαιμον, εἴτε ἄρρης | εἴτε θῆλυς, κατὰ τοῦ βαρβαριθα χενμβρα βα| ρουχαμβρα καὶ κατὰ τοῦ αβρατ Αβραcαξ ||[364] cεcενγεν βαρφαραγγης καὶ κατὰ τοῦ αωια | μαρι ἐνδόξου καὶ κατὰ τοῦ μαρμα⟨ρ⟩εωθ | μαρμαραυωθ μαρμαραωθ μαρεχθανα | αμαρζα· μαριβεωθ·

C [12] ὅτι ὁρκίζω cε κατὰ τοῦ ὀνόματος τοῦ φοβεροῦ καὶ τρομεροῦ, οὗ ἡ γῆ ἀκούcαcα | τὸ ὄνομα ἀνοίγεται, οὗ οἱ δαίμονες ἀκούοντες τὸ ὄνομα ἔμφοβοι τρέμουcι, οὗ οἱ ποταμοὶ καὶ | θάλαccαι ἀκούουcαι τὸ ὄνομα ἔμφοβοι φοβοῦνται, οὗ αἱ πέτραι ἀκούουcαι τὸ ὄνομα ῥήccονται. ὁρκί|ζω cε, νέκυc δαίμων, ὅcτις ποτὲ εἶ εἴτε ἄρcης εἴτε θήλια, κατὰ τοῦ βαρβαραθαμ χελουμβρα |[16] βαρουχαμβρα Ἀδωναίου καὶ κατὰ τοῦ αβραθ Αβραcαξ cεcενγεν βαρφαραγγη καὶ κατὰ τοῦ Ιαω ιωα πακεπτωθ πακεβραωθ cαβαρβαριαωθ μαρει ἐνδόξου καὶ κατὰ τοῦ μαρμαραιωθ καὶ | κατὰ τοῦ μαρμαραωθ μαρμαραυωθ μαρμαραχθα αμαρζα μαρειβαιωθ.

W$_1$ [28] [ὅτι ἐξορκίζ]ω cε, νεκυδέμων, κατὰ τοῦ ὀνόματος τοῦ τρο|[μεροῦ κ]αὶ φοβεροῦ, οὗ ἡ γῆ ἀκού{ο}ουcα τὸ ὄνομα ἀνύγετε {[αν]ụ[γε]τε ουν οι δεμονες} οὗ οἱ δέμονες ἀκούοντες τὸ ὄνο|μα ἔμφοβοι τρέμουcιν, οὗ οἱ ποταμοὶ καὶ ἑ θάλαccαι, ἀκού|[32][ο]ντες τὸ ὄνομα ἔμφοβοι τρέμουcι, ⟨οὗ αἱ πέτραι ἀκούουcαι τὸ ὄνομα⟩ ῥήcονται. ὀρ[κί]|ζω cε, νεκυδέμων, ἴτε ἄρcης ἴτε θήλια, κατ[ὰ τοῦ] | βαρβαραθαμ χαλουμβρα βαρουχ Ἀδωναίου | θεοῦ καὶ κατὰ τοῦ Αβραcαξ βραωcα \`βα´βαρβαριαωθ |[36] cαβαρβαριαωθ cεcενγε βαρβαραφαραγ' γης μαρι|ονιοξας καὶ κατὰ τοῦ μαρμαραχθα μαλμαρζα μαριβα|[ρι]ọθ.

W$_2$ [14] ἐξορκίζω cε γὰρ | κατὰ τοῦ ἁγίου ὀνόματος, οὗ φρί|[16]cι τὰ ὄρη καὶ τρέμι τὰ δεμόνια. --- |[32] ἐξορκίζω cε γὰρ κα|τὰ τοῦ ἐνδόξου ὀνόματος | ⟦οβ⟧ οβαχ καὶ κατὰ τοῦ βαρβα|ραθαμ βαρουχ βαρουχα |[36] βαρουχ Ἀδωναίου θεοῦ | cαβαραaμ χαβαρα|αμ | cαβαρα-

αμ χαβαραα̣μ [ ] |40 'Αδωναιΐου Αβραcαξ | cεcενγε φαραγγηc Ιαω |
Ιαω μεμβρεωθι τεφρε|ωθι ιαρβατιαω αρβατιαοθ |44 ακραμμαχαμαρει ακραμμα|χαμαρει ἐνδόξω μαμαρα|ωθ μαρμαριουωθ μαρμα|ιοθ μαρμα⟦ρ⟧ι`α΄οθ χθαμα |48 αμαζε μαριβαριοθ.[3]

L [11] ἐξορκίζω cε, νεκύδαιμον |[12] 'Αντίνοε, κατὰ τοῦ ὀνόματος [τοῦ] τρομεροῦ καὶ φοβεροῦ, οὗ ἡ γῆ ἀκούcαcα τοῦ ὀνό|ματος ἀνυγήcεται, οὗ οἱ δαίμονες ἀκούcαντες τοῦ ὀνόματος ἐνφόβως φοβοῦνται, | οὗ οἱ ποταμοὶ καὶ πέτραι ἀκούcαντες ῥήcc̣[οντα]ι· ὁρκίζω cε, νεκύδαιμον 'Αντίνοε, | κατὰ τοῦ βαρβαραθαμ χελουμβρα βαρο̣υ̣[χ] Αδωναι καὶ κατὰ τοῦ Αβραcαξ καὶ |[16]κατὰ τοῦ Ιαω πακεπτωθ πακεβραωθ cαβαρβαφαει καὶ κατὰ | τοῦ μαρμαραουωθ καὶ κατὰ τοῦ μαρμαραχθα μ̣αμαζαγαρ̣.

For detailed comparisons between the parallels, cf. the critical apparatus, below pp. 116f., nn. on lines 18ff. In general, the original version probably contained some form of the four clauses οὗ ἡ γῆ --- οὗ οἱ δαίμονες --- οὗ οἱ ποταμοὶ καὶ αἱ θάλαccαι --- οὗ αἱ πέτραι. With the exception of W_2's abbreviated version, all of our texts contain the first two, only M and C have the last two in full.

In this adjuration Ailourion threatens the *nekydaimon* and compels it to obey by the power of "the name fearful and dreadful." Threats against a divinity occur in ancient prayer (F. Heiler, *Das Gebet* [München/Basel 1969] 83ff.; H.S. Versnel in *Faith Hope and Worship* [ed. Versnel, Leiden 1981] 37ff., esp. 40 with n. 162) and are constantly employed in magic; e.g., τέλεcον, δαῖμον, τὰ ἐνθάδε γεγραμμένα. τελέcαντι δέ cοι θυcίαν ἀποδώcω, βραδύναντι δέ cοι κολάcειc ἐπενεγκῶ, ἃc οὐ δύναcαι ἐνεγκεῖν (*PGM* IV 2094ff.; cf. Hopfner, OZ I §§ 787-801; B. Olsson in *ΔΡΑΓΜΑ Martino P. Nilsson --- dedicatum* [Skrifter Utgivna av Svenska Institutet i Rom, Acta Series Altera I, 1939] 374ff.; Versnel, *loc. cit.*). Sometimes the operator warns that if his wishes are not performed, the processes of nature will be disturbed or destoyed by his magic: ἐὰν δὲ παρακούcητε καὶ μὴ ταχέωc τελέcητε ὃ λέγω ὑμῖν, οὐ δύνεται ὁ ἥλιος ὑπὸ γῆν, οὔτε ὁ ῞Α̣δηc οὔτε ὁ κόcμος οὐκ ἔcτιν (W_4 9ff. with Wortmann's n. *ad loc.* p. 92f.; similarly *PGM* XII 55ff.; cf. XXXIV 1ff.; LVII 2ff.). This type of threat is

[3] For the beginning of the first threat in W_2 14 and its continuation in 32, see above p. 18.

implicit in two other contexts: when, as in the passage under consideration, the operator claims to know the great god's secret name which can confound the elements and make demons tremble, or when he through the ἐγώ εἰμι formula professes actually to be the all-powerful demiurge on whom the continuity of the cosmos depends (cf. below p. 94 on ἐγώ εἰμι, esp. Kropp III §§ 251ff. and Wortmann p. 92f.). We will again turn to this theme of cosmic disruption after some further observations on the general topos of threats.

The concept of human beings threatening gods through magic raises theological problems concerning divine power and freedom, well expressed by Lucan (VI 492ff.):

quis labor hic superis cantus herbasque sequendi
spernendique timor? cuius commercia pacti
obstrictos habuere deos? parere necesse est,
an iuvat? ignota tantum pietate merentur,
an tacitis valuere minis? hoc iuris in omnis
est illis superos, an habent haec carmina certum
imperiosa deum, qui mundum cogere quidquid
cogitur ipse potest?

Iamblichus defends the practice, which he considers chiefly Egyptian, by asserting that threats are directed against demons, not gods (*de Myst.* VI 5-7, esp. p. 246, 2ff. and p. 249, 2ff. Parthey [pp. 186 and 188 Des Places; much of this section cited below p. 74]; cf. Olsson, *op. cit.* p. 375 with n. 4). Although (as in our text) such is often the case, gods too are threatened; cf. *PGM* IV 2903 and above pp. 40f.; XII 117ff. and below p. 75; Lucan VI 730ff. cited below p. 73; further examples collected by Hopfner in *Über die Geheimlehren von Jamblichus* (Leipzig 1922) p. 247ff. and *OZ* I §§ 787ff. The authority of threats often rests on a powerful name. In some cases the name is used to legitimate a particular threat (e.g., *PGM* XII 137ff.). In our text the threat itself consists in the effect of uttering the supreme name; the name *is* the threat (cf. Lucan VI 730ff. [cited below p. 73], esp. 732f. and 744f.).

Magical documents often celebrate the immense power of the supreme name and the deity who bears it in a manner similar to that in M and its parallels; e.g., *PGM* XII 239ff.: ἐπάκουϲόν μου, κύριε, οὗ ἐϲτιν | τὸ κρυπτὸν ὄνομα ἄρρητον, ὃ οἱ δαίμονεϲ ἀκούϲαντεϲ πτοοῦνται, οὗ καὶ ὁ ἥλιοϲ βαρβαρειχ || αρϲεμφεμφρωθου τὸ ὄνομα ⟨ἀκούων ἵϲταται⟩, οὗ ἡ γῆ ἀκούϲαϲα ἑλίϲϲεται, ὁ ᾍδηϲ ἀκούων ταράϲϲεται, | ποταμοί, θάλαϲϲα, λίμναι, πηγαὶ ἀκούουϲαι πήγυνται, αἱ πέτραι ἀκούϲαϲαι ῥήγυνται (⟨ἀκούων ἵϲταται⟩ Koenen; cf. *PGM* XIII 872f.). Similarly, *PGM* IV 3069ff.; XII 117ff.; XIII 871ff.; XXI 1ff.; Aud. 242.43ff.; 271.32ff.; amulet in Cod. Par. 2316, 316r ss. [Reitzenstein, *Poim.* p. 295]; Pradel 24.6f.; further parallels and bibliography in Wortmann p. 73; Hopfner, *OZ* I § 689. Two stylistic features are especially striking. First, later religious feeling, as expressed, e.g., in the hymns of Proclus and the *Orphic hymns*, popularized such accumulation of relative sentences as one means of accrediting deities with as many epithets as possible (cf. NT Heb. 1.2ff.). Classical authors employed this technique with more restraint (Norden, *Ag. Th.* 168-72). Second, our text (and its parallels) and many of the other above-cited passages stress the pervasive authority of the mighty name over all nature by enumerating the various parts of the cosmos which tremble before it (or as in the case of the δαίμονεϲ, the inhabitants of a certain part, i.e., ᾍδηϲ). E.g., in our text: γῆ, δαίμονεϲ, ποταμοί, θάλαϲϲαι, πέτραι; in the above-cited *PGM* XII 239ff.: δαίμονεϲ, ἥλιοϲ, γῆ, ᾍδηϲ, ποταμοί, θάλαϲϲα κτλ.; cf. Aud. 242.43f.: εἴπω ϲοι καὶ τὸ ἀληθινὸν ὄνομα ὃ τρέμει Τάρταρα γῆ βυθὸϲ οὐρανὸϲ Φορβαβορφορβαβορφ κτλ. On the Egyptian side, we may compare Borghouts *AEMT* # 127 (p. 87f.): "If his name is pronounced on the border of the river, then it will dry up. If his name is pronounced on the earth, then it will produce a flame." While this device cannot strictly be called polar expression (see above p. 53), it includes polar elements (e.g., γῆ-θάλαϲϲα and γῆ-οὐρανόϲ, see Kemmer *op. cit.* [above p. 53] p. 160f.), and has the same purpose of exhausting a concept (in this case, "cosmos").

With this thought of the divine name disrupting and terrifying all of nature we may compare descriptions of the power of *carmina* ("spells") in Roman poetry: *carmina sanguineae deducunt cornua lunae,* | *et revocant niveos solis euntis equos;* | *carmine dissiliunt abruptis faucibus angues,* | *inque suos fontes versa recurrit aqua* (Ovid *Am.* II 1.23-26; cf. *ibid.* I 8.5-18; Verg. *Ec.* 8.69-71; Tib. I 8.19-21; Prop. I 1.19-24; Hor. *Epod.* 5.45-46; Lucan VI 499-506; Petron. 134.12). It is on this point that the author of the Hippocratic treatise περὶ ἱερῆϲ νούϲου condemns magicians for impiety in that by claiming to control nature with their spells, they usurp what belongs only to gods: δυϲϲεβέειν ἔμοιγε δοκέουϲι καὶ θεοὺϲ οὔτε εἶναι νομίζειν οὔτ' ἐόνταϲ ἰϲχύειν οὐδὲν --- εἰ γὰρ ἄνθρωποϲ μαγεύων τε καὶ θύων ϲελήνην τε καθαιρήϲει καὶ ἥλιον ἀφανιεῖ καὶ χειμῶνα καὶ εὐδίην ποιήϲει, οὐκ ἂν ἔγωγέ τι θεῖον νομίϲαιμι τούτων εἶναι, ἀλλ᾽ ἀνθρώπινον, εἰ δὴ τοῦ θείου ἡ δύναμιϲ ὑπὸ ἀνθρώπου γνώμηϲ κρατέεται καὶ δεδούλωται (Littré vol. 6 p. 360; for an excellent discussion of this and other texts which condemn as impious any human claim of power over the elements, see Wilamowitz, *Euripides Heracles* [Darmstadt³ 1959] on line 1232 [vol. 3 pp. 248ff.]).

That governing and intimidating the cosmos is indeed the divine prerogative is evident, e.g., in the opening lines of Lucretius (*Aeneadum genetrix* --- *quae mare* --- *quae terras* --- *concelebras* --- *te, dea, te fugiunt venti, te nubila caeli* | *adventumque tuum* --- *quoniam rerum naturam sola gubernas* etc. [1-21]) and especially in descriptions of Yahweh in Jewish apocalypse, which bear striking similarities to our text: ἀπειλῶν θαλάϲϲῃ καὶ ξηραίνων αὐτὴν καὶ πάνταϲ τοὺϲ ποταμοὺϲ ἐξερημῶν --- τὰ ὄρη ἐϲείϲθηϲαν ἀπ᾽ αὐτοῦ, καὶ οἱ βουνοὶ ἐϲαλεύθηϲαν· καὶ ἀνεϲτάλη ἡ γῆ ἀπὸ προϲώπου αὐτοῦ --- αἱ πέτραι διεθρύβηϲαν ἀπ᾽ αὐτοῦ (LXX Nahum 1.4-6; cf. Is. 13.9-10; Ezek. 32.7-8; Joel 2.10; 3.3-4 quoted in NT Acts 2.19-20; Amos 8.9; cf. in NT, Mk. 13.24; 2Pet. 3.10; Rev. 6.12-17). Similarly, when Jesus, having cried out, died on the cross, ἡ γῆ ἐϲείϲθη, καὶ αἱ πέτραι ἐϲχίϲθηϲαν (Mat. 27.51; not in other gospels). For further parallel material, see Pradel 40-42. One aspect of Iamblichus' justification of threats in Egyptian religion (cf. above p. 70) hinges on the middle/later Platonic doctrine that the gods have given the *daimones* custody over the various spheres of nature, and thus it is actually the latter group who are affected by threats against it (*de Myst.* VI 6, p. 247,5ff. Parthey = p. 187 Des Places). His argument, of course, presupposes an objection similar to that of περὶ ἱερῆϲ νούϲου.

Central to this concept of assuming authority over nature through the great name is the Egyptian technique of threatening invoked deities and *daimones* with the disclosure of divine secrets; cf. esp. this Egyptian spell, where, in the context of threats against Osiris, the operator says:

> As for that chest of acacia-wood, which is in charge of Horus, the lord of Letopolis, the name of whose contents one does not know how to pronounce—that tongue, those eyes, that wind-pipe departing from the pharynx, those vital parts of Osiris—it is not I who have said it, it is not I who have repeated it. It is this magic that comes for NN born of NN that has said it,

that has repeated it. And it has told the mysteries of Osiris, it has told the nature of the gods, and the Ennead is its servant in the great place.

(Borghouts, *AEMT* # 10, p. 8f.)

In Lucan VI 730ff. similar themes are cast into Greek and Roman myth:

Tisiphone vocisque meae secura Megaera,
non agitis saevis Erebi per inane flagellis
infelicem animam? iam vos ego nomine vero
eliciam Stygiasque canes in luce superna
destituam; per busta sequar per funera custos,
expellam tumulis, abigam vos omnibus urnis.
teque deis, ad quos alio procedere voltu
ficta soles, Hecate pallenti tabida forma,
ostendam faciemque Erebi mutare vetabo.
eloquar inmenso terrae sub pondere quae te
contineant, Hennaea, dapes, quo foedere maestum
regem noctis ames, quae te contagia passam
noluerit revocare Ceres. tibi, pessime mundi
arbiter, inmittam ruptis Titana cavernis,
et subito feriere die. paretis, an ille
conpellandus erit, quo numquam terra vocato
non concussa tremit, qui Gorgona cernit apertam
verberibusque suis trepidam castigat Erinyn,
indespecta tenet vobis qui Tartara, cuius
vos estis superi, Stygias qui perierat undas?

In this passage Erichtho warns that, by saying the true name(s) of the Erinyes, she will expose the hounds of Styx to the sunlight (732-34; similarly also Pluto, 742f.) and reveal other secrets of the underworld gods (e.g., the true appearance of Hekate 736ff., the secret food of Proserpina 739ff.; cf. in the Egyptian text magic revealing "the nature of the gods"). In 744ff., Erichtho describes as the greatest mystery the supreme god who inhabits a Tartarus so deep and inaccessible that the normal *inferi* are *superbi* by comparison,* whose name causes the earth to tremble, but who himself need not fear any underworld power.

Significantly, Iamblichus argues that the continuity and serenity of the cosmos depends on such secrets remaining concealed; thus the demons, who have custody over nature, fear even the suggestion of their disclosure: μένει δὲ καὶ ἡ τῶν ὅλων ζωὴ καθαρὰ καὶ ἀδιάφθορος, ἐπειδὴ τὰ ἀπόκρυφα ζωογόνα τῶν λόγων κάλλη τῆς Ἴσιδος οὐ κάτεισιν εἰς τὸ φαινόμενον καὶ ὁρώμενον σῶμα. ἀκίνητα δὲ διατελεῖ πάντα καὶ ἀειγενῆ, διότι οὐδέποτε ἵσταται ὁ τοῦ ἡλίου δρόμος· τέλεια δὲ καὶ ὁλόκληρα διαμένει πάντα, ἐπειδὴ τὰ ἐν Ἀβύδῳ ἀπόρρητα οὐδέποτε ἀποκαλύπτεται· οἷς οὖν ἔχει τὴν σωτηρίαν τὰ ὅλα (λέγω δὲ ἐν τῷ τὰ ἀπόρρητα κεκρυμμένα ἀεὶ διατηρεῖσθαι καὶ ἐν τῷ τὴν ἄφθεγκτον τῶν θεῶν οὐσίαν μηδέποτε τῆς ἐναντίας μεταλαμβάνειν μοίρας), τοῦτο οὐδ' ἄχρι φωνῆς ἀνεκτόν ἐστι τοῖς περιγείοις δαίμοσιν ἐπακούειν ὡς ἄλλως ἔχον ἢ βέβηλον γιγνόμενον, καὶ διὰ τοῦτο ἔχει δύναμίν τινα πρὸς αὐτοὺς ὁ τοιοῦτος τρόπος τῶν λόγων (*de Myst.* VI 7, p. 248, 5ff. Parthey [p. 187f. Des Places]).

Magical texts employ similar language in describing the true name(s) as mystery (e.g., κρύπτον *PGM* I 217; XXIIb 20; IV 1610; κρύπτον ἄρρητον XII 237, 240; XIII 763; ἄφθεγκτον XIII 1000; VII 560; see in general Blau 124).

Thus, by revealing the name of the supreme god, the operator assumes the power of the supreme mystery which carries with it the most potent threat of cosmic disaster. For the name to have its desired effect, however, his knowledge of it must be precise and complete: ἐπικαλοῦμαί σου τὸ ὄνομα, τὸ μέγιστον ἐν θεοῖς· ὃ ἐὰν εἴπω τέλειον, ἔσται σεισμός, ὁ ἥλιος στήσεται, καὶ ἡ σελήνη ἔνφοβος ἔσται (*PGM* XIII 871ff.). Concern to say the name perfectly generates the impulse to multiply names and epithets; in our text, e.g., the "name" is actually six names (each preceded by κατὰ τοῦ), further augmented and amplified by magical *logoi*.

One general comment should be offered concerning the etymologies of the magical names in 16ff. Several contain the element *arba* or by metathesis *abra*, which is probably the transliteration of ארבע, "four." *Arba* became a euphemism for the Tetragram, the Hebrew divine name with the four letters יהוה, and as such compounds with other names of Yahweh, such as Adonai, אדני (see below pp. 94f. on Βαρβαδωναι § K 40f.), El, אל (Αβραηλ, Delatte/Derchain 10, 469 with n.), and esp. Iao, יהו (αρβαθιαω/αβραθιαω, which A. Jacoby interprets as "die Vierzahl des [Namens] Jao" [*HDA* I 568 s.v. Arbatel; cf. *idem*, *ARW* 28, 1930, 273 n. 8]; *PGM* IV 1414; V 117f., 479; VI 35; XIII 79, 146, 452, 592; XXXVI 350; Bonner # 284, p. 300; see Perdrizet 77f.; J.M.R. Cormack, *HTR* 44 [1951] 33; esp. Fauth 65ff. Cf. also βαρβαθιαω [W_4 4 and n. p. 92; *PGM* V 355; III 267; Delatte/Derchain 460 (βαρβαθιηαωθ); Robinson, *Fest. Rand* 245 line 3 with n. p. 249], and in our text cαβαρβατιαωθ [below p. 81]). S. Eitrem (*Forhandlinger i videnskapsselskapet i Kristiania* 1921, 1, p. 15) explains the second word of the combination αβρα μαροια (*PGM* IV 3022) as possibly Μαρία (cf. also *PGM* vol. 3 p. 238B s.v. Μαρία; T. Hopfner, *AO* 3 [1931] 347f.). It is more likely a variation of μαρι, מרי, the Aramaic "(my) Lord" (cf. below p. 81 on μαρι ἐνδόξου). For other variations on *arba*, cf. F. Maltomini, *SCO* 29 (1979) 79 (on line 36). See also nn. below on βαρβαριθαμ line 16, pp. 76f.; βαρουχαμβρα 17, p. 77; αμβραθ Αβραcαξ 17, pp. 77f. Fauth (71f., 79ff., 97, and *passim*) observes that in connection with various designations for Yahweh, *arba* refers not only to the *Vierheit* of his supreme name, but also to that of his nature as solar *pantocrator*, the number "4" often expressing the idea of cosmic totality (e.g., in phrases such as the four corners of the earth, the four sectors of heaven, the four cτοιχεία, etc.).

14 ὅτι cε ἐξορκίζω κατὰ κτλ.: a common form for adjurations; cf. ὅτι ὁρκίζω ὑμᾶc κατὰ τοῦ ὑπὸ γῆν ἀνανεάζοντοc, Aud. 155a.40f.; similarly Aud. 155b.16f.; 159a.14f.; 161.38f.; etc. (cf. Aud. index p. 534 s.v. ὅτι ὁρκίζω *sine verbo praecedente*; *PGM* vol. 3 p. 92 s.v. ἐξορκίζω).

15 οὗ οἱ δαίμονεc --- τρέμουcιν: similarly NT James 2.19: cὺ πιcτεύειc ὅτι εἷc ἐcτιν ὁ θεόc; καλῶc ποιεῖc· καὶ τὰ δαιμόνια πιcτεύουcιν καὶ φρίccουcιν (on which see M. Dibelius, *Jakobusbrief* [Göttingen 1964] *ad loc*., 196f. [Eng., Philadelphia 1976, 159f.]; A. Deissmann, *Bib. Stud.* 288). However, not only the demons fear the name of the great god: ἐπάκουcόν μου, ὅτι μέλλω τὸ μέγα ὄνο⟨μα⟩ λέγειν· Αωθ, ὃν πᾶc θ(εὸc) προcκυνεῖ καὶ πᾶc δαίμων φρίccει, ᾧ πᾶc ἄγγελοc τὰ ἐπιταccόμενα ἀποτελεῖ (*PGM* XII 117ff.). In general cf. also *Pist. Soph.* IV 143 (Schmidt/MacDermot p. 373); Proclus *hymn* I 27f. Vogt; Enoch 69.14; Iamblichus' arguments, above pp. 70, 72, and 74.

16 αἱ πέτραι --- ἀκούcαντεc: similarly *PGM* XXXVI 263. There was an increasing tendency in later Greek to use masculine for feminine participles; cf. esp. Kapsomenakis 40ff. n. 2; also Gignac II 130f.; Mandilaras § 877; BDR § 136.3. W.S. Barrett (*contra* Wilamowitz) doubts the evidence for this phenomenon in the classical period (*Euripides Hippolytos* [Oxford 1964] 366ff.).

16-17 κατὰ τοῦ βαρβαριθαμ βαρβαριθααμ χελομβρα βαρουχαμβρα Ἀδωναίου: parallels: κατὰ τοῦ βαρβαριθα χενμβρα βαρουχαμβρα (P 362f.); κατὰ τοῦ βαρβαραθαμ χελουμβρα βαρουχαμβρα Ἀδωναίου (C 15f.); κατ[ὰ τοῦ] βαρβαραθαμ χαλουμβρα βαρουχ Ἀδωναίου θεοῦ (W_1 33ff.); κατὰ τοῦ βαρβαραθαμ βαρουχ βαρουχα βαρουχ Ἀδωναίου θεοῦ (W_2 34ff.); κατὰ τοῦ βαρβαραθαμ χελουμβρ̣α βαρ̣ο̣υ̣[χ] Αδωναι (L 15). Ἀδωναίος (אדני,"Lord"; om. P) is the first of the six names; it is preceded by various forms of the *βαρβαριθα-logos*. Cf. κατὰ τοῦ βαρβαραθαμ βαρουχ βαρουχα Ἀδωναίου θεοῦ (W_3 2f.); κατὰ τῶν cῶν ὀνομ[άτων βα]ρβαραθαμ χελουβ̣αμ βαρουχ [Ἀδωναίου] (*PGM* III 108ff.); κατὰ τοῦ βαρβαραθαν βαροχ Αβρααμ (W_6 4ff.); cf. also Ιαω Cαβαωθ Αδων[αι βαρβαραθαμ] βαρουχα βαρου⟦βα⟧χ (W_3 11f.). The following magical gems in Delatte/Derchain preserve various parts of the formula: χελωμβρα (502); βαρουχ αβραα αβραμα (507); βαρβαραθειω --- χελομβραμ βαρουχαβραμ (516); βαρβαραθειω --- χελομβρα βια̣ο̣υ̣χ αβραμ --- χελμβρα βαρουχα (520); βαρουχαβραμ (521); cf. also βαρβαρ[αθαμ Ἀ]δων̣α̣[ίου (*PGM* LXVII 10). In most of these texts (exc. L, W_6, gems 502 and 507) some form of *sesengen barpharanges* (see below pp. 78f.) follows either immediately or after other formulae.

The Hebraic character of the *barbaritha-logos* is evinced by its connection with Adonai in most instances, by its individual elements (see below), and perhaps by *PGM* III 119, ἐξορκίζω cε κατὰ τῆc ἑβραϊκῆc φωνῆc, which seems to refer to the above cited III 109f.; see Preisendanz's n. on 110.

16 βαρβαριθαμ: see preceding n. for the parallels. Apart from its use in the *barbaritha-logos*, this word occurs above line 3 (p. 41) as a *signum* of Adonis and in *PGM* LXVII 10 with the Hebrew *Adonai(os). Barbar*, a common element in magical words, is probably a play on Hebrew ארבע, *arba*, "four" (see above pp. 74f.). Thus βαρβαριθα(μ)/βαρβαραθα(μ) is perhaps ארבע אתה, "Thou art *arba*." Another possibility is *arba* + Aramaic אתא which may be interpreted either "*Arba* has come" or "Come *arba*" (cf. μαραναθα, NT 1Cor. 16.22; Kuhn in *TDNT* IV 466ff.; cf. also μ̣[α]ριθα, Xer. Corp. inv. 51/4740 DUO, line 5f. [ed. by C.A. Faraone, R. Kotansky, *ZPE* 75, 1988, 258 with n. p. 261]). Cf. also the Hebrew-Kabbalistic divine name *Ar-ar-i-ta*, an acrostic abbreviation for seven words which mean, "One, the beginning of his unity, the beginning of his uniqueness, his change is one" (A. Jacoby, *HDA* I 567f. s.v.; S. Seligmann, *Hessische Blätter für Volkskunde* 20 [1921] 11).

17 βαρουχαμβρα: so P and C; W_1, W_2, and L omit -αμβρα, linking βαρουχ directly with *Adonai(os)* (see below). For these and other parallels, see above (p. 76) on κατὰ τοῦ βαρβαριθα etc. βαρουχ is most likely ברוך, "blessed" (so A. Jacoby, n. on P 362f.). αμβρα (similarly αμβραθ with Αβρασαξ below) seems to be a variation of ארבע, "four" = (the name of) Yahweh (see above pp. 74f.); thus, "Blessed be *arba*" (in general see F. Maltomini, *SCO* 29 [1979] 110; cf. also βαρβαρουχ [Kropp II 6.24, p. 17], a contraction of αρβα βαρουχ?).

βαρουχ (variously spelled) also compounds with other Hebrew divine names: βαρουχ Αδωναι (W_1 W_2 L; *PGM* V 480; W_1 3 [cf. also *PGM* XLV 3f.]); βαρουχ Ιαω (Xer. Corp. inv. 51/4740 DUO, line 1, ed. Faraone/Kotanski *op. cit.* [see above p. 76] 258 with n. p. 259, but I disagree with their conclusion that βαρουχ is usually independent; cf. ⟨β⟩αραχ Ιαω Bonner # 284.3f., p. 300 with n.) βαρουχιηλ (*Test. Sol.* VIII 6, p. 33, 1; probably ברוכי אל, "blessed of God"; cf. βαρακιηλ discussed by E. Peterson, *Rhein. Mus.* 75, 1926, 399 and other angel names ending in *-iel* which he lists, 393ff.); Σαβαω βαρυχ (Southesk gem # 56 cited by A. Delatte, *Amulettes mithriaques* [*Musée Belge* 18, 1, 1914] p. 35); βαρουχα (Delatte/Derchain 520; part of the *barbaritha-logos* in W_2 35, W_3 3 and 12 [-α is perhaps יה, "God"; cf. βαρου --- χα, pap. 1.4 in Maltomini, *op. cit.* p. 64 with nn. on lines 2-4 p. 70 and line 4 p. 71]. For *barroucha* in Coptic texts, cf. Stegemann XXVIII 2 [p. 52]; Kropp II 43.93 [with n. p. 159] and 128. Similarly *Baruchia*, *ibid.* 72 col. 2.3 [p. 239]; *Baracha* [ברכה, "blessing"], *ibid.* 40.33 [p. 136]; cf. also the dekan name *Baroche* in the *Tabula Aristobuli* # 18 [Gundel, W., *Dekane* 406f.]). βαρουχ also occurs apart from any of the above compounds; e.g., pap. 7.6 in Maltomini, *op. cit.* p. 99; *P. Bad.* V 140.3 (p. 405). For various combinations with ברוך in the Hebrew Bible, see BDB 138B s.v. [ברך] 2a.

αμβραθ Αβρασαξ: first word lacking in W_1, W_2, L. The etymology of Αβρασαξ is uncertain (in general see *Jewish Encyclopedia* I 129f. s.v.; Dornseiff, *Alphabet* 42f.; for its numerical value see P 332 above p. 10 with n. 40). The name, like other magical words (cf. above pp. 74f.), may be derived from Heb. ארבע, "four", i.e., (the name of) Yahweh (A.A. Barb in *Hommages à Waldemar Deonna* [Col. Latomus 28, 1957] 68ff.; A. Jacoby, *HDA* I 99 s.v. Abrasax; K. Rudolph, *Die Gnosis* [Göttingen 1980] 332f. = Eng. [Edinburgh 1983] 311). The same word precedes Αβραcαξ in P 363 (αρβατ; probably the fem. construct form ארבעת, as often with Iao [above pp. 74f.; cf. Fauth 71]), C 16 (αβραθ; same form with metathesis), and our text (αμβραθ; with metathesis and, as in βαρουχ αμβρα above, development of μ before labial β [cf. Gignac I 118; Threatte 488ff.]). It is not surprising to find *arba/abra*, which is usually joined to the different names of Yahweh, here attached to Abrasax, since Iao-Adonai-Abrasax are frequently invoked together as designations of the supreme solar god; cf., e.g., *PGM* III 76f.; VII 221, 649; XXXVI 42; XII 74; Delatte/Derchain 128, 149, 211, 362, 379; Kropp II 48.38f.; Fauth 74 with n. 76. For the Abrasax/Yahweh syncretism in Basilidian Gnosis, see K. Rudolph *loc. cit.*

cεcενγεν βαρφαραγγηc: so spelled in P 364; cεcενγεν βαρφαραγγη (C 16); cεcενγε βαρβαραφαραγ'γηc (W_1 36); cεcενγε φαραγγηc (W_2 41, cεcενγενφαρανγηc Bonner # 357 [p. 314], cεcενγενφαρανγη # 233 [p. 292]); om. L. For other spelling variations, cf. Kopp III § 671. These common *voces magicae* often occur with or near the *barbaritha-logos* or similar formulae (so M; cf. *PGM* III 110; W_3 4; Delatte/Derchain 516, 520, 521), with αβλαναθαναλβα ακραμμαχαμαρει (*PGM* III 79f.; IV 981f.; VII 312; *An. Ath.* 550. 14f.; Youtie/Bonner "Beisan" obv. frag. 1.25 [p. 55/621]; Perdrizet 73, lines 4-6), in solar connections, including that of Horus-Apollo (*PGM* II 108, 122, 174; III 155, 217; IV 1025; Bonner p. 201f.), and in other contexts. Various forms of it occur in Coptic and Aramaic/Jewish magic; see Kropp II p. 271; Scholem 85, line 10 with n. p. 89; 99f. The latter (p. 98 and n. 16) also cites an Aramaic incantation bowl edited by J.A. Montgomery (*Aramaic Incantation Texts from Nippur* [Philadelphia 1913] 146), which reads, "In the name of Pharagin bar Pharagin, before whom trembles the sea and behind whom the mountains tremble" (cf. our text above lines 14-16). On the grounds of the Jewish evidence, Scholem (97f. with n. 15) explains our words as the name of a demon with an Aramaic patronym: "Sesengen son (*bar*) of Pharanges." He (p. 100) and more recently W. Fauth (*ZDMG* 120 [1970] 254f.) have compared the formula with *Ssm bn Pdršša*, a divine/demonic name found in various Semitic magical texts, which displays the following similarities: 1. *Ssm* is most likely the same name or of the same root as ϲεϲεν(γεν) (m/n interchange is common in certain Semitic languages [Fauth, *op. cit.* 252 with n. 266 and cf. below p. 104 on ϲαταμα]); 2. the second name is a patronym, but with the Hebrew form *bn* rather than Aramaic *br*; 3. *Ssm bn Pdršša* has strong solar affiliations, especially with regard to Horus-Apollo (Fauth, *op. cit.* 246-55). The provenances and meanings of the actual names ϲεϲενγεν and φαραγγηϲ remain obscure. Scholem (97 n. 15) has rightly discounted earlier proposals for Hebrew and Greek etymologies (Heb. *šišim gibborim* [see OT Song of Songs 3.7] + Pharaoh, Perdrizet 79; "the ravine [φάραγξ] of Baaras," which, according to Josephus [*Bel. Jud.* VII 180ff.], produced a magical plant; see Hopfner, OZ I §§ 507, 754; Kopp III p. 672f.; Kropp III § 211).

Ιαω Cαβαωθ: This Greek version of the common Hebrew יהוה צבאות "Lord of hosts," is fairly frequent in our literature (*PGM* IV 1538; V 479; XII 207; *al.*). *Sabaoth*, which is lacking at this point in M's parallels, originally in the OT designated Yahweh as lord of the armies of Israel and (later) of the heavenly hosts, i.e., stars, angels, etc. (BDB s.v. צבא 4). Aquila translates it ϲτρατιῶν, LXX often δυναμέων. In much of the LXX, however (esp. the Minor Prophets), it is interpreted more generally as an ascription of Yahweh's might and rendered παντοκράτωρ (Thackeray 8f.). In this light, it is not difficult to see how in magic *Sabaoth* often ceased to function as an appendage to various Yahweh names and became a divine/magical name in its own right (*PGM* VII 605, 1012; IV 3052f.; IX 7; III 219; M § K 46 below; etc. Cf. Bonner 136; M. Smith, *JANES* 16/17 [1984/85] 210).

Iao is actually not the transcription for יהוה, but for a shorter form, יהו, which does not occur in the Hebrew Bible (except as an element in proper names) but in Jewish magic, Aramaic ostraca, and elsewhere; cf. Ganschinietz in *RE* IX 699 s.v. Iao; L. Blau in *Jewish Encyclopedia* XII 119A-20A s.v. Tetragrammaton; Hopfner, OZ I § 743; Fauth 68f. It is one of the most (if not the most) frequently used names of power in Greco-Egyptian magical texts (see Ganschinietz, *op. cit.* 698ff. [esp. 709-13] and O. Eissfeldt, *Zeitschrift für Missionskunde und Religionswissenschaft* 42 [1927] 161ff. [*Kleine Schriften* I 150ff.]). For Iao in non-magical Hellenistic, Greco-Jewish, and Patristic literature, see Deissmann, *Bib. Stud.* 322; Eissfeldt, *op. cit.* 180f. (*Kl. Sch.* I 166f.); E. Norden in *Festgabe von Fachgenossen und Freunden A. von Harnack* (Tübingen 1921) 298ff.; *PGM*

Eng. p. 335 s.v. There were other Greek versions of the Tetragram; cf. next n. on ιαεω and below p. 103 on αϊα. The form ιω (often a prefix) has been taken as a variation of Ιαω or as Egyptian/Coptic *eio*, "ass", i.e., Seth (W. Fauth, *Oriens Christianus* 57 [1973] 106-120, and for *eio*/*io* in particular, *ibid.* 113f.; R.W. Daniel, *ZPE* 50 [1983] 151; Youtie/Bonner "Beisan" obv. frag. 1.7f., 25f. with n. p. 61/627; Griffiths on *Is. et Os.* 30 [p. 409f.]; cf. Eissfeldt, *op. cit.* p. 183 [*Kl. Sch.* I 168]. For Seth's identification with Yahweh, see above p. 33; Griffiths, *loc. cit.* and n. 5; thus with βαρβαθ*ιαω* (above, p. 75) cf. βαρβαραθ*ειω* Delatte/Derchain 520.

Ιαεω: lacking in the parallels; cf. *PGM* VII 584, 598, 608; VIII 96; LIX 4(?); cf. also the *ιαεω-logos* palindrome (below pp. 105ff.). According to Ganschinietz (*RE* IX 700 s.v. Iao), this is a more precise transcription of יהו than Ιαω, the ε being the normal way of representing Heb. ה. The form possibly arose from the impulse to make the transcription have four letters as does YHWH (A. Jacoby, *ARW* 28 [1930] 276 n. 3).

18 πακενψωθ πακενβραωθ: lacking in P, W_1, W_2; πακεπτωθ πακεβραωθ (C 17, L 16); cf. πακεπτωθ πα[κεπθωθ] (*PGM* XII 186 with Eitrem's supplement; more likely πα[κεβραωθ] on the basis of our text and parallels); πακερβαω (VII 328). Cf. also the common πακερβηθ which, as our words, is associated with Yahweh in formulae such as Ιαω πακερβηθ (*PGM* VII 646; cf. I 304; note similarity of -βηθ with Heb. בית, "house"). Similarly, ιωερβηθ ιωπακερβηθ (*PGM* III 71f., 116f., etc.), but these words primarily belong to Seth; cf. above on ιω esp. Daniel *loc. cit.*; also R. Wünsch, *Sethianische Verfluchungstafeln aus Rom* (Leipzig 1898) 88 and 90; for πακερβηθ see further F. Maltomini, *Aegyptus* 59 (1979) 281. In M the element -ενβραωθ resembles αβραωθ (*PGM* IV 1214, 3020; V 133; cf. αμβραθ for αβραθ above p. 78), which may be a play on αρβαθιαω or Cαβαωθ (cf. above pp. 74f. and p. 79 respectively, and for αβραωθ see P. Moraux, *Une défixion judiciaire au musée d' Istanbul* [Mem. Ac. Roy. Belge LIV 2, 1960] 33f.).

cαβαρβατιαωθ cαβαρβατιανη cαβαρβαφαι: om. P. Variations of only the first word occur in three of the parallels: cαβαρβαριαωθ, C 17; βαβαρβαριαωθ cαβαρβαριαωθ, W_1 35f.; ιαρβατιαω αρβατιαοθ, W_2 43. cαβαρβαρφαει in L 16 resembles the third. With the entire formula, cf. esp. *PGM* IV 1241ff.: cαβαρβαρβαθιωθ cαβαρβαρβαθιουθ cαβαρβαρβαθιωνηθ σαβαρβαρβαφαϊ. The element σαβαρβα, common to all three words in our text, is perhaps Σαβαωθ + αρβα (see above p. 79 and pp. 74f. respectively).

σαβαρβατιαωθ: cf. Σαβ Αβρα Ιαω (Delatte/Derchain 30); Ζαβαρβαθιαω (*PGM* VIII 96, X 6); σαβαθιουθ, below § K 44 (p. 101) and the corresponding σαρβαθιουθ, P 388; cf. also βαρβαθιαω (above p. 75). The element -ιαωθ equals Ιαω; the final θ may have developed on the analogy of Σαβαωθ (Baudissin "Iao" 194f.; cf. esp. Ιαωθ Σαβαωθ, *PGM* V 479). On this point and for various other interpretations of the significance of medial and final θ in magical words, see Peterson, *EIC ΘEOC* 97-103. Thus, σαβ(αωθ)-αρβατ-ιαωθ (for αρβατ as the fem. construct of *arba*, see above p. 78).

σαβαρβατιανη: perhaps σαβ(αωθ)-αρβ(α)-ατιανη, the final element probably a corruption of Αδωναι (Heb. "Lord"); cf. in our text βαρβαδωναι, § K 40f. (below p. 94); βαρβαραιωνη (*PGM* XIII 768).

σαβαρβαφαι: cf. βαρβαραϊ (*PGM* IV 1008). αι may stand for αϊα, a palindromic form of the Heb. Tetragram (see below on § K 46, p. 103). It could also be the possessive morpheme "my," as in *Adon-ai* (lit. "my Lord"); cf. Ιαω αι (*PGM* IV 1035, 1076; Ganschinietz in *RE* IX 701 s.v. Iao).* I am not sure how to account for the preceding φ.

μαρι ἐνδόξου: so P 365 (and see Preisendanz's n.); μαρει ἐνδόξου, C 17; ακραμμαχαμαρει ἐνδόξω, W_2 44f.; μαριονιοξαc, W_1 36f. (-ονιοξαc is a case of a Greek word corrupted to a *nomen barbarum*; cf. below pp. 104f. on αθερεcφιλαυω); lacking in L. Cf. μαρι μαρι αρι, *An. Ath.* 581.13-14; μαρμαριμαρι, Kropp II 15.3 (p. 57); μαρι μαριη μαρει, *Pist. Soph.* IV 142 (Schmidt/MacDermot 370.18); ⲱ ⲡⲉⲝⲥ ⲁ ⲙⲁⲣⲓ, Stegemann XLV 1.6 (p. 70). μαρι is probably Aramaic מרי, "(my) Lord" (cf. Heb. *Adonai*).

18 μαρμαραωθ - - - 19 κατὰ τοῦ μαρμαραυωθ: Only in M are the *marmar-* words separated by the two Osiris names. Parallels: κατὰ τοῦ μαρμαρεωθ μαρμαραυωθ μαρμαραωθ (P 365f.); κατὰ τοῦ μαρμαραιωθ καὶ κατὰ τοῦ μαρμαραωθ μαρμαραυωθ (C 17f.); μαμαραωθ μαρμαριουωθ μαρμαιοθ μαρμα⟦ρ⟧ι`α´οθ (W_2 45ff.); κατὰ τοῦ μαρμαραουωθ (L 16f.); lacking in W_1. In other magical texts, μαρμαραωθ: *PGM* XII 187; Kropp II 47.4,7 (p. 178); Aud. 242.17; Delatte/Derchain 222; *Test. Sol.* XVIII 28 and 33 (new fragments of these passages edited by R.W. Daniel in *P. Rainer Cent.* 39, p.

298f. and nn. p. 300); μαρμαραυωθ: *PGM* IV 946f., 1591; XII 231; Delatte/Derchain 212, 460. For the Aramaic etymology מר מריות, "lord of lords" and others, see C. Brockelmann, *Bonner Jahrbücher* 104 (1899) 193; Hopfner, OZ I § 746; Bonner 154.* In the *Test. Sol.* μαρμαραωθ is the name of the 24th and 29th dekan angel (Gundel, W., *Dekane* 79). In our spell, in the context of Iao, Adonai, and Abrasax, it is probably intended as another name for Yahweh and as such occurs in Syrian liturgy (cf. Kropp III § 206). For Yahweh as "Lord of lords" in the Bible, see Deut. 10.17; Ps. 136.3 (MT); cf. also Enoch 9.4; NT ITim. 6.15.

18f. ουcερβεντηθ: I find no other attestations. ουcερ is Osiris (for Osiris in magical texts, cf. Hopfner, *AO* 3 [1931] 120ff.; R.W. Daniel, *ZPE* 19 [1975] 263). I owe to Mr. R. Kotansky the suggestion that βε may represent the Egyptian *ba*, "life," "being," often with the idea of self-manifestation or disclosure; thus, "Gestaltfähigkeit" (see E.M. Wolf-Brinkmann, *Versuch einer Deutung des Begriffes "b3" anhand der Überlieferung der Frühzeit und des Alten Reiches* [Diss. Basel 1968] 7-9). *Ba* occurs as an element in magical words in its Coptic form *bai* (βαινφνουν, *PGM* XIII 809; βαινχωωωχ, IV 973; see L. Koenen, *ZPE* 8 [1971] 203; R.W. Daniel, *ZPE* 19 [1975] 253; Crum 28A s.v. ⲃⲁⲓ; further below p. 102. *Bai* is phonetically equivalent to our βε [Gignac I 191ff.]). In Egyptian texts the word compounds with names of gods as an epithet formula (e.g., Osiris is the "*ba* of Re," Re is the "*ba* of Nun," etc.; see L.V. Zabkar, *A Study of the Ba Concept in Ancient Egyptian Texts* [Studies in Ancient Oriental Civilization 34, Chicago 1968] 11-15; cf. cὺ εἶ ἡ ψυχὴ τοῦ δαίμονος τοῦ Ὀcίρεως, *PGM* IV 2987). Thus, ουcερβεντηθ may be *wsir-b3-ntr*, "Osiris is the *ba* of God," or perhaps "*ba* of the gods," understanding the last element as Coptic plural *ěntēr*, "gods" (Crum 230B s.v. ⲚⲞⲨⲦⲈ; cf. φνουθι νινθηρ, "God of gods," in *PGM* IV 1643 and XXXVIII 16; see *PGM* vol. 3 p. 229B s.v. πνουτε). In either case, ρ is replaced by θ, a common appendage to magical words; see above p. 81.*

19 ουcερπατη: tab. ουεερπατη; ε/c is a standard letter confusion (F.W. Hall, *Companion to Classical Texts* [Oxford 1913] 158; H.C. Youtie, *The Textual Criticism of the Documentary Papyri, Prolegomena* [London² 1974] 68.). The element -πατη is perhaps Egyptian *pḥty*, "strength." Crum (284B) notes that the Coptic equivalent ⲠⲀϨⲦⲈ appears in various Greco-Egyptian proper names; e.g., Ἀπάθηc, Ψεναπάθηc (or -τηc), Cεναπάθηc (or -τηc); cf. s.vv.

in Preisigke, *Namenbuch* and D. Foraboschi, *Onomasticon Alterum Papyrologicum*. With the interpretation of ουcερπατη as "Osiris is strength," cf. the etymology of Osiris' name in Plutarch *Is. et Os.* 37 as ὄβριμοc, "mighty" (Egyptian *wsr*; see the comments of Hopfner [vol. II p. 174] and Griffiths [p. 442] *ad loc*).

μαρμαραχθα: repeated only in our text; so spelled in C 18, W_1 37, L 17; μαρεχθανα (P 366); χθαμα (W_2 47). The name is applied to God in Jesus' prayer in *Pist. Soph.* IV 142 (Schmidt/MacDermot 370.13). Cf. also compounds involving the Egyptian solar figure Harachte, e.g., in M, αμουραχθη (§ K 46) and its parallel αμαραχθι in P 390 (see below p. 103); thus our word may mean "Lord (Aramaic *mar-* ; cf. above pp. 81f.) Harachte." This explanation does not contradict the connection with Yahweh in *Pist. Soph.*, since magical names and formulae often evince an underlying syncretism of sun deities with Yahweh (see below on βαρβαδωναι lines 40f. [pp. 94f.]; § A, the *ιαεω-Logos* [pp. 105-08]; §§ C and E, αβλαναθαναλβα ακραμμαχαμαρει [pp. 108-10 esp. Peterson ref. on p. 110]; cf. also Fauth 72-75).

αμαρδα: αμαρζα (P 367, C 18, and *PGM* XII 178); αμαζε (W_2 48); μαλμαρζα (W_1 37); μαμαζαγα̣ρ̣ (L 17); cf. μαρζα below § K 29 (p. 89).

μαριβεωθ: so in P 367; μαρειβαιωθ (C 18); μαριβα[ρι]ω̣θ (W_1 37f.); μαριβαριοθ (W_2 48); lacking in L. Here also the Aramaic *mari* may be involved (see above on μαρι ἐνδόξου p. 81).

19-26: Second Command to the νεκυδαίμων

M [19] μή μου παρακούcῃc τῶν |[20] ἐντολῶν, νεκυδαίμων, ὅcτιc ποτ' εἶ εἴτε ἄρρην εἴτε θήλεια, ἀλλ' ἔγειρέ μοι cεαυτὸν καὶ ὕπαγε εἰc πᾶν τόπον, εἰc πᾶν ἄμφοδον, | εἰc πᾶcαν οἰκίαν, καὶ κατάδηcον Κοπρίαν, ἣν ἔτεκε μήτηρ Ταῆcιc, ἧc ἔχειc τὰc τρίχαc τῆc κεφαλῆc, Αἰλουρίωνι, ᾧ ἔτεκε | μήτηρ ὀνόματι Κοπρία, ὅπωc μὴ βινηθῇ μηδὲ πυγιcθῇ μήτε ἡδονὴν ποιήcῃ ἄλλῳ νεανίcκῳ ἢ ἑτέρῳ ἀνδρί, ἀλ|λὰ μηδὲ δυνηθῇ μήτε φαγεῖν μήτε πιεῖν μήτε ὕπνου τυχεῖν μήτε ἡcυχάζειν τῇ ψυχῇ ἢ τῇ διανοίᾳ ἐπιζητοῦcα διὰ παντὸc ἡμέ|[24]ρηc καὶ νυκτὸc Αἰλουρίωνα, ὃν ἔτεκε μήτηρ ὀνόματι Κοπρία, φιλοῦcα ἐρῶcα ἐξ ὅληc καρδίαc ἐξ ὅλου πνεύματοc ὡc τὴν ἑαυ|τῆc ψυχὴν Κοπρία, ἧς ἔχεις τὰς τρίχας, φιλοῦσα ἔρωτι θείῳ μέχρι θανάτου Αἰλουρίωνα, ὃν ἔτεκε μήτηρ ὀνόματι Κοπρία· ἤδη | ἤδη ταχὺ ταχύ.

P [367] μή μου παρακούσῃς, |[368] νεκύδαιμον, τῶν ἐντολῶν καὶ τῶν ὀνομάτων, | ἀλλ' ἔγειρον μόνον σεαυτὸν ἀπὸ τῆς ἐχούσης | σε ἀναπαύσεως, ὅστις ποτὲ εἶ, εἴτε ἄρρης εἴτε θῆ|λυς, καὶ ὕπαγε εἰς πάντα τόπον, εἰς πᾶν ἄμφοδον, |[372] εἰς πᾶσαν οἰκίαν καὶ ἔνεγκόν μοι τὴν δεῖνα, καὶ κα|τάσχες αὐτῆς τὴν βρῶσιν καὶ τὴν πόσιν, καὶ | μὴ ἐάσῃς τὴν δεῖνα ἄλλου ἀνδρὸς πεῖραν λαβεῖν | πρὸς ἡδονήν, μηδὲ ἰδίου ἀνδρός, εἰ μὴ ἐμοῦ |[376] μόνου, τοῦ δεῖνα, ἀλλ' ἕλκε τὴν δεῖνα τῶν τριχῶν, τῶν | σπλάγχνων, τῆς ψυχῆς πρὸς ἐμέ, τὸν δεῖνα, πά|σῃ ὥρᾳ τοῦ αἰῶνος, νυκτὸς καὶ ἡμέρας, μέ|χρι οὗ ἔλθῃ πρὸς ἐμέ, τὸν δεῖνα, καὶ ἀχώριστός |[380] μου μείνῃ ἡ δεῖνα. ποίησον, κατάδησον εἰς τὸν | ἅπαντα χρόνον τῆς ζωῆς μου καὶ συναναγ|κασον τὴν δεῖνα ὑπουργὸν εἶναί μοι, τῷ δεῖνα, καὶ μὴ | ἀποσκιρτάτω ἀπ' ἐμοῦ ὥραν μίαν τοῦ αἰῶνος. |[384] ἐάν μοι τοῦτο τελέσῃς, ἀναπαύσω σε ταχέως.

C [18] μή μου πα|ρακούσῃς, νέκυς δαίμων, ὅστις ποτὲ εἶ, καὶ ὕπαγε ἰς πάντα τόπον καὶ ἰς πᾶν ἄμφο|[20]δον καὶ εἰς πᾶσαν οἰκίαν καὶ ἔνεγκέ μοι Ἡρωνοῦν, ἣν ἔτεκεν Πτολεμαΐς, καὶ κατάσχες αὐτῆς | τὸν βροτὸν καὶ τὸν ποτόν, μὴ ἐάσῃς Ἡρωνοῦν ἄλλου ἀνδρὸς πεῖραν λαβεῖν εἰ μὴ ἐμοῦ | μόνου Ποσιδωνίου, ὃν ἔτεκεν Θσενουβάσθις, ἕλκε ται⟨ν⟩ (i.e., τὴν)* Ηρωνοῦν τῶν τριχῶν καὶ τῶν | σπλάγχνων αὐτῆς πρὸς ἐμὲ Ποσιδώνιον πᾶσαν ὥραν τοῦ αἰῶνος, νυκτὸς καὶ ἡμέρας, |[24] μέχρι οὗ ἔλθῃ Ἡρωνοῦς πρὸς ἐμὲ Ποσιδώνιον καὶ ἀδιαχώριστόν μου αὐτὴν ποιήσῃς μέ|χρι θανάτου, ἵν' ἔχω αὐτὴν Ἡρωνοῦν, ἣν ἔτεκεν Πτολεμαΐς, ὑποτεταγμένην ἐγὼ Πο|σιδώνιος, ὃν ἔτεκεν Θσενουβάσθις, ἰς τὸν ἅπαντα χρόνον τῆς ζωῆς μου. ἤδη | ἤδη ταχὺ ταχύ· ἐὰν τοῦτό μοι ποιήσῃς, ἀπολύσω σε.

W$_1$ [38] μή μου παρακούσῃς, νεκυδαίμων, ὅστις ποτ' οὖν | [εἶ, κ]αὶ ἔγειρέ μοι σεαυτόν, ὅτι ἐξορκίζω σε κατὰ τῆς κυρίας |[40] [Ἑ]κάτης Ἀρτέμιδος κτλ.*

W$_2$ [48] ὁρκίζω | σε, μὴ παρακούσῃς τῶν ὀνο|μάτων, ἀλλὰ ἐξέγειρε σεαυ|τὸν καὶ ὕπαγε εἰς πᾶν τόπον, |[52] ὅπου ἐστὶ Ματρῶνα, ἣν ἔτε|κεν Ταγένη, ἧς ἔχις τὴν οὐ|σίαν, καὶ ἄπελθε πρὸς αὐτὴν |

καὶ κατάσχες αὐτῆς τὸν ὕ{πν`ον´}|56πνον,* τὸ ποτόν, τὸν βρο-{τὸν}|τὸν καὶ μὴ ἀφῇς Ματρῶναν, | ἣν ἔτεκεν Ταγένη, ἧς ἔχις | τὴν οὐςίαν, ἄλλου ἀντρὸς |60 φιλίαν ἔχιν καὶ ςτοργήν, | εἰ μὴ Θεοδώρω, ὃν {ετ}ἔτε|κεν Τεχῶςις. ἕλκε τὴν | Ματρῶναν τῶν τριχῶν, |64 τῶν ςπλά⟨γ⟩χνων, τῆς ψυχῆ`ς´, | τῆς καρδίας, ἕως ἔλθῃ πρὸ`ς´ | Θεόδωρον, καὶ ἀχώριςτον | αὐτὸν ποίηςον μέχ⟨ρ⟩εις θα|68νάτου νυκτὸς καὶ ἡμέραις | πάςᾳ ὥρᾳ τοῦ αἰῶνος. | ἤδη ἤδη ταχὺ ταχὺ ἄρτι ἄρ`τι´. | ἄμ μοι τοῦτο τελέςῃς, |72 λύςω ςε ταχέως.

L 17 μὴ παρα|κούςῃς, νεκύδαιμον Ἀντίνοε, ἀλλ' ἔγειραί μοι ςεαυτὸν καὶ ὕπαγε εἰς πᾶν τό|πον, εἰς πᾶν ἄμφοδον, εἰς πᾶςαν οἰκείαν καὶ ἄγαγέ μοι τὴν Πτολεμαΐδα, |20 ἣν ἔτεκεν Ἀϊᾶς, τὴν θυγατέρα Ὠριγένους· κατάςχες αὐτῆς τὸ βροτόν, | τὸ ποτόν, ἕως ἔλθῃ πρὸς ἐμὲ τὸν Σαραπάμμωνα, ὃν ἔτεκεν Ἀρέα, | καὶ μὴ ἐάςῃς αὐτὴν ἄλλου ἀνδρὸς πεῖραν λαβεῖν εἰ μὴ ἐμοῦ μόνου | τοῦ Σαραπάμμωνος. ἕλκε αὐτὴν τῶν τριχῶν, τῶν ςπλάγχνων, |24 ἕως μὴ ἀποςτῇ μου τοῦ Σαραπάμμωνος, οὗ ἔτεκεν Ἀρέα, καὶ ἔχω | αὐτὴν τὴν Πτολεμαΐδα, ἣν ἔτεκεν Ἀϊᾶς, τὴν θυγατέρα Ὠριγένους, | ὑποτεταγμένην εἰς τὸν ἅπαντα χρόνον τῆς ζωῆς μου, | φιλοῦςάν με, ἐρῶς[ά]ν μου, λέγουςάν μοι ἃ ἔχει ἐν νόῳ. ἐὰν τοῦτο |28 ποιήςῃς, ἀπολύςω ςε.

All the parallels at this point incorporate material similar to part of the first command (above pp. 51ff.). Thus, with P 369-72 (ἔγειρον μόνον --- τὴν δεῖνα) cf. 347-50 (ἀνέγειρέ μοι --- ἆξον τὴν δεῖνα); with C 19-20 (νέκυς δαίμων --- Πτολεμαΐς) cf. 7-8 (νέκυς δαίμων --- Πτολεμαΐς); W_1 38ff. repeats only ἔγειρέ μοι ςεαυτόν from the earlier part (16-21) and then proceeds with the adjuration of Artemis/Hekate (cf. above p. 18); with W_2 50-54 (ἐξέγειρε --- οὐςίαν) cf. 12-22 (ἔγειρέ μοι --- αὐτῆς [with ἐξορκίζω --- δεμόνια interrupting; see above p. 18]); with L 18-20 (νεκύδαιμον ---Ὠριγένους) cf. 6-8 (τῷ δαίμονι --- Ὠριγένους); with M 20-26 (νεκυδαίμων --- ταχύ) cf. 6-14 (⟨ἔγειρέ μοι⟩ --- χρόνον). M prolongs the repeated material with ὅπως μὴ βινηθῇ κτλ., omitting the rest of the second command as it occurs in P, C, L, and W_2. Since W_1 also omits most of this material and W_2 includes it, it is likely that the handbook(s) of these two texts and perhaps some of the other handbooks offered optional spells at this point (on such options, see above pp. 6f.).

In the following synopsis of variations between the two corresponding sections of our text, the present passage is labled M_2 and the earlier M_1 (so also in the textual appendix, below pp. 113ff.). Much of M_2 is iterated in § K 30ff. (below pp. 88ff.). The comments which follow the chart treat a few points where M_2 differs from M_1.

	M_1		M_2
	om.	19	μή μου παρακούςῃς τῶν ἐντολῶν
8	ἑτέρῳ --- ἄλλῳ	22	ἄλλῳ --- ἑτέρῳ
9	εἰ μὴ --- ὀνόματι Κοπρία		om.
9f.	διὰ παντός	23f.	transposed after ἐπιζητοῦςα with ἡμέρας καὶ νυκτός added
10	εὐςταθεῖν ἢ	23	om. (possibly haplography before ἡςυχάζειν)
	ταῖς φρεςὶ		τῇ διανοίᾳ
	μήτηρ Κοπρία		μήτηρ ὀνόματι Κοπρία
	ἕως οὗ --- (12) ὀνόματι Κοπρία		om. (perhaps haplography caused by ὀνόματι Κοπρία before φιλοῦ-ςα)
12	ψυχῆς	24	καρδίας
12f.	φίλτροις --- ἐρωτικοῖς	24f.	ὡς τὴν ἑαυτῆς ψυχήν
13	Αἰλουρίωνα --- Κοπρία	25	transposed after θανάτου Κοπρία --- φιλοῦςα
13f.	ἀπὸ τῆς ςήμερον --- χρόνον		μέχρι θανάτου
	om.	25f.	ἤδη ἤδη ταχὺ ταχύ

19f. μή μου παρακούςῃς τῶν ἐντολῶν: L 17f. has the shortest version, μὴ παρακούςῃς; cf. μή μου παρακούςῃς (C 18f., W_1 38); μὴ παρακούςῃς τῶν ὀνομάτων (W_2 49f.); μή μου παρακούςῃς, νεκύδαιμον, τῶν ἐντολῶν καὶ τῶν ὀνομάτων (P 367f.). Magical texts employ παρακούειν with the late meanings "fail to heed," "disobey," for commands or threats. The former sometimes, as in M, takes the form of a μή + subjunctive prohibition followed by ἀλλά and an imperative (μή μου παρακούςῃς, ἀλλὰ ἀνάπεμψον, *PGM* XIVa 10; μή μου παρακούςητε, ἀλλὰ τάχιον ποιήςατε, W_4 22f.; cf. F. Maltomini, *SCO* 29 [1979] 110f. [on line 8]); the latter is often expressed as a condition (ἐὰν δέ μου παρακούςῃς, κατακαήςεται ὁ κύκλος [*sc.* τοῦ ἡλίου], καὶ cκότος ἔςται καθ' ὅλην τὴν οἰκουμένην, *PGM* XII 55f.; ἐάν με παρακούςῃς --- ἐρῶ τῷ μεγάλῳ θεῷ --- καὶ τὰ κρέατά cου δώcει φαγεῖν τῷ ψωριῶντι κυνί, XII 140f.; similarly, W_4 9f.; *PGM* IV 290f.; cf. also *PGM* VII 691f., 893; XIV 22; *paretis* in Lucan VI 744 (cited above p. 73). For threats in general, see above pp. 69ff.

24f. ὡc τὴν ἑαυτῆc ψυχὴν: Tab. has ΨΥΧΗΝC. The scribe, having first written ψυχῆc under the influence of ἑαυτῆc, corrected it to ψυχήν. This use of ψυχή as a near-equivalent of a personal or reflexive pronoun has some classical precedent, e.g., in expressions meaning "to gratify oneself": χαίρετ', ἐν κακοῖc ὅμωc | ψυχῇ διδόντεc ἡδονὴν καθ' ἡμέραν (Aesch. *Pers.* 840f.); τὴν ⟨δ'⟩ ἐμὴν ψυχὴν ἐγὼ | οὐ παύcομαι δρῶν εὖ (Eur. *Cycl.* 340f.); cf. κελεύει cε βαcιλεὺc ἐκ μὲν τούτου τοῦ χρυcίου εὐφραίνειν τὴν cεαυτοῦ ψυχήν, ἐπεὶ καὶ cὺ τὴν ἐκείνου εὔφρανac (Ael. *Var. Hist.* I 32); *pater nunc intus suo animo morem gerit* (Plaut. *Amph.* 131); further examples in Gow's n. on Theoc. 16.24 (II p. 310); Dodds, *Greeks and Irrat.* 138. Cf. also μηδεὶc κρατείτω τῆc ἐμῆc ψυχῆc ποτε (Soph. *OC* 1207 with R.C. Jebb's n. *ad loc.*); ἡ δ' ἐμὴ ψυχὴ πάλαι | τέθνηκεν (*Ant.* 559f.); ψυχὴ γὰρ ηὔδα πολλά μοι μυθουμένη (*Ant.* 227); similarly, the Homeric θυμόc in *Il.* XI 407 *et al.*

The expansion of this idiom in later times probably owes much to Semitic influence, as in Hebrew, where נפש often means "self" (Jacob in *TDNT* IX 620 s.v. ψυχή). E.g., in the LXX: προcάγωγέ μοι [*sc.* τὴν βρῶcιν] - - -, τέκνον, ἵνα εὐλογήcῃ cε ἡ ψυχή μου (Gen. 27.25); ἐδικαίωcεν τὴν ψυχὴν αὐτοῦ Ιcραηλ (Jer. 3.11). Compare Luke's version of Jesus' famous maxim (9.25, τί γὰρ ὠφελεῖται ἄνθρωποc κερδήcαc τὸν κόcμον ὅλον ἑαυτὸν δὲ ἀπολέcαc ἢ ζημιωθείc;) with that of Mark (8.36, τί γὰρ ὠφελεῖ ἄνθρωπον κερδῆcαι τὸν κόcμον ὅλον καὶ ζημιωθῆναι τὴν ψυχὴν αὐτοῦ;). For other NT examples, parallels, and discussion, see Bauer s.v. ψυχή 1 sect. f; Turner, *Syntax* 43; C.F.D. Moule, *An Idiom Book of NT Greek* (Cambridge 1968) 185; G.B. Winer, P.W. Schmiedel, *Grammatik des neutestamentlichen Sprachidioms* (Göttingen[8] 1898) § 22.18b with n. 33 (p. 214f.). In papyri this meaning of ψυχή is especially common in letters: τῷ δεςπότῃ μου καὶ ἀδελφῷ καὶ κυρίῳ τῆς ψυχῆς μου Κοπρέᾳ, *P. Lond.* III 1244.1 (p. 244) = G. Ghedini, *Lettere Cristiane* (Milan 1923) p. 215 with n. p. 217 (same text also published in M. Naldini, *Il Cristianesimo in Egitto* [Florence 1968] p. 250 and cf. p. 50 with n. 5); cf. also Bonner 185; J.H. Moulton, G. Milligan, *The Vocabulary of the Greek Testament* (London 1930) s.v. ψυχή 3.

25 μέχρι θανάτου: also in § K 39. The purely temporal meaning "until the time of death" is appropriate in this context, but otherwise rare (cf. C 24f. and W_2 67f. [above pp. 84f.]; Pseud. Luc. *Amor.* 47; cf. also Plutarch *Numa* 10.2; Philo *Decal.* 114). The phrase μέχρι/ἄχρι θανάτου normally denotes degree, not time (see Bauer, s.v. μέχρι).

25f. ἤδη ἤδη ταχὺ ταχύ: This common formula either marks the end of a spell (*PGM* IV 1924; VII 248, 254, 259; X 50; XII 143; XIXa 54; XXXVI 84, 114; P. Köln inv. no. 5514.11f., 5512.18f. [ed. R.W. Daniel, *ZPE* 19, 1975, 251, 259]; etc.) or the closing of a section of a spell (so our text; cf. § K 39-40 below; *PGM* III 35, 85; IV 2037; VIII 52; XII 58; XIXa 15; etc.).

The remainder of § J (26-28) consists of a combination of letters and obscure magical signs known as χαρακτῆρες. On the χαρακτῆρες in general cf. Youtie/Bonner "Beisan" 75/641; Hopfner in *RE* Supp. IV 1183ff.; *idem, OZ* I §§ 819f. For the χαρακτῆρες in P, see above p. 19 n. 58.

Commentary § K

Synopsis: Following a series of vowels and *voces magicae* (29-30), lines 30-40 iterate with some alteration and abbreviation § J 19-26, which in turn corresponds to § J 6-14 (i.e., M_2 and M_1 respectively; cf. above pp. 85f.). In lines 40-47 the Michigan tablet (alone of the five) preserves the second threat, corresponding to P 385-94 (see above pp. 16f. and the general discussion of structure, pp. 18ff.).

29-40: *Voces Magicae* and Iteration of Parts of § J (M_2)

[29]αεο ... ωαηωαιυαυεωιαεωμαρζα | μαριβεωθ. μή μου παρακούςῃς τῶν ἐντολῶν, | νεκυδαίμων, ὅςτις ποτ' εἶ, ἀλλ' ἔγειρέ μοι

cεαυτόν |[32] καὶ ὕπαγε εἰc πᾶν τόπον εἰc πᾶν ἄμφοδον | εἰc πᾶcαν οἰκίαν καὶ ἄξον Κοπρίαν, ἣν ἔτε|κε μήτηρ Ταῆcιc, ἧc ἔχειc τὰc τρίχαc, Αἰλουρι|ῶνι, ᾧ ἔτεκε μήτηρ ὀνόματι Κοπρία, πυρου|[36]μένην καιομένην τηκομένην τὴν ψυχὴν | τὸ πνεῦμα τὴν γυναικείαν φύcιν, φιλοῦcαν | ἐρῶcαν ἔρωτι θείῳ Αἰλουρίωνα, ὃν ἔτεκε | μήτηρ ὀνόματι Κοπρία, μέχρι θανάτου· ἤδη |[40] ἤδη ταχὺ ταχύ.

29 αεο --- ιαεω: for the significance of vowels in magic, see below on §§ B G H, p. 110. The series ends with the Hebrew divine name ιαεω, on which see above p. 80.

29-30 μαρζα μαριβεωθ: similarly, αμαρδα μαριβεωθ before μή μου παρακούcῃc above § J 19, and see nn. p. 83. With μαρζα cf. also μαραδθα P 392 (see above p. 12); μαρατα *PGM* XVI 10; μ̣[α]ριθα̣ (cf. above p. 76 n. on 16); Μαρζουνη (or Μαρζουν ἡ) IV 2547.

30-40: The variations between M_2 (see synopsis above) and the present passage (labeled M_3) are summarized as follows:

M_2	M_3
20 εἴτε ἄρρην εἴτε θήλεια	om.
21 κατάδηcον	33 ἄξον
τῆc κεφαλῆc	om.
22 ὅπωc μὴ --- (24) Κοπρία	35 πυρουμένην (cf. § J 11) --- (37) φύcιν
24 ἐξ ὅληc --- (25) φιλοῦcα	om.
25 μέχρι θανάτου	39 transposed after ὀνόματι Κοπρία

33 ἄξον: cf. κατάδηcον, § J 21 (and 7). The sigmatic aor. of ἄγειν is rare in the classical language (KB 2.347; Veitch s.v.) and occurs mainly in compound in the NT (BDR § 75) and LXX (Helbing 90f.; Thackeray 233). Mayser (I 2, 144) gives one compound form, διάξῃ{cθε} (*P. Tebt.* I 22.16), from the Ptolemaic papyri. The simplex is much more common in the Roman and Byzantine periods, esp. in the magical papyri, where it is used considerably more than ἤγαγον (Barber 61f.; Gignac II 290(-91) with nn. 5 and 6; *PGM* vol. 3 p. 49A and B); cf. *PGM* IV 1591, 1915; VII 305, 309; XIXa 50; XXXVI 110, 311; etc.).

35-37 πυρουμένην --- φύσιν: This section seems to replace ὅπως μὴ βινηθῇ --- Κοπρία of § J 22-24. In general, for the effect of erotic magic on the soul or heart ("burning," etc.) see above on ἐξ ὅλης ψυχῆς κτλ. § J 12, pp. 63f. For the specific wording here, cf. ναί, κύριε δαῖμον, ἄξον, καῦσον, ὄλεσον, πύρωσον, σκότωσον [και]ομένην, πυρουμένην, κέντει βασανιζομένην τὴν ψυχήν, τὴν καρδίαν τῆς Κάρωσα (*PGM* XIXa 50f.); ἄξετέ μοι --- τὴν δεῖνα --- καιομένην, πυρουμένην, ἀεροπετουμένην (XXXVI 125ff.); cf. *ibid.* 110f.; 200. Intensification through accumulation of synonyms is common; see above p. 63.

36f. τὴν ψυχὴν τὸ πνεῦμα τὴν γυναικείαν φύσιν: with the last cf. *PGM* XXXVI 82f.: ἕως ἂν ἔλθῃ φιλοῦσα ἐμὲ τὸν δεῖνα καὶ τὴν θηλυκὴν αὐτῆς φύσιν τῇ ἀρσενικῇ μου κολλήσῃ (also *ibid.* 113f. and 150). φύσις (or φύσεις) can in fact mean αἰδοῖα, esp. the female organ, without a qualifying adjective (P 318, 326 [see above p. 9]; *PGM* XXXVI 324; LXII 103; etc. See LSJ s.v., VII 2; Henderson, *Muse* 5). The three items together recall Paul's trichotomy, τὸ πνεῦμα καὶ ἡ ψυχὴ καὶ τὸ σῶμα, in 1Thess. 5.23 (see esp. A.J. Festugière, *L' Idéal Religieux des Grecs et l'Évangile* [Paris 1932] 196ff.), with our τὴν γυναικείαν φύσιν representing τὸ σῶμα. Cf. also Aud. 41a.8f.: τούτους ἀναθεμα[τί]ζομεν σῶμα πνεῦμα ψ[υ]χὴν [δι]άνοιαν φρόνησιν κτλ. (Audollent places a high dot after ἀναθεματίζομεν and apparently assumes a verb in the lacunae which follow in lines 12f.); Youtie/Bonner "Beisan" obv. frag. 1.23 (p. 55/621); Kagarow 36 s.vv. *Asyndeta und Polysyndeta.*

We have seen that the grouping of words like "soul," "heart," "mind," "spirit," etc., often serves the purposes of stylistic intensification, and thus such terms are frequently interchangeable (e.g., in the parallel groups of M_1 and M_2 [see above p. 86], διανοίᾳ line 23 replaces φρεσί 10; καρδίας 24 replaces ψυχῆς 12). The union of πνεῦμα and ψυχή at this point in our spell (cf. also line 12) deserves special consideration because of the importance of these ideas in various philosophical and theological systems which at times treat the two words as synonyms and at times sharply discriminate between them. In Presocratic and Stoic thought, ψυχή became closely associated with πνεῦμα, the former being conceived as air or breath (with Anaximenes frag. 2 Diels-Kranz [I p. 95] cf. Eur. *Suppl.* 530-34; see also G.S. Kirk, J.E. Raven, M. Schofield, *The Presocratic Philosophers* [Cambridge[2] 1983] 158f.; H. von Arnim, *Stoicorum Veterum Fragmenta* II

[Leipzig 1903] p. 217ff. [fragg. 773ff.]; Dodds, *Greeks and Irrat.* 174 n. 112; Kleinknecht in *TDNT* VI 336 s.v. πνεῦμα). Similarly in later periods, New Testament authors and magical texts at times scarcely differentiate between πνεῦμα and ψυχή (μεγαλύνει ἡ ψυχή μου --- καὶ ἠγαλλίαcεν τὸ πνεῦμά μου, NT Lk. 1.46f.; ἀκούω --- ὅτι cτήκετε ἐν ἑνὶ πνεύματι, μιᾷ ψυχῇ, Phil. 1. 27; τὸ πνεῦμά cου --- cου ἡ ψυχή, *PGM* IV 627, 630; for Hebrew and the LXX, see Jacob, *loc. cit.* [above p. 64] and Hatch, *op. cit.* [above p. 64] p. 104 respectively). Thus either cῶμα/ψυχή (NT Mat. 6.25; cf. Kemmer, *op. cit.* [above p. 53] p. 161f.) or cῶμα/πνεῦμα (1Cor. 7.34; cf. *PGM* I 177f.) function as a polarism to circumscribe the whole person (cf. also cώματα --- νοόc NT Rom. 12.1f.).

Paul often employs πνεῦμα as he and other writers use ψυχή (cf. above pp. 87f.) as a near-equivalent to a personal or reflexive pronoun (ἀνέπαυcαν γὰρ τὸ ἐμὸν πνεῦμα καὶ τὸ ὑμῶν [i.e., με καὶ ὑμᾶc], 1Cor. 16.18; similarly 2Cor. 2.13, 7.13; Gal. 6.18; Phil. 4.23; Philem. 25; see R. Bultmann, *Theologie des Neuen Testaments* [Tübingen[3] 1958] 207 [Eng. vol. I, New York 1951, 206]). In other Pauline contexts πνεῦμα approaches the Greek concept of νοῦc or the modern idea of "conscience" (τίc γὰρ οἶδεν ἀνθρώπων τὰ τοῦ ἀνθρώπου εἰ μὴ τὸ πνεῦμα τοῦ ἀνθρώπου τὸ ἐν αὐτῷ, 1Cor. 2.11; cf. Rom. 8.16; Bultmann *op. cit.* 208f. [Eng. vol. I 207]. For Origen's conception of πνεῦμα as cυνειδόc see A. Henrichs, L. Koenen, *ZPE* 5 [1970] 186 n. 223). In 1Cor. 14.14f., however, νοῦc is contrasted with πνεῦμα, the latter signifying the emotive/ecstatic element expressed through *glossolalia.* Sometimes Paul elevates πνεῦμα to a position superior to ψυχή (ἐγένετο ὁ πρῶτοc ἄνθρωποc Ἀδὰμ εἰc ψυχὴν ζῶcαν· ὁ ἔcχατοc Ἀδὰμ εἰc πνεῦμα ζῳοποιοῦν, 1Cor. 15.45, implied also in the ψυχικόc and πνευματικόc terminology in this passage and 2.13ff.; see Bultmann, *op. cit.* 205 [Eng. vol. I 204]). Similarly Didymus the Blind, in his allegory of the almond in Eccles. 12.5 (based on the above-cited 1Thess. 5.23), interprets the outer and inner husks as cῶμα and ψυχή, and the innermost edible part as πνεῦμα (*Kommentar zum Ecclesiastes* [Eccl.T.] 357.26-358.8, ed. G. Binder, L. Liesenborghs VI, [PTA 9, 1969] 214f.). Elsewhere Didymus speaks of the identity of πνεῦμα and ψυχή (*Psalmenkommentar* [Ps.T.] 139.6-9, ed. M. Gronewald III [PTA 8, 1969] p. 50; see also *Der Psalmenkommentar von Tura Quaternio IX* [Papyrologica Coloniensia I, 1964], ed. A. Kehl, p. 84, with commentary, p. 161ff.).

It is uncertain whether we should assign some particular connotation to πνεῦμα in our text, such as νοῦς, or simply take it and ψυχή together as a periphrasis of the inward life (in contrast to φύσιν). The basic point, however, is obvious enough: our spell demands that the ἔρως θεῖος overtake Kopria's entire being, which here, as elsewhere (cf. § J 10, 12, 23, 24), is analyzed into various anthropological categories.

40-47: Second Threat against the νεκυδαίμων

M 40 ἐγώ εἰμι βαρβαδωναιαι | βαρβαδωναι, ὁ τὰ ἄςτρα κρύβων, ὁ τὸν οὐ|ρανὸν κρατέων, ὁ τὸν κόςμον ἀληθεύων· | ιατθεουν ιατρεουν ςαλβιουθ Αωθ |44 Αωθ ςαβαθιουθ ιατ΄θεραθ Αδωναιαι | ιςαρ ςυρια βιβιβε βιβιουθ νατθω | Ϲαβαωθ αιαναφα αμουραχθη ςαταμα | Ζεύς αθερεςφιλαυω.

P 385 ἐγὼ γάρ εἰμι βαρβαρ Αδωναι ὁ τὰ ἄςτρα κρύ|βων, ὁ λαμπροφεγγὴς οὐρανοῦ κρατῶν, | ὁ κύριος κόςμου αθθουϊν ϊαθουϊν ςελ|388βιουωθ· Αωθ ςαρβαθιουθ ιαθθιεραθ | Αδωναι ια ρουρα βια βι βιοθη αθωθ | Ϲαβαωθ ηα νιαφα αμαραχθι· ςαταμα· | ζαυαθθειη ςερφω κτλ.

40 ἐγώ εἰμι: Magical literature employs this common formula with names of the great gods (Κρόνος, *PGM* XII 233; Ἑρμῆς, IV 2999; Ἀφροδείτη, XII 232; Ἶςις, XII 234; Ὄςιρις, XII 234; Ἥλιος, XII 232; Ὧρος, IV 1075; Θωυθ, V 247 and cf. IV 394; Ερεςχιγαλ, LXX 5; Αβραςαξ, LXIX 2; πρόςωπον of Iao Sabaoth Adonai, Kropp II 47.11,11 [p. 183]), with more general words for deity (ὁ θεός, *PGM* XII 230; [ὁ κύρ]ιος, III 343f.; ὁ υἱός, IV 535), with deified abstractions (ἡ αλήθεια, *PGM* V 148 and cf. NT Jn. 14.6; ἡ πίςτις, XII 228; ἡ χάρις, V 156), with Biblical characters (Αδαμ, *PGM* III 145f.; Μωυςῆς, V 108f.), with magic words/*nomina barbara* (*PGM* XXIIb 34f.; XXXVI 169f.), and with divine attributes in the form of adjectives (ὁ ἰςχυρότερος, *PGM* XIII 202f.; ὁ μέγας, XII 110), participles (ὁ ποιῶν, *PGM* XIII 281; ὁ γεννῶν, V 154f.) and relative sentences (οὗ ἐςτιν ὁ ἱδρὼς ὄμβρος, *PGM* V 151f.; ᾧ ςυνήντηςας, XII 92). The formula occurs at times in series one after the other (*PGM* V 145ff.; XII 227ff.), at times in isolated instances (IV 2999; XXIIb 34f.). The common magical word ανοχ/ανοκ, which represents the Coptic first pers. personal pronoun (Crum 11B; cf. Heb. אנכי), sometimes stands for ἐγώ (εἰμι); e.g., ανοκ πε βαινχωωωχ,* "I am the soul of darkness," *PGM* LXXIX 2 (see A.A. Barb, *Hommages à Waldemar Deonna* [Col. Latomus 28, 1957] 74f.; A. Jacoby, *ARW* 28 [1930] 271ff.).

On the usage and interpretation of "I am" in various religious traditions, see Norden, *Ag. Th.* 183-201, 210-20; Stauffer in *TDNT* II 343-54 s.v. ἐγώ; R.E. Brown, *The Gospel According to John* vol. I (Garden City NY, 1966) 533ff.; and esp. R. Bultmann, *Das Evangelium des Johannes* (Göttingen 1950) 167f. n. 2 (Eng. [Oxford 1971] 225f. n. 3). For our purposes we may note two broad categories, the first being when a deity employs it as a formula of self-revelation by which he communicates his name, attributes, activities, etc. Cf., e.g., in the LXX the periphrasis of the divine name as ἐγώ εἰμι ὁ ὤν (Ex. 3.14) and the numerous "I (am)" sayings of Yahweh in Isaiah (43.3,11,15; 44.6,24; 45.5; 48.12; *et al.*). In the NT cf. the Christological ἐγώ εἰμι in the Fourth Gospel (6.35,48; 8.12; 14.6; 15.1; etc.) and Revelation (1.8,17; 21.6; etc.). Outside Judaism and Christianity, this use of ἐγώ εἰμι occurs frequently in the Greek Isis hymns (e.g., the Memphite aretalogy from Cyme [J. Bergman, *Ich bin Isis*, Acta Universitatis Upsaliensis, Hist. Relig. 3, Uppsala 1968, p. 301f.] vv. 3a, 5-10, 41-42, 49, *et al.*) and occasionally in the *Hymni Homerici* (e.g., III 480 [Apollo]; VII 56 [Dionysus]; εἰμι only in II 268 [Demeter]) and other Greek literature (Hom. *Od.* XI 252; Ar. *Pl.* 78). Norden (*Ag. Th.* 183) characterizes the formula as basically "unhellenisch."

According to A.D. Nock (*Gnomon* 21 [1949] 224 [*Essays* 706f.]), there is no genuine native example of the purely revelatory "I am" in ancient Eg. literature (similarly D. Müller, *Ägypten und die griechischen Isis-Aretalogien*, Abh. Leipzig, Aka. Berlin, Philol.-hist. Kl. 53.1, 15-17). However, Eg. funerary and magical texts and the later Greco-Egyptian magic abound in examples of what we may designate as the second type, the formula of identification (Bultmann, *loc. cit.*), in which a mortal equates himself with a god; e.g., *Bk. of the Dead* 17.1: "I am Atum, who made the sky and created what exists while I existed alone in the deep. I am Re," etc. (ed. T.G. Allen, The Univ. of Chicago Oriental Institute Publications 82, 1960, 88). Norden (*Ag. Th.* 218f.) interprets these statements as apotropaic; i.e., the dead, by identifying himself with a great god as he approaches the underworld, repels harmful *daimones*. Morenz, however, believes that the deceased through the "I am" predication magically usurps divine power and so gains immortality (*Äg. Rel.* 242 [Eng. 230f.]). In Greek magical texts the sense is occasionally apotropaic: ἐὰν ἐξέρχηται (*sc.* ὁ κολαστής), λέγε ⟨αὐ⟩τῷ· ἐγώ εἰμι Ερεσχιγαλ --- καὶ οὐδὲ ἓν δύναται κακὸν αὐτῇ γενέσθαι (*PGM* LXX 5f.). Usually, however, as in M and P, a spell-operator uses ἐγώ εἰμι in the context of adjurations/invocations (ἐξορκίζω σε, ἐπικαλῶ σε, etc.) and/or commands (ἔλθε, ἔγειρε, etc.) to legitimate his claim of power over the invoked demons and to threaten them into submission (e.g., *PGM* XII 226-38; V 139ff., 247ff.; LXIX 2; on threats in general cf. above on § J 14ff. pp. 69ff.). For parallels from Coptic and Eg. magic, see Kropp III §§ 251-52; Massart, *Leid. Mag. Pap.* 63f. n. 38 respectively.

The distinction, however, between the two main types of "I am" predication becomes less rigid when we realize that we are concerned with a religious milieu in which man becoming god, e.g., as in the deification of the Eg. king and the previously discussed transformation of the dead into Osiris (above p. 49), was regarded as sacred reality and not mere role-play. On this basis Bergman (*op. cit.*, 219-24) rejects Müller's and Nock's characterization of the revelation formula as non-Egyptian. He in fact maintains, I think correctly, that the "I am" of identification, as used by kings in royal proclamations, by the dead in funerary texts, and by spell-operators in magic, functioned also as a revelation formula, i.e., a means by which the gods manifested themselves in men. For the popular practitioner of magical spells, the practical (legitimating/threatening) dimensions of "I am" no doubt played the dominant role; but in its deeper significance and in its origins within Eg. religious experience, the formula of identification was perhaps primarily an instrument of divine self-disclosure.

40f. βαρβαδωναιαι βαρβαδωναι: for -αιαι see below on Αδωναιαι line 44 p. 101. P's spelling βαρβαρ Αδωναι also in *PGM* XII 90. Cf. χαρχαρ Αδωναι, *PGM* IV 2772; Αραθ Αδωναι, XIII 147, 453, 592; Αραθυ 'Αδωναΐε, *ibid.* 80. Αραθ and χαρχαρ have been explained as the dekan names Aroth and Charcham respectively (Gundel, W., *Dekane* 77 [# 5], 48, 289 n. 4; Gundel, H.G.,*Weltbild* 21, 23; denied by A. Jacoby [for Αραθ], *PGM* vol. 3, 215C and Preisendanz [for χαρχαρ], *GGA* 201, 1939, 140). Our βαρβ- (βαρβαρ- P) may be a variation of one of these names. More likely βαρβαδωναι is a play on αρβα- Αδωναι; *arba* = Heb. "four" = (the name of) Yahweh. Adonai is the common אדני, "Lord," a frequent surrogate for the Tetragrammaton. *Arba* is often connected with words denoting Yahweh; cf. above pp. 74f. and esp. the form βαρβαθιαω there cited. The participial epithets which follow make obvious that *Barbadonai* is the sun god; for the syncretism of Yahweh with solar deities, see above p. 83.

41f. ὁ --- κρύβων, ὁ --- κρατέων, ὁ --- ἀληθεύων: These phrases display both characteristics which, according to Norden (*Ag. Th.* 202-03), distinguish the oriental/Semitic style of participial predication from the more purely Gk., namely 1. the use of the article with the participles; 2. a penchant for parallel construction which results in strings of participial clauses used like relative sentences (ἐγὼ κύριος ὁ θεός --- ἐγὼ ὁ κατασκευάσας φῶς καὶ ποιήσας σκότος, ὁ ποιῶν εἰρήνην --- ὁ ποιῶν πάντα ταῦτα, LXX Is. 45.6f.; εὐλόγει --- τὸν κύριον --- τὸν εὐιλατεύοντα --- τὸν ἰώμενον --- τὸν λυτρούμενον κτλ., LXX Ps. 102 [MT 103].1ff.; cf. *ibid.* 103 [MT 104].2-4; NT Rev. 3.7; *PGM* I 205ff.; IV 3048ff.; Norden, *Ag. Th.* 204f., 380-83. See *ibid.* p. 202 n. 1 and 167 n. 1 for examples of the more classical style).

41 ὁ τὰ ἄστρα κρύβων: same as P 325f. On the late κρύβειν for κρύπτειν (back-formed from the 2 aor. pass. ἐκρύβην) see Gignac II 284 and n. 2; BDR § 73.1; s.v. κρύπτω in Bauer. We have already seen the motif of "hiding" or "concealing" the stars in the common topos of witches drawing down the moon and stars by spells (cf. Hor. *Epod.* 5.45f. and other material cited above p. 2 n. 6 and p. 71) and in the Jewish apocalyptic image of the darkening of the heavenly bodies on judgment day: καὶ κατακαλύψω --- οὐρανὸν καὶ συσκοτάσω τὰ ἄστρα αὐτοῦ, LXX Ezek. 32.7; cf. NT Lk. 23.44f. and other Biblical parallels cited above p. 72. Κρύπτειν/κρύβειν is not used in these texts. It is, however, a common astronomical term for the "concealing" or (in passive) "disappearing" of the stars either through heliacal setting (Ptolemaeus *Phas.* 5, vol. II p. 8 Heiberg) or eclipse: ἡ μὲν σελήνη, προσγειοτάτη οὖσα, --- πάντα τὰ πλανώμενα, τινὰ δὲ καὶ τῶν ἀπλανῶν, κρύπτει, ἐπειδὰν μεταξὺ τινος αὐτῶν καὶ τῆς ὄψεως ἡμῶν ἐπ' εὐθείας καταστῇ, αὐτὴ δὲ ὑπ' οὐδενὸς ἄστρου κρύπτεται (Theon Smyrnaeus, ed. E. Hiller [1878], 193, 2ff., as cited by Oepke in *TDNT* III 959 s.v. κρύπτω; cf. LSJ s.v. κρύπτω and κρύψις); similarly in a magical invocation to Selene: καὶ κρύψει σὸν φῶς Ἥλιος πρὸς τὸν νότον, *PGM* IV 2312f. Thus, the sense may be that *Barbadonai* causes the stars to set, occulting them by his greater glory. This solar-astronomical interpretation does not preclude the apocalyptic background mentioned earlier. Images from the two spheres are sometimes mingled; e.g., Chrysostom *hom.* 14.10 *in Rom.*, Migne *PG* 60.538: (the return of Christ will be such) ὡς καὶ τὴν σελήνην καὶ τὸν ἥλιον καὶ ἅπαν κρύπτεσθαι φῶς ὑπὸ τῆς αὐγῆς ἐκείνης καταλαμπόμενον (see Lampe 781A s.v. κρύπτω).

41f. ὁ τὸν οὐρανὸν κρατέων: for other examples of non-contracted -εω verbs, cf. [ὑμᾶς ἐπικα]λέομε, Aud. 189a.1; καλέω, 15.52; καλέουσι, *PGM* IV 2770f.; μεσουρανέοντος, *ibid.* 173 (but μεσουρανοῦντος, 762). Similarly in Romanos' *Cantica*, καλέεις, 50 ιη′ 3 (Maas/Trypanis p. 436); τρομέοντες, 43 λα′ 1 (*eidem* p. 350). Scholars explain tendencies toward non-contraction in Romanos and other late Greek authors as poeticism and/or ionicism (K. Mitsakis, *The Language of Romanos the Melodist* [Byzantinisches Archiv 11, Munich 1967] §§ 31-32, 340; cf. P. Maas, *Byzantinische Zeitschrift* 16 [1907] 572 [*Kleine Schriften* p. 333f.]). Gignac (I 311) notes that in general, ε sometimes develops before a back vowel (e.g., μεταβαλεόμενος, *P. Oxy.* XII 1470.12; ποστησέω [for ἀποστήσω], *P. Tebt.* II 397.32), and according to L.R. Palmer (*Grammar of the Post-Ptolemaic Papyri*, p. 12), this tendency is especially evident following a liquid or nasal (thus the preference in late Greek for the open genitives ὀρέων and χειλέων). It is therefore possible that such a phonological environment may account for the presence of ε rather than non-contraction, especially in cases such as καλέω and μεσουρανέοντος; one at least suspects that the two processes helped each other along.

κρατεῖν with the accusative normally means "defeat," "conquer"; with the genitive (and occasionally accusative, e.g., Aesch. *Supp.* 254f.) "rule," "be master of" (in general, see KG 1.368f. [Anm. 16]; S. Witkowski, *Glotta* 6 [1915] 20). Thus, the parallel reading of P 386: ὁ λαμπροφεγγὴς οὐρανοῦ κρατῶν, "the bright ruler of heaven." In later times the verb with accus. (less often with gen.) frequently denotes "hold (in one's hand)," "possess," and thus, "have in one's power," "maintain," "preserve" (e.g., in a cosmological vein much like our text, the epithet of Christ in NT Rev. 2.1: ὁ κρατῶν τοὺς ἑπτὰ ἄστερας ἐν τῇ δεξιᾷ αὐτοῦ [cf. also 1.16,20]). Cf. κατέχειν: καὶ σὲ τὸν οὐράνιον κόσμον κατέχοντα, Μιχαηλ, *PGM* I 300f. (cf. III 212); ἐξορκίζω σε κατὰ τοῦ κατέχοντος τὸν κόσμον, XII 58f., cf. 71; with both verbs (hymn to Christ by

Mary): Ἥλιε, Υἱέ, --- πῶϲ ϲε χερϲὶ κατέχω, τὸν κρατοῦντα τὰ ϲύμπαντα, Pitra XXIX 2, λϛʹ p. 229; cf. *ibid.* 1, ιϛʹ, p. 225. In legal language, κρατεῖν and κατέχειν are used synonymously with the meaning "have right of ownership over" (*P. Oxy.* II 237, viii 22, 34 with nn. *ad locc.* [pp. 175, 179]; *ibid.* I 131.5; J.H. Moulton, G. Milligan, *The Vocabulary of the Greek Testament* [London 1931] s.v. κρατέω).

In the Egyptian context, the sun god must repeatedly defeat Apophis, the serpent-like enemy of the gods, who daily tries to impede the progress of the solar bark. By so doing he "maintains" heaven as his domain and "preserves" it from the forces of chaos which Apophis personifies (for the various versions of the myth, see *P. Bremner-Rind* 22.1ff., trans. by R.O. Faulkner, *JEA* 23 [1937] 166-85, 24 [1938] 41-53; Morenz, *Äg. Rel.* 81 [Eng. 77]; E. Hornung and A. Badawy in *Lex. Äg.* I 350f. s.v. Apophis; Bonnet 52Bf. s.v. Apophis; cf. also J.F. Borghouts, *JEA* 59 [1973] 114ff.; Griffiths on *Is. et Os.* 36 [p. 440]).

42f. ὁ τὸν κόϲμον ἀληθεύων ιατθεουν ιατρεουν ϲαλβιουθ κτλ.: cf. ὁ κύριοϲ κόϲμου αθθουϊν ϊαθουϊν ϲελβιουθ κτλ., P 387f. In M we must attempt to explain: 1. the peculiarity of ἀληθεύων; 2. the omission of αθθουιν, the first word of the magical *logos* which follows (this *logos* is also attested in *PGM* LXII 21f.: αθουιν αθουιν αθουιν ιαθαουιν ϲιβελθιουθ ιατητ ατατητ Αδωνε). With regard to the second problem, the similarity of ἀληθεύων and αθθουιν probably caused the omission of the latter through haplography. The reverse may have occurred in the tradition of P, and if so, a subsequent scribe may have tried to make sense of the resultant ὁ τὸν κόϲμον αθθουιν κτλ. by changing the Greek phrase to the rather safe, generalizing ὁ κύριοϲ κόϲμου. In the case of M, it is also possible that the original participle was lost and ἀληθεύων represents a scribe's attempt to recover it from αθθουιν. It seems, however, unlikely that αθθουιν would have been "normalized" into a word which in this phrase is inexplicable from a Greek point of view. To understand its usage, we must turn to Near Eastern/Egyptian cosmological ideas.

ἀληθεύειν is usually intrans., "tell the truth," "speak truthfully." Among the rarer transitive meanings are "rightly foretell" (τὰϲ δέκα ἡμέραϲ ἠλήθευϲε Xen. *An.* V 6.18), "prove something true," "verify" (ὡϲ ἀληθεύοιϲ τοὺϲ ἐπαίνουϲ αὐτῶν, Lucian *Ind.* 20; πῶϲ γὰρ [*sc.* ὁ φιλάνθρωποϲ] ἂν τοὔνομα ἀληθεύοι, "--- make good his name," Themistius *Or.* I 4c). None of these basic senses of the word helps explain its usage in our text, where it seems to describe some activity of creating or governing the cosmos. ἀληθεύων may in fact represent a Greek rendering of an essentially Semitic conception. A small number of Hebrew verbs mean both "establish" (i.e., "found" or "create") and, in an ethical sense, "verify"; e.g., Heb. כונן (po'lel of [כון]; BDB 466bf.): "*Confirm* the work of our hands" (Ps. 90.17); "The Lord *established* the heavens" (Prov. 3.19). Similarly the niph. of [אמן] (BDB 52Bf.) may mean "verified" (e.g., words, Gen. 42.20) or "established" (e.g., a house and kingdom, 2Sam. 7.16). In our text ἀληθεύων may thus reflect an attempt to translate such an idiom so as to preserve the implicit notion of truth, viz., "who establishes the cosmos in accordance with truth." Cf. esp. in this regard Is. 44.26, where the LXX translates ישלים (hiph. of שלם, BDB 1022B) with ἀληθεύων in the phrase τὴν βούλην τῶν ἀγγέλων αὐτοῦ ἀληθεύων, "(*sc.* Yahweh) verifying the will of his messengers" (or "angels"). The root meaning of שלם is "be complete," "be finished" (e.g., the work of building the temple, 2Chron. 5.1, LXX cυνετελέcθη) and thus the hiph. means "perform," "accomplish." The LXX translators, however, perceived here an ethical force in the hiph. form; perhaps through ἀληθεύων they meant to convey "performing the counsel of his messengers, and thus verifying it" or "proving it true," i.e., as being in accordance with his own βούλη (cf. J.F. Schleusner, *Novus Thesaurus Philologico-criticus* [Glasgow^2 1822] I 119, s.v. ἀληθεύω, where he compares the German *wahr machen*). Such an understanding of the word would be easily adapted to a Hebrew cosmological context; the Genesis account has Yahweh affirming the ethical quality of each creative act with the statement, "He saw that it was good."

ἀληθεύειν may also imply various aspects of Eg. creation theology and cosmology. Since the word is basically concerned with speaking truth, it may suggest in our text the concept common to many ancient Near Eastern cultures of creation through speech (for the Eg. versions, see J. Zandee in *Verbum: Essays on Some Aspects of the Religious Function of Words dedicated to H.W. Obbink* [Studia Theologica Rheno-Traiectina 6, 1964] 33ff.; G. Maspéro, *Études de mythologie et d' archéologie égyptiennes* II, 260ff., 373ff. [*non vidi*; cited in W. Otto, *Priester und Tempel im hellenistischen Ägypten* I, Leipzig/Berlin 1905, p. 15 n. 3]). Cf. esp. the Memphite creation narrative of the "Shabaka stone," where Ptah is said to create through his heart (thought) and tongue (speech): "The mighty Great One is Ptah, who transmitted [life to all gods], as well as (to) their *ka's* through this heart ... and through this tongue" (J.B. Pritchard, *Ancient Near Eastern Texts* [Princeton 1969] p. 5, § 53). Similarly, "All the divine order ... came into being through what the heart thought and the tongue commanded" (*ibid.* p. 5, § 55). Also, Ptah creates things by pronouncing their names: "Whereas the Ennead of Atum came into being by his semen ... the Ennead (of Ptah), however, is the teeth and lips in his mouth, which pronounced the name of everything, from which Shu and Tefnut came forth" (*ibid.*). A similar concept is involved in a creation account involving Atum (*ibid.*, p. 4 and n. 8). ἀληθεύειν τὸν κόcμον may therefore mean creating the world order through speaking what is in the heart or by uttering the true name.

Basically the same idea is expressed in the concept of creation through *maat* (Eg. *m3't*), variously rendered "truth," "rightness," "order," etc. At an early date *maat* acquired a particular connection with the creator-god (Amon-)Re (Bonnet 430Af.; W. Helck in *Lex. Äg.* III 1111 s.v. *maat*; H. Ringgren, *Word and Wisdom*, [Lund 1947] 46, 50f.). In her personified form, *Maat* accompanies Re in his trek across heaven and as his navigator (with Thoth) plots out the course of the solar bark (Ringgren, *op. cit.* 46 and n. 6; Budge, *Gods* I 417f.). Re frequently bears the title "Lord of *maat*" (e.g., J. Assmann, *Ägyptische Hymnen und Gebete* [Zürich/München 1975] # 87C.62 [p. 201]; Morenz, *Äg. Rel.* 136f. [Eng. 129f.]) and is in fact her creator, who established her as the ordering principle of the cosmos (Assmann, *op. cit.* 87G.197 [p. 206]; Morenz, *Äg. Rel.* 120, 137 [Eng. 113, 130]). Since, however, the cosmic order is constantly threatened by the forces of chaos personified in the serpent monster Apopis (see above p. 97), Re must daily subdue these powers to maintain *maat* as the universal canon (Ringgren, *op. cit.* 50). Such is the "establishing" or "verifying" expressed by our ἀληθεύων.

Thus, by way of summary, the three participial clauses portray the sun god *Barbadonai* as the one who conceals the stars by the glory of his rising, who preserves the heavens by defeating Apophis, and who by this victory establishes the cosmos in truth.

43f. ιατθεουν --- Αδωναιαι: with M's and P's versions of this *logos*, cf. that of *PGM* LXII 21f. (cited above p. 97).

ιατθεουν ιατρεουν --- ιατ'θεραθ: ιατ/ιαθ introduce several magical words; e.g., ιατμωμι, *PGM* IV 1631; ιατμων, IV 1626f.; ιαθθα, P 392; ιαθαφθω, XIII 919 (Preisendanz divides differently); ιαθιν, IV 275. With our ιατθεουν cf. ιαθουιν, P 387; ιαθαουιν, *PGM* LXII 22. The second element in each of these words (-θεουν, -θουιν, -θαουιν) closely resembles Θιοῦιν, Copt. ΤΙ-ΟΥΙ, Eg. *t3 w'.t*, "the one," a common name for Isis and other deities; cf. Vanderlip 31 (on hymn I 23); Griffiths, *Isis Book*, 167. I find no parallels for ιατρεουν; possibly a corruption of ἰατρεύων, "healer"; cf. Apollo's epithet ἰατρός (Drexler in Roscher 2.1, 90 s.v. *Iatros*). -θεραθ in the third word ιατ'θεραθ resembles the common element -θαρα- (see F. Maltomini, *SCO* 29 [1979] 84); e.g., ζαρακαθαρα Aud. 267.10; cανκανθαρα, *PGM* II 33; βαθαρα, I 153; esp. similar to our word, θατθαραθαυθωλθαρα, XXXIX 1. The apostrophe between double consonants becomes common at the beginning of the third cent. A.D. (E.G. Turner, *Greek Manuscripts of the Ancient World* [*Institute of Classical Studies Bulletin Supp.* 46, 1987^2] 11 with n. 50); in magical texts cf., e.g., ἀναγ'κacθῶ, *PGM* XII 143; γλωτ'τῶν, VIII 34; cεcεγ'γεν, XXXVI 244; βαρφαραγ'γηc, VII 979 (*PGM* vol. 2 p. 269 s.v. Doppelkonsonanten); and specifically with our word cf. ιατ'θαννουιτα, *PGM* VII 327.

43 cαλβιουθ: cf. cελβιουωθ, P 387f.; cελβιουc, *PGM* XII 102; cιβελθιουθ, LXII 22; cαλβαθβαλ, Aud. 237.2. cελ/cαλ introduce many magical words: cελετηα, *PGM* XII 103; cελεπηλ, XII 104; cαλβαναχαμβρη, VIII 83f.; cαλβαχθι, IV 1489; etc. For -βιουθ cf. βιβιουθ, line 45 below and n. *ad loc.* (pp. 101f.); cf. also βιου there cited.

43f. Αωθ Αωθ: only once in P 389. The word usually occurs, as here, in connection with names for Yahweh and/or other Hebrew names; e.g., the *Αωθ-logos*: Αωθ Αβαωθ βαcυμ Ιcακ Cαβαωθ Ιαω Ιακωπ, *PGM* IV 1376f.; similarly V 134f. See also Aud. 271.1ff.: Αωθ Αβαωθ, τὸν θεὸν τοῦ Αβρααν καὶ τὸν Ιαω τὸν τοῦ Ιακου, Ιαω Αωθ Αβαωθ --- ἄκουcον τοῦ ὀνόματοc ἐντείμου καὶ φ[οβ]εροῦ καὶ μεγάλου· cf. *ibid.* 38-39; Delatte/Derchain 416, 487. For Αωθ in other contexts, cf. *PGM* IV 3030; VII 567; XII 118; and esp. XIXa 1-2, where (as in our text) it is followed by βιβιου(θ): cαμι cαμιc οφορ ανουιφω χθεθωνι νουηριωθ Αωθ ουωρ τενοχ τενοχ βιβιου βιβιου κτλ. Blau (p. 105) explains the word as an abbreviation of Cαβαωθ (on which see n. on Ιαω Cαβαωθ, § J 17 p. 79 above).

44 cαβαθιουθ: cf. cαρβαθιουθ, P 388; cαβαρβαρβαθιουθ, *PGM* IV 1241f.; see also above on cαβαρβατιαωθ, § J 18 p. 81.

ιατ'θεραθ: cf. above on ιατθεουν ιατρεουν p. 100.

Αδωναιαι: the final -αι may stand for ε (Gignac I 193), in which case we would have the vocative of the declinable 'Αδωναῖοc (*PGM* VII 979; VIII 61; etc.). Αδωναιαι, however, could also be one of the many plays on the indeclinable Αδωναι; e.g., Αδωναιει, *PGM* XXVIIIb 4; Αδωναια, XLV 4, 5; Αδωνεαι, XII 63; etc.; cf. esp. above line 40 βαρβαδωναιαι, which cannot be vocative, and the n. on that word (pp. 94f.) for the meaning of *Adonai.*

45 ιcαρ cυρια: cf. ια ρουρα, P 389. cυρια may refer to the θεὸc Cυρία, i.e., 'Αταργάτιc, a Syrian earth goddess and mother of the gods closely related to the Phoenician Astarte, Aramaic Atar, and Babylonian Istar. Some such name may be intended by our ιcαρ. To my knowledge, the *Dea Syria* is not invoked in this form in other magical texts. She is addressed as κυρία θεὰ Cυρία in a *defixio* from Delos (ed. Ph. Bruneau, *Recherches sur les cultes de Delos* [Paris 1970] 649-53). She also appears with the name Cημέα (see in general Roscher IV 660-62, where Höfer cites inscriptional and literary evidence; for magic, see F. Maltomini, *SCO* 29 [1979] 120 on pap. 13.3; [Cη]μέα χθονία, *PGM* III 29; and the *Cημέα-logos*, *PGM* V 428ff., *DMP* VII 28 [p. 62], Bonner 196f. Cημέα βαcιλεῦ in *PGM* III 206 [see Preisendanz's n. *ad loc.*] is problematic). The μήτερα θεῶν in Aud. 72.17 may also refer to her (A. Abt, *ARW* 14 [1911] 148f., esp. 149 n. 2; Kagarow 63). The Syrian Goddess is identified with Hera, Aphrodite, Isis, and others (Lucian, *de Syria Dea* 32; Griffiths on *Is. et Os.* 15 [p. 326f.]; Cumont in *RE* IV 2236ff. s.v. Dea Syria; Höfer in Roscher IV 1631f. s.v. Syria).

βιβιβε βιβιουθ νατθω: cf. βια βι βιοθη αθωθ, P 389, so Preisendanz; but the words should probably be divided βια βιβιοθ ηαθωθ, since the second word corresponds to our βιβιουθ. Cf. also βιβιου, which occurs, e.g., in the *cιεπη-logos* (ανοχ αιεφε cακτιετη βιβιου βιβιου cφη cφη νουcι νουcι κτλ., *PGM* XIII 806f.; similarly II 123f.; I 239f.) and in other combinations (doubled: Οὔcειρι --- Φθα --- Ἶcιc --- βιβιου βιβιου cφη cφη κτλ., *PGM* XII 80f.; Αωθ ουωρ τενοχ τενοχ, βιβιου βιβιου, μουαυ μουαυ κτλ., XIXa 2. Not doubled: βιβιου ουηρ αψαβαρα, *PGM* XIII 325; βιου βιου βιβιου, P. Köln inv.

no. 5512.3-4 [ed. R. Daniel, *ZPE* 19, 1975, 258]; cf. Aud. 269a.14; *DMP* VI 26 [p. 54] and VIII 6 [p. 64]). For final θ in magical words, see above p. 81.

Karl Fr. W. Schmidt (*Philologische Wochenschrift* 55 [1935] 1183) explains βιβιου as Eg. *b3-b3.w*, "soul of souls" (cf. also Hopfner, OZ I § 694 and II § 224; on *b3*, "ba" see below). It may also be connected with the *vox magica* and dekan name Βιου (cf. above cited P. Köln inv. no. 5512.3-4, on which see Daniel, *op. cit.*, 260; *PGM* V 484f. [*cιεπη-logos*]; XIII 1058; XVI 63) or with the related dekan Πτιβιου; see K. Preisendanz, *GGA* 201 (1939) 143f.; Daniel, *loc. cit.*; Gundel, W., *Dekane* 77 (## 34 and 36) and 233f.; Gundel, H.G.,*Weltbild* 21f.

I find no parallels for βιβιβε and νατθω. The former may be *b3 b3 b3*, "three times *ba*." Cf. *voces magicae* consisting of repetitions of ⲂⲀⲒ, the Coptic form of *ba*: βια βαϊβαϊ, *PGM* IV 1587 (βια [also in P] is probably metathesis for βαι, and thus we would have *b3 b3 b3*); βαιβειζωθ (ηβαι βεβ[ọ]θ), V 7 (so Preisendanz divides the words, but the suggestion in his note, that η is ἤ, is probably correct; thus two optional Grecizations of *b3-b3.w* are offered); βαϊ βαιτοκαρακωπτο --- βαϊ, IV 2697f.; cουβαιβαι, *Pist. Soph.* IV 142 (Schmidt/MacDermot 370.14). The Eg. concept of *b3* (*ba*, "essence," "soul"), when applied to divinities, designates the manifestation of their divine being and power (L.V. Zabkar in *Lex. Äg.* I 590f. s.v. *Ba*; cf. above p. 82). The import, therefore, of βιβιουθ and βιβιβε may resemble predications such as "lord of lords" (cf. μαρμαραωθ above p. 82) and τριcμέγιcτοc respectively.

46 Cαβαωθ: Heb. צבאות cf. above on § J 17 (p. 79).

46f. αιαναφα αμουραχθη cαταμα Ζεύc αθερεcφιλαυω: cf. ηα νιαφα αμαραχθι cαταμα ζαυαθθειη cερφω κτλ., P 390f. These formulae resemble a *logos* preserved mainly in magical gems (in the following examples I italicize the words most like those in our text): *Αιαναχφα* Αμοραχοι Cαλαμαζα Βαμαιαζα, Delatte/Derchain 473; Αιαναγβα *Αμοραχθει* Cαλαμαξα Βαμεαζα, 472; Αιαναγβα Αμοραχει *Cαδαμαζα* Βαμεαζα, Le Blant 232 (cited by Delatte/Derchain p. 322); Αιανακβα *Αμοραχθει* Cαλαμαξα Βαμεαζζα *φύλαξον* (see discussion below p. 105) 477; cf. also 475, 476, 478, 479; Bonner p. 95f. and # 284.5 p. 300; H. Philipp, *Mira et Magica* (Mainz 1986) 118 (n. on # 190). For an analysis of the different spellings of the individual words, cf. Delatte/Derchain p. 322. Some of the elements occur also in Bonner ## 217, 271,

396 (pp. 289, 298, 321f.) and Delatte/Derchain 367, 516 rev. The resemblance between this *logos* and our formula ends after cαταμα. The -ζα, which forms the ending of Cαλαμαζα/Cαδαμαζα, is Ζεύc in our text and the first syllable of ζαυαθθειη in P (the ms. of P has a colon between cαταμα and ζαυαθθειη showing that the scribe understood them as separate words). Since Cαλαμαζα and its variants are well established in the *logos* of the amulets, possibly cαταμα (M and P) and probably Ζεύc (M only) represent a tendency to normalize this obscure *nomen barbarum* into more recognizable forms.

46 αιαναφα: cf. ηα νιαφα, P 390. Αϊα (Heb. "I am," Exodus 3.14) is attested as a form of the Hebrew divine name by both Origen and Theodoret (Baudissin "Iao" 184 and n. 3; *Jewish Encyclop.* XII 119A s.v. Tetragrammaton; Deissmann, *Bib. Stud.* 326). Cf. Αϊα αϊνρυχαθ, *PGM* XIII 331 with n. *ad loc.* (see also addendum to this passage in vol. 2 p. 268). I have no explanation for -ναφα.

αμουραχθη: similarly αμοραχθι/-ει Bonner # 284.5, p. 300; Delatte/Derchain 284, 472, 476, 477; αμοραχοι, 473; αμαραχθι/-ει, P 390; *PGM* XVI 9; Delatte/Derchain 478 (-ειc), 479; αμαρχθα, *PGM* XIII 987. The element -ουραχθη and the corresponding elements in the parallels probably represent Eg. *Ḥr-3ḫ.t*, *Harachte*, "Horus of the Horizon," a Heliopolitan designation for Re-Horus (Bonnet 269A s.v. *Harachte*; Eitrem's translation of P's αμαραχθι, "Hor *im* Horizont" [*PGM* vol. 3 p. 216A] seems rather to be based on *Harmachis* [*Ḥr-m-3ḫ.t*], the name of the great sphinx of Giza, which represented *Harachte* [Bonnet 269B]). See also above on μαρμαραχθα p. 83.

Harachte also came to be used of other deities, esp. Amon, to emphasize their solar-cosmic aspects (J. Assmann in *Lex. Äg.* II 959f. s.v. *Harachte* and the texts cited in nn. 32-35). It is thus important to note that in the three cases of the word in *PGM* (cf. above), as also in our tablet, the context is that of a world creator or κύριοc κόcμου (see Delatte/Derchain p. 322). In our text the prefix αμ- probably represents Amon. Cf. Ἶcιc αχθι, *PGM* XII 81; cαραχθι, I 136 and ζαραχθω, VII 511 (Sar(apis)- achte?).

cαταμα: same as P 390; cf. Preisendanz's n. *ad loc.*, where Cατανᾶ (voc. of Cατανᾶc), "Satan" is suggested (for decl. see BDR § 55(1)b; Bauer s.v.). For the possibility that cαταμα evinces a normalizing tendency, see above. There are very few cases of ν > μ which cannot be explained as assimilation (cf. Threatte 491; Schwyzer, "Vulgärsprache" 252; Gignac I 119, and his "improper" category p. 167). E.g. μόμων (i.e., νόμων), *P. Aberd.* 16.6f.;* Μελαμθίου (i.e., Μελανθίου), Aud. 70.2f.; ἐπὴμ (i.e., αἰπὺν) ἀφ', *PGM* VII 119 (Homeric quote); (αὐ)τὸμ καί, Wünsch 84b.2. In the case of Cαταμᾶ for Cατανᾶ, F. Legge (*PSBA* 23 [1901] 47 n. ¶) suggests Coptic influence where the interchange is common; cf. W. Worrell, *Coptic Sounds* (Ann Arbor 1934) 114; he notes (as does Threatte, *loc. cit.*, for Greek) that some examples are due to copying mistakes. For *m/n* in Aramaic, see W. Fauth, *ZDMG* 120 (1970) 252 with n. 266.

With respect to magic, Satan occurs most frequently in Coptic texts, usually in the context of being exorcised (*PGM* IV 1238; Kropp II 47.8, 16 [p. 181]) but occasionally as an invoked deity (Kropp II 8.14-21 [p. 21], 9.2 [p. 23], and see III §§ 14-15, 165-66); cf. a Greek formula on a gold tablet: ἐξορκίζω cε, ὦ cατανᾶ (ed. F. Lénormant, *Mélanges d' archéologie* III, 1853, 150 [cited by Preisendanz in n. on *PGM* IV 1238]). For the development of Seth as a Satan figure, see H. C. Youtie, *Studies ... in Honor of A.C. Johnson* (Princeton 1951) 189-92 (*Scriptiunculae* I 525-28); Griffiths on *Is. et Os.* 27, p. 389.

47 Ζεύς αθερεcφιλαυωc: We could also interpret Ζεῦ cαθερεcφιλαυω; cf. ζαυαθθειη cερφω, P 391 (ζαυ, i.e., Ζεῦ ?). For the likelihood that Ζεύc here is a normalization of the last syllable of Cαλαμαζα, see above p. 103. In *PGM* Zeus is associated with Helios-Sarapis (II 89; IV 1715; V 4f.; XXXIc 1f.; LXXIII 1; LXXIV 1), with Iao-Adonai-Abrasax (I 300ff.; V 471f.; IV 2773), with the chiefly solar figure Damnameneus (IV 2773; III 81 and 101 [χευ for Ζεῦ? see *PGM* vol. 3 p. 221A]), and others. His name also appears in more traditionally Greek/Homeric contexts and phrases (e.g., [after a Homeric quote] ἀνέβη Ζεὺc εἰc ὄροc χρυcοῦν, IV 825; τῷ τῆc Λητοῦc καὶ Διὸc υἱῷ, II 10; cf. IV 1473; VI 46).

I can find no parallels for the word(s) following Zeus. The element αθερ may be the Eg. goddess Hathor, as in other formulae (Αθερνεβουνι, *PGM* VII 495 and Delatte/Derchain 345; Αθερνεκληcιχ, *PGM* VII 494 and cf. Delatte/Derchain 335, 345). Possibly αθερεc- is a corruption of Zeus' epithet αἰθέριοc (e.g., Aristotle *Mu.* 401a 17; cf. C.F.H. Bruchmann, *Epitheta Deorum* [Suppl. Roscher, Leipzig 1893] 123B s.v. For an example of how a Greek epithet may degenerate into a *nomen barbarum*, cf. Preisendanz's n. on Βαρζου φερβα, *PGM*

IV 2693, where it is suggested that these words arose from Μαρζουνη φοβερά in line 2547. Similarly, our φιλαυω may be a corruption of φύλαξον which follows the *αιαναφα-logos* in Delatte/Derchain 477 (cited above p. 102); cf. above p. 81 on W_1 36 (s.vv. μαρι ἐνδόζου).

§§ A-H: *Voces Magicae* and Vowel Combinations

These formulae as a whole resemble the continuation of the *praxis* section of P 406ff. (above p. 13; cf. p. 19) with considerable additions, some of which occur also in *PGM* XIXa 16ff. (see below p. 106 fig. 3).

§ **A:** The *ιαεω-logos* palindrome is also written as a heart-shaped *Schwindeform* in P 409ff. (7 lines only; see above p. 13) and *PGM* XIXa 16ff. (below p. 106 fig. 3; see above p. 1 n. 2 for the *Schwindeform* in general). The formula (with peculiar spelling) is divided into four wing-shaped *Schwindeformen* (cf. §§ C and E) in *PGM* XXXVI 115-33 (see below, p. 107 fig. 4).

In addition to the *Schwindeform*, the *ιαεω-logos* is connected with other magical figures and drawings; e.g., within the *ouroboros*, "tail swallowing serpent" (cf. above p. 38) in *PGM* VII col. 17 (see vol. 2, Taf. I Abb. 4) and between the two concentric circles of a magical ring made from tracing a chain link in *PGM* V 357 (see vol. 1, Taf. III Abb. 6). It is sometimes abbreviated (esp. in *praxis*), e.g., *PGM* VII 1022: γράψον ⟨γράμματα⟩ νθ′, *ιαεω-λόγον* ("the *iaeo* formula" or "*iaeo* etc." [K. Preisendanz, *Philologische Wochenschrift* 33, 1913, 510ff.]); cf. ιαεω λό(γοc), *PGM* III 77, 269; V 361f., 366; ιαεωβαφρενεμουν λό(γοc), I 195; IV 3071f.

The formula most often appears in specifically solar contexts (*PGM* I 140f., part of ὁ λόγοc ὁ λεγόμενοc --- πρὸc ἥλιον, which begins in 132; τὸ δὲ λεγόμενον πρὸc ἥλιον οὐδὲν ζητεῖ εἰ μὴ ιαεωβαφρενεμουν λό(γοc), I 194f.; after χαῖρε Ἥλιε [1017] in VII 1022; with Helios-Sarapis: Delatte/Derchain 100; Kropp II 13.8-10? [p. 31]; with the chiefly solar figure Damnameneus: Kropp *ibid.* 9-10; Delatte/Derchain 432. Cf. in general also Bonner 204; Kropp III § 210) and in invocations/adjurations of Ιαω (of which ιαεω is a variation; cf. above p. 80) and other Jewish divine names (ὅτι ὁρκίζω cε Ιαω, Cαβαωθ, Αδω-

Fig. 3: PGM XIXa 16ff. (to p. 105)

16 Αβρασαξ ιαεωβαφρενεμουνοθιλαρικριφιαευεαιφιρκιραλιθονυομενερφαβωεαι Βαινχωωωχ
ωυοιηεα αεωβαφρενεμουνοθιλαρικριφιαευεαιφιρκιραλιθονυομενερφαβωεα αεηιουω Δαμναμενευ
υοιηεαω εωβαφρενεμουνοθιλαρικριφιαευεαιφιρκιραλιθονυομενερφαβωε εηιουωα αμναμενευ
οιηεαωυ ωβαφρενεμουνοθιλαρικριφιαευεαιφιρκιραλιθονυομενερφαβω ηιουωαε μναμενευ
20 ιηεαωυο βαφρενεμουνοθιλαρικριφιαευεαιφιρκιραλιθονυομενερφαβ ιουωα[εη] αμενευ
ηεαωυοι Ιαω αφρεν[εμου]νοθιλαρικριφιαευεαιφιρκιραλιθονυομενερφα ουωαε[ηι] ω αμενευ
εαωυοιη Ιαω φρεν[εμο]υνοθιλαρικριφιαευεαιφιρκιραλιθονυομενερφ υωαεηι[ο] υω μενευ
αωυοιηε ιωια ρενεμ[ο]υνοθιλαρικριφιαευεαιφιρκιραλιθονυομενερ ιαω αωι ωαεηιου ουω ενευ
24 αιωιαωιιι ααα ω ενεμ[ου]νοθιλαρικριφιαευεαιφιρκιραλιθονυομενεν
ωω ιιι οοο υυυ ωωω νεμ[ου]νοθιλαρικριφιαευεαιφιρκιραλιθονυομεν ωια αιω ιαω ιιι ααα ιουω νευ
ωια αωι αιω ωια ωια εμ[ου]νοθιλαρικριφιαευεαιφιρκιραλιθονυομε η ωωω ιιιι οοο υυυ ωω
ιιι ααα εεε ηηη ιιιι οοοο [μου]νοθιλαρικριφιαευεαιφιρκιραλιθονυομ ωιαιωιαιωωιαωια[ω] ηιουω ευ
28 ουυυυυωωωωωωω [ου]νοθιλαρικριφιαευεαιφιρκιραλιθονυο ιιι ααα εεε ηηη ιιιι οο[ο]ο εηιουω υ
αβλαναθαναλβα [υ]νοθιλαρικριφιαευεαιφιρκιραλιθονυ ο υυυυ ωωωωωω[ω] αεηιουω
βλαναθαναλβα νοθιλαρικριφιαευεαιφιρκιραλιθον ακραμμαχαμαρι συρημενη βακερβηθ [πακερβ-]
λαναθαναλβα οθιλαρικριφιαευεαιφιρκιραλιθο κραμμαχαμαρι ηθ Αβρασαξ Αρσαμω αχιωνουθ
32 αναθαναλβα θιλαρικριφιαευεαιφιρκιραλιθ ραμμαχαμαρι ανουφι Αωθ ζωι ζωφ χμουιε α-
ναθαναλβα ιλαρικριφιαευεαιφιρκιραλι α αμμαχαμαρι χωρ αρχιτωρ ιαηθ αρνθιμοριαμ
αθαναλβα λαρικριφιαευεαιφιρκιραλ εε μμαχαμαρι βιωχ βιωχ αφρου φιλα βραυπωπα
ω θαναλβα α αρικριφιαευεαιφιρκιρα ηηη μαχαμαρι ..χουχ ηευρηνιθεπαλασωχ
36 υω αναλβα [ε]α ρικριφιαευεαιφιρκιρ ιιιι αχαμαρι ...ιω μουισρω ρωσ μουισρω
ουω ναλβα [ηε]α ικριφιαευεαιφιρκι οοοοο χαμαρι ..βαλβα..... ..αιαω παγου-
ιουω αλβα [ιηε]α κριφιαευεαιφιρκ υυυυυυ αμαρι ρη παaγουρη μα..ψυλω παρναβ
ηιουω λβα οιηεα ριφιαευεαιφιρ ωωωωωωω μαρι λο αρκαβερρωθ μαρμαριιλησα
40 εηιουω βα υοιηεα ιφιαευεαιφι ααααααα αρι ριανυρρησον χοριγτρηε ανωχ πρ
αεηιουω α ωυοιηεα φιαευεαιφ [εεεε]εε ρι ηχθενιθ ασωχ νυχευνεχαπεα
ουοιβηλ ουαιβηλ ουαι ιαιωθω βαρραβαυ ιαευεαι [ηηηη]η ι παιχωρσαρι ασισινηιθ ανασωχ
Σεμεσιλαμ Αβρασαξ ορχραθ βιουρα ζαζερ αευεα [ιιιι] ρη ευνι φωρ φωρ Αβαωθ δωι δωι
44 μαβε χαχαρ Ζασ χλαβαταρ Αωθ Αρουηρ χω ευε [οο]ο κολυφμυωθ επονχωθ σευεισηι Σηθ
βλαθαθ αληθ βηιγαμα χραειω μευααωηωθ υ υυ βοιλωθ τελεσφευχα... ασωρετηριωνιχ φυγρισ σχηικ
ηιουω εηιουω ηιουω ιουω[ουω] ουωωααεαεη ω παντα παρερειθωσδ... φαρχηλαμα διναχαρπαυλι
αεηι αεηιο αεηιου αεηιουω... βαρα ουααμου ποδρυφοριφ θωρι ζωρι ων αω Αβρασαξ Φονοβουβοηλ Ιαω
48 χμηχεεμεαυ αραρεβαιχι φια[νο]χω

Fig. 4: Wing-shaped *Schwindeformen* in *PGM* XXXVI 115-133
(to p. 105)

115	ιαεω	νοθειλαριιιαη
116	ιαε	οθειλαριιιαη
	ια	ειλαριιαη
	ι	ιλαριιαη
	βαφρενδεμουν	λαριιαη
120	βαφρενδεμου	αριιαη
	βαφρενδεμο	ριιαη
	βαφρενδεμ	ιιαη
	βαφρενδε	ιαη
124	βαφρενδ	αη
	βαφρεν	η
	βαφρε	φιρκιαλι
	βαφρ	ιρκιαλι
128	βαφ	ρκιαλι
	βα	κιαλι
	β	ιαλι
		αλι
		λι
		[ι]

Between the two columns is a drawing of a demon, the *sesengen-logos*, and an erotic spell (see *PGM* vol. 2, Taf. III Abb. 16).

ναι, Αβραcαξ, καὶ κα⟨τὰ⟩ τοῦ μεγάλου θεο[ῦ] Ιαεω λό(γοc), *PGM* III 76f.; cf. III 269; VII 584f.; LXI 9; Delatte/Derchain 516, 521; Kropp II 13.10 [p. 31 and see line 6]; cf. also *PGM* IV 3071f.). It is sometimes associated with αβλαναθαναλβα ακραμμαχαμαρει, as in our text (*PGM* III 77; VII 1022; LIX 9; Kropp II 13.10 [p. 31; see line 6]; cf. Delatte/Derchain 432; *PGM* III 59f. [both αβλαναθ. only]) and with cεcενγεν βαρφαραγγηc (*PGM* III 77; XXXVI 115ff.; Delatte/Derchain 516, 521; Kropp II 13.10 [p. 31]). For its occurrence in various other associations, cf. P 398f. (above p. 12); Delatte/ Derchain 122 (Anubis and Isis), 194 (Thoth).

Especially significant for our text and parallels is an amulet (Delatte/Derchain 330) which depicts Ares armed and holding Aphrodite bound by a chain; on the reverse is the *ιαεω-λογοc* (spelled ιαηω etc. and lacking the final five letters). This portrayal closely resembles the instructions of P's *praxis* (296ff.; cf. above pp. 8f. with n. 37) which prescribes the making of two effigies, one of Ares with a sword, the other of a bound woman (representing the one to be charmed) kneeling before him.

Karl Fr. W. Schmidt (*GGA* 196 [1934] 177f.) explains the word as the Jewish divine name ιαεω (cf.above p. 80) + Egyptian *f3j. f-rn-imn 'd mr (= rw)-R' (m-) k3r. f*, "Iaeo is the bearer of the secret name, the lion of Re secure in his shrine" (cf. also *idem*, *GGA* 193 [1931] 443f.; T. Hopfner, *AO* 7 [1935] 119). This etymology accommodates two of the more important contexts where the name occurs, the solar and the Hebraic. The two, of course, are often identical (on the syncretism of Yahweh and solar gods, see above p. 83).

§§ **C and E**: The palindrome αβλανα-θ-αναλβα occurs most often in close connection with ακραμμαχαμαρει. As in our text, the two words are in *Schwindeform* in *PGM* XIXa 29 left, 30 right ("wing shaped"; see fig. 3 above p. 106), XVIIa 1ff. right ("egg shaped") and XXXIII 1ff. ("heart shaped" [with peculiar spelling]; for both see p. 109 figure 5). Not in *Schwindeform*, αβλαν. ακραμ. occur most commonly with Ιαω, Cαβαωθ, Αδωναι, and other Hebrew names; e.g., *PGM* III 79, 150; IV 982, 3030; V 63; VII 311f., 647f., 1020f.; VIII 61; XXXV 23f.; XXXVI 43; LIX 2f.; Kropp II 13.6 (p. 31); 43.121 (p. 153); 50.12f. (p. 211); 53 (p. 214); Youtie/Bonner "Beisan" obv. frag. 1.25 (p. 55/621; ιω = Ιαω?); Perdrizet 73, lines 4ff.; Robinson, *Fest. Rand* 245f. (lines 2, 7f.); P. Berol. inv. 21165.1 (ed. Wm. Brashear, *ZPE* 17 [1975] 28); etc. For less Hebraic or non-Hebraic associations, cf., e.g., *PGM* XII 112, 157, 183; XVIIc 1; XXXVI 227f. For the frequent connection of αβλ. ακρ. with *sesengen-barpharanges*, cf. above p. 78.

The two words also occur apart from each other; αβλαναθαναλβα: *PGM* III 341; V 476; XII 63; XIII 818; Kropp II 47.1,9 (p. 176); 48.64 (p. 202); Delatte/Derchain index p. 351 (16 examples); Aud. index p. 500 (8 examples); ακραμμαχαμαρει: *PGM* III 223, 508; VII 217f., 220-220b; Kropp II 34.14 (p. 116); Delatte/Derchain 284, 416, 460, 510; Aud. 242.7f. (ὁ θεὸϲ ὁ τῶν οὐρανίων ϲτερεωμάτων δεϲπότηϲ); *Pist. Soph.* IV 136 (p. 354, 12 Schmidt/MacDermot).

The etymology of the two words remains obscure; cf. the explanation of F. J. Dölger (*Sol Salutis* [Münster in Westf. 1925] 361) of ϲαλβαναχαμβρη (*PGM* VIII 83f., 102; III 474) as αλβανα (Heb. הלבנה, "the moon") + χαμα (חמה, "sun") + ρη (Eg. god Re). The same elements may account for our αβλανα (me-

Fig. 5: "Egg" and "Heart-shaped" *Schwindeformen* in *PGM* XVIIa 1ff. (a) and XXXIII 1ff. (b)

(to p. 108)

(a)

α α
βα ακ
λβα ακρ
αλβα ακρα
ναλβα ακραμ
αναλβα ακραμμ
θαναλβα ακραμμα
αθαναλβα ακραμμαχ
ναθαναλκα ακραμμαχα
αναθαναλβα ακραμμαχαμ
λαναθαναλβα ακραμμαχαμα
βλαναθαναλβα ακραμμαχαμαρ
αβλαναθαναλβα ακραμμαχαμαρι
βλαναθαναλβα ακραμμαχαμαρ
λαναθαναλβα ακραμμαχαμα
αναθαναλβα ακραμμαχαμ
ναθαναλβα ακραμμαχα
αθαναλβα ακραμμαχ
θαναλβα ακραμμα
αναλβα ακραμμ
ναλβα ακραμ
αλβα ακρα
λβα ακρ
βα ακ
α α

(b)

αβλαναθαναβλαναμαχαραμαραχαραμαρα[χ
βλαναθαναβλαναμαχαραμαραχαραμαρα
λαναθαναβλαναμαχαραμαραχαραμαρ
etc. until μαχα
αχ
α

tathesis) - χαμα - ρει, the difficulty being that ακραμμα is left unsolved. Scholem (p. 97) interprets ακρα as imperative of the Aramaic *aqar* (עקר), "uproot," often used in spells with regard to destroying evil spirits (see his n. 13 for examples); μαχαμαρει, מכמרי, "nets," which in Aramaic magical texts came to mean captivating spells (cf. κατάδεςμοι). Thus, "Uproot magical spells."

Other attempts at Hebrew etymologies are as follows. αβλαναθαναλβα: אב לנו אתה, "You are our father" or, "Father, come to us" (Kopp III § 581; cf. Hopfner *OZ* I § 732; Robinson, *Fest. Rand* 250; Scholem p. 94 and n. 3; cf. also *Abba Abba Ablanathanaphla akramachamari*, Kropp II 50.12 [p. 211], which suggests that אב, "father," may be [or at least was thought to be] involved); αβλα acrostic for אתה ברוך לעולם אדני, "You are blessed forever, Lord," then ναθαν for the palindromic Biblical name Nathan (M. Ginsburger in Perdrizet 78; cf. Robinson, *Fest. Rand* 250f.; *PGM* vol. 3, p. 212A s.v.); for further bibliography on the word, see F. Maltomini, *Aegyptus* 59 (1979) 280; for its solar/Jewish applications see Peterson, *EIC ΘEOC* 98f. and in general cf. above p. 83 on μαρμαραχθα. ακραμμαχαμαρει: Kopp (IV §§ 681, 749) analyzes it either as κραμ αχαμαρι (קרם החמרי), "*liga amuletum meum*," or ακραμνι καμαρι (אקרמני קמרי) "*protegit me amuletum meum*" (cf. Hopfner, OZ I § 735). A. Barb suggests אקרא ממעמקים, "I call from the depths" (*Klassische Hexenkunst* [1933] 15 [*non vidi*, cited in Scholem 97 n. 12]).

§§ **B G H:** The seven vowels, representing the seven planets, were thought to have magical significance and were used as magical formulae in various combinations and groups (cf. tables in Roscher III 2.2533f. s.v. Planeten; Dornseiff, *Alphabet* 35ff., 82f.; Hopfner, OZ I §§ 150-51, 770-75; R.W. Daniel, *ZPE* 50 [1983] 153; Blau 141ff.; e.g., *PGM* XIXa 25ff. right and 17ff. left [see fig. 3 above p. 106]; VII 307ff.; XIII 890ff., 988ff.; etc. [see *PGM* vol. 3 reg. XIV, pp. 281-84]). These sections of M correspond to P as shown in Figure 6 (see below p. 111).

§§ **D and F**: The two groups of the seven vowels are written together as a palindrome, αεηιουω-ωυοιηεα, e.g., in *PGM* I 139; III 152; X 29ff. (in a diagram). As such they occur as a heart-shaped *Schwindeform* in P. Mich. inv. no. 6666.7ff. (ed. R.W. Daniel, *ZPE* 50 [1983] 150) as follows:

αεηιουωωυοιηεα
εηιουωωυοιηε
ηιουωωυοιη
ιουωωυοι
ουωωυο
υωωυ
ωω

In our text the two groups are separated into two heart-shaped structures and flank the *ιαεω-Schwindeform*. Cf. the wing-shaped structures in *PGM* XIXa 35ff. (left) and 21ff. (right) surrounding ιαεω etc. (fig. 3 above p. 106); cf. also *PGM* LXII 96-102; XIII 557-559, 905-11.

Figure 6

Comparison of M §§ B G H and P 412ff.[4]

(to p. 110)

P 412ff. (lft)	M§B	P 412ff. (rt)	M§§ G&H[5]
αω	αω	ιι*	} ριιο-εω
εα	εα	οεω*	
ιω	ιω	οιεε*	θι-εο
υο	υο	οευι*	αε-ιι
ιο	ιο	οευυ*	οε-οο
οε*	ε ο	ιαυυ*	υα-υυ
ιωαε	ιωαε	υυαα	υυ-αα
εοηι	εοηι	οιιι	οι-ιι
υαου	υαου	υαεε	υα-εε
ιαωι*	ιοωι	εωαυ	εω-αυ
αηαη	αηαη	οουι	οο-υι
ηιοι*	ηιου	ηηεα	ηη-εα
ωιυα	ωιυα	ααια	αα-ια
αωοε	αωοε	ιιιω	ιι-ιω
υιωη	υ̣ι̣ω̣η̣	εεαω	εε-αω
εοαωα	εο̣α̣ωα	ηηαω*	ηη-ιε
υαυα*	υαυαιο	ηιηε*	ηι-ηι
ιοηιιη*	υοηιη	οαη ι*	ωα-υι
—*	ιαουα	ηιυι*	ηι-ου
ιαωι	ιαωι	ηηοι*	ηη-υα
αο αο*	ιαο αο	υααι*	ηε-ιο
υυοι	υυοι	ηιια	ηι-ια
—*	ιιυιι	ααωω	αα-ωω

[4] In this table the asterisk (*) marks variation between M and P.

[5] In M, § G is separated from § H, being at a slightly lower point on the tablet (see above p. 22). §§ G and H combined correspond to P's right column.

TEXTUAL APPENDIX

When we speak of proposing an hypothetical archetype for our six texts, we mean the archetype of however many handbooks[1] were involved. For reasons already mentioned (above p. 7), such a procedure is extremely complicated. As the *magus* sat before his handbook, he had to consider his client's particular needs and also, perhaps, how much he wanted to pay.[2] The *magus* could thus augment or abbreviate material in accordance with his judgment concerning the most effective formulae for the situation; the magical books themselves encouraged such liberties (cf. above pp. 6f. with n. 30). Since therefore practical considerations could override the impulse to preserve the exact form of the text, we can never be entirely certain that any tablet faithfully represents its exemplar. I do not therefore set forth the following archetype (abbrev. ω) and critical apparatus with any pretense of suggesting an "original text." I offer it rather as a helpful study in detailed comparison and as a tool for discerning possible textual relationships.

For ω I utilize only material which covers points II.A (M 2-4), II .B (M 4-6), II.C 1 (M 6-10), part of II.C 2 (M 14-16), and part of II.C 3 (M 20-22) in the synopsis of P on pp. 15f. above, `since these portions are common to all six texts. I have not included the second half of II.C 2, since it consists almost entirely of *nomina barbara*, which are not helpful for our purposes. In II.A I note only the more interesting spelling variations of divine and magical names.

As explained above (p. 85), all the texts repeat in the second command the section of the first command corresponding to M 6-8. Only M, however, also repeats (in abbreviated form) 8-14 in 22-26, of which 8-10 (abbrev. M_1) and 22-24 (M_2; M = their agreement) correspond to ω 14 (ὅπωc) --- 18 (δεῖνα). In the apparatus I note the beginning and end of this section in which M and M_2 are taken

[1] P is a handbook; the 5 tablets were copied from handbooks; in general, see above pp. 6ff.

[2] Scribes were paid by the line (see E.G. Turner, *Greek Manuscripts of the Ancient World* [Univ. of London, *Institute of Classical Studies, Bulletin Supp.* 46, 1987²] p. 1); the same may have been true for *magi*. The fact that our five tablets vary considerably in length may thus reflect financial considerations.

into account with ♦. I have used Jordan's new text of W_1 and his corrections of W_2 and C and compared (and occasionally preferred) Wortmann's *editio princeps* and readings suggested by L. Koenen. In the final proofs I also had access to R.W. Daniel and F. Maltomini's recent editions of these texts and L.[3] In listing the evidence from all the texts, I resolve itacism and other spelling variations only where I think necessary.

Hypothetical Archetype

(II.A) παρακατατίθεμαι ὑμῖν τοῦτον τὸν κατάδεσμον θεοῖς καταχθονίοις, Πλούτωνι υεσεμιγαδων καὶ Κόρῃ Περσεφόνῃ Ερεσχιγαλ καὶ Ἀδώνιδι τῷ καὶ βαρβαριθα καὶ Ἑρμῇ καταχθονίῳ Θωουθ φωκενσεψευ αρεκταθου μισονκταικ καὶ Ἀνούβιδι κραταιῷ ψηριφθα τῷ τὰς κλεῖδας ἔχοντι τῶν καθ' Ἅιδους, (II.B) | καὶ δαίμοσι καταχθονίοις θεοῖς ἀώροις τε καὶ ἀώραις, μέλλαξί τε καὶ παρθένοις, ἐνιαυτοὺς ἐξ ἐνιαυτῶν, μῆνας ἐκ μηνῶν, ἡμέ-

1 παρακατατιθεμαι (-ομαι C) CLP : παρακατατιθημι W : παρατιθημι M τουτον τον καταδεσμον LPW_1 : τον καταδεσμον τουτον MW_2 : om. C 1-2 καταχθονίοις: χθονιοις P και θεαις καταχθονιαις post καταχθονιοις add. C 2 Πλούτωνι : και Πλ. W_1 : om. P υεσεμιγαδων P : υεσεμιγαδωθ C : υεσσεμιγαδων ορθω Βαυβω W_1 : τε και Κορη υεσεμμειγαδων M : omm. LW_2 και om. W_1 Κορη και Περσεφονη W_2 2-5 Ερεσχιγαλ --- Αδους om. W_2 3 Αδωνιζι M και$_2$ omm. PW_1 βαρβαριωνηθ (sic Jordan: ηρα...πυωνηθ Wortmann) W_1 και$_3$ om. P Ερμια W_1 4 Θοουθ C : Θωουωθ M φωκενσεψευ LM : φωκενταζεψευ PW_1 : om. C αρεκταθου μισονκταικ LMP : omm. CW_1 αλβαναχαμβρη post μισονκταικ add. P 4-5 καρτερω W_1 5 ψηριφθα: ψηριχθα κανχενε[...]θ W_1 : ψιρινθ P Αδου P (Αδ̣[C) : Αδους πυλων W_1 6 [δεμ]ο̣ς[ι in W_1 (sic Koenen : [τοι]ς Jordan : [τοις] Wortmann : δεμονες W_2 καταχθονίοις: χθονιοις M θεοις LMPW_1 : νεκροις W_2 : om. C αωροις CLMP : om. W αωραις CLMP : αωροις W 6-7 μελλαξι τε (τε om. L) και παρθενοις CLMPW_1 : παρθενοις και μελλαξι W_2 7-9 ενιαυτους --- τοπω τουτω om. W_2 7 ενιαυσιους W_1 : ενιαυτοις L μῆνας: μηνες W_1 (Wortmann) : μηναςι L 7-8 ἡμέρας : ημεραις LW_1

[3] See "List of Abbreviations" (p. 131f.) s.vv. C, L, W_1 and W_2. Professor Koenen and I have had access to photographs of the two Wortmann tablets provided by the University of Cologne, West Germany. As is evident from the following apparatus, many questions concerning the readings of these difficult documents remain. W = the agreement of W_1 and W_2.

ρας ἐξ ἡμερῶν, νύκτας ἐκ νυκτῶν, ὥρας ἐξ ὡρῶν. ὁρκίζω πάντας τοὺς δαίμονας τοὺς ἐν τῷ τόπῳ τούτῳ συνπαραςταθῆναι τῷ δαίμονι τούτῳ.
(II.C 1) | διέγειρέ μοι σεαυτόν, νεκυδαίμων, ὅςτις ποτὲ εἶ, εἴτε ἄρσης εἴτε θήλεια, καὶ ὕπαγε εἰς πᾶν τόπον καὶ εἰς πᾶν ἄμφοδον καὶ εἰς πᾶσαν οἰκίαν καὶ κατάδησον τὴν δεῖνα, ἣν ἔτεκεν ἡ δεῖνα, ἧς ἔχεις τὴν οὐσίαν, ἐμοὶ τῷ δεῖνα, ὃν ἔτεκεν ἡ δεῖνα, ὅπως μὴ βινηθῇ, μὴ πυγισθῇ, μηδὲν πρὸς ἡδονὴν ποιήσῃ ἄλλῳ ἀνδρὶ εἰ μὴ ἐμοὶ μόνῳ τῷ δεῖνα, ὃν ἔτε-

---

8 νυκτας εκ νυκτων CMW_1, post ωρων transpos. L : om. P νύκτας : νυκτες L : νυκτεκτε W_1 ωρασι L : ωρεσι W_1 ἐξ$_2$ om. L εξορκιζω σε M **9** τους$_1$ om. P **9-10** συνπαραστηναι L : συνπαραστατε C **10** δαίμονι : νεκυδαιμονι M τούτῳ : τουτω Αντινοω L : om. M εγειρε μοι σεαυτον post οστις ποτε ει \`κ̣α̣μ̣η⟦ ̣⟧ς´ νεκυδαιμων transpos. $W_2$ : om. M διεγειρε CL : εγειρε W (cf. M 20) : και ανεγειρε P post σεαυτον add. απο της εχουσης σε αναπαυσεως W νεκυδαίμων : νεκυς δαιμων C : \`κ̣α̣μ̣η⟦ ̣⟧ς´ νεκυδαιμων in transpos. supra indicata W_2 : omm. LMPW_1 **10-11** οστις ποτε (ποτ P) ει CMPW_2 : omm. LW_1 **11** ειτε αρσης (αρρην P) ειτε θηλεια (θηλυς P) CMP : omm. LW και om. W_2 πᾶν : παντα CP **12** και$_1$ et και$_2$ omm. LM και εις παν καπηλιον post οικιαν add. W αξον και (κ. om. W_1) ante καταδησον add. PW_1 αξον post καταδησον add. P **13** την δεινα P : Ηρωνουν C : Πτολεμαιδα L : Κοπριαν M : Ματρωναν W ετεκεν om. P ἡ δεῖνα : δεινα P : Πτολεμαις C : Αιας L : μητηρ Τασις M : Ταγενη W ἧς --- οὐσίαν : την θυγατερα Ωριγενους L : om. C την ουσιαν P : τας τριχας της κεφαλης αυτης (α. om. M) MW_2 ε τριχες της κεφαλης αυτης ταυτην post ουσιαν add. W_1 **13-14** ἐμοὶ τῷ δεῖνα : εμοι Ποσιδωνιω C : Αιλουριωνι M : φιλουσαν με τον δεινα P : επι φιλια Θεοδωρω (lege -ρου) W_2 : omm. LW_1 **14** ον --- δεινα omm. LW_1 ὃν : ω M η δεινα P : Θσενουβασθις C : μητηρ ονοματι Κ̣οπρια M : Τεχωσις W_2 ♦**14-17** ὅπως --- εὐσταθεῖν : ποιησον την Ματρωναν υποταγηναι Θεοδωρω μη δ̣αμη (μὴ δ̣αμῇ scripsi : μηδ̣αμῇ Jordan et Daniel-Maltomini : μὴ ε̣ὐ̣ς̣τ̣α̣[θ]ῇ̣ Wortmann) εκτος Θεοδωρ̣ω W_2 **14** voce ὅπως omissa μη βινηθητω μη πυγισθητω P μη$_2$: μηδε M post πυγισθη add. μη λαικαση C et ut vid. W_1 μηδεν CL : μηδε P : μητε M et fortasse W_1 **14-15** προς (πρ. om. M) ηδονην ποιηση CLMP : αφρο⟨δι⟩σιακον επιτελεση W_1 **15** αλλω (εταιρω L) CL : μετ αλλου ανδρος P : ετερω νεανισκω η αλλω ανδρι (αλλω --- ετερω M_2) M : μεθ ετερου μη [αλ]λω αντρι συνελθις (lege ανδρι συνελθη) W_1 **15-16** ει --- η δεινα$_1$ om. M_2 **15** εμοι (εμ. om. M_1) μονω CLM_1 : μετ εμου μονου P : om. W_1 τῷ δεῖνα : του δεινα P : Ποσιδωνιω C : τω Σαραπαμμωνι L : Αιλουριωνι M_1 : Θεοδωρω W_1 **15-16** ον --- η δεινα$_1$ omm. CP **15** ὃν : ω M_1

(II.C 2) κεν ἡ δεῖνα, ἵνα μὴ δυνηθῇ ἡ δεῖνα μήτε φαγεῖν μήτε πιεῖν, μὴ στέγειν, μὴ καρτερεῖν, μὴ εὐσταθεῖν, μὴ ὕπνου τυχεῖν ἐκτὸς ἐμοῦ τοῦ δεῖνα, | ὅτι ϲε ἐξορκίζω, νεκυδαίμων, κατὰ τοῦ ὀνόματοϲ τοῦ φοβεροῦ καὶ τρομεροῦ, οὗ ἡ γῆ ἀκούϲαϲα τὸ ὄνομα ἀνοιγήϲεται, οὗ οἱ δαίμονεϲ ἀκούϲαντεϲ τὸ ὄνομα ἔμφοβοι τρέμουϲιν, οὗ οἱ ποταμοὶ καὶ αἱ θάλαϲϲαι ἀκούϲαντεϲ τὸ ὄνομα ταράϲϲον-

---

16 ἡ δεῖνα$_1$: Αρεα L : μητηρ ονοματι Κοπρια M$_1$: Τεχωϲιϲ W$_1$ ινα μη CP : και μη L : αλλα μητε (lege μηδε) M : [αλλ]α̣ μ̣η̣ W$_1$ (sic Koenen : [αλλ]α μ̣[η] Daniel-Maltomini : [ιν]α μ[η] Wortmann : [κα]ι̣ μ̣η̣ Jordan) δυνηθη MP : δυνηται C : [δυ]νηθητω πωποτε W$_1$: αφηϲ L η δεινα$_2$ P : Ηρωνουϲ C : Ματρωνα χωριϲ Θεοδωρο`υ´ W$_1$: αυτην L : om. M μητε (μη C : om. L) φαγειν μητε (μη CL) πειν (πειν - φαγ. P) CLMP: om. W$_1$ **16-17** μη ϲτεγειν L : μη ϲτεργειν CP : omm. MW$_1$ **17** μὴ καρτερεῖν : μητε εξελθειν L : om. M μη ευϲταθειν CW$_1$: μητε ευϲταθειν post τυχειν δια παντοϲ M$_1$ (ad δ. π. v. infra) : μη ευϲταθηϲαι P : omm. LM$_2$ post ευϲταθειν (τυχειν M$_2$) add. η (M$_1$: μητε M$_2$) ηϲυχαζιν τη ψυχη η τεϲ φρεϲι (τ. φρ. M$_1$: τη διανοια M$_2$) M μη$_3$ CP : μητε L M : μηδε (μηδε|δε aut μηδε̄|δε W$_2$)* W τυχειν LMPW$_1$: τυγχανειν C : τυγχανη W$_2$ post τυχειν (vel τυγχανη) add. η δεινα P, δια παντοϲ M$_1$, νυκτοϲ [η ημεραϲ Ματ]ρωνα ην ετεκεν Ταγενη ου ιϲιν ε (lege ηϲ ειϲιν αι) τριχεϲ [τηϲ κεφαληϲ] αυτηϲ W$_1$, Ματρωνα νυκτοϲ και ημεραιϲ (lege -ραϲ) W$_2$ **17-18** ἐκτὸϲ --- δεῖνα : επιζητουϲα δια παντοϲ ημεραϲ και νυκτοϲ (δια --- νυκ. om. M$_1$) Αιλουριωνα ον ετεκεν μητερ ονοματι (ονομ. om. M$_1$) Κοπρια M : εκτοϲ Θεοδωρω (lege -ρου) post μηδαμη (v. supra ad 14-17) transpos. W$_2$ εκτοϲ εμου CLP : χωριϲ W$_1$ **18** του δεινα P : Ποϲιδωνιου C : του Ϲαραπαμμωνοϲ ου ετεκεν Αρεα L : Θεοδωρου ον ετεκε Τεχωϲιϲ W$_1$♦ οτι CMP et W$_1$ ut vid. (in lacuna rest. Jordan) : om. W$_2$ ϲε post εξορκιζω (ορκιζω C) transpos. CLW νεκυδαιμων MW$_1$: νεκυδαιμον Αντινοε L : γαρ W$_2$: omm. CP **18-19** κατα --- φοβερου και τρομερου (τρ. κ. φο. LW$_1$) CLMPW$_1$: κατα του αγιου ονοματοϲ W$_2$ **19-20** ου --- ανοιγηϲεται om. W$_2$ **19** ακουϲαϲα LPW$_1$ M (in M post ονομα) : ακουουϲα C το ονομα CMW$_1$: του ονοματοϲ LP **19-20** ανοιγηϲεται LMP : ανοιγεται CW$_1$ **20-22** οὗ --- ῥήϲϲονται : ου φριϲϲι τα ορη και τρεμει τα δεμονια W$_2$ **20** ακουϲαντεϲ LPM (in M post ονομα) : ακουοντεϲ CW$_1$ το ονομα CMW$_1$: του ονοματοϲ LP ενφοβου P : ενφοβωϲ L τρεμουϲι(ν) CMW$_1$: φοβουνται L : φοβηθηϲονται P **21-22** αι θαλαϲϲαι --- ταραϲϲονται omm. LP **21** αι om. C ακουϲαντεϲ M (post ονομα) : ακουουϲαι C : ακουοντεϲ W$_1$ post ονομα add. εμφοβοι CW$_1$ **21-22** ταραϲϲονται M : φοβουνται C : τρεμουϲιν W$_1$

ται, οὗ αἱ πέτραι ἀκούςαςαι τὸ ὄνομα ῥήςςονται. ὁρκίζω ςε, νε-
(II.C 3) κυδαίμων, εἴτε ἄρςης εἴτε θήλεια, κατὰ τοῦ (mw) --- | μή μου
παρακούςῃς τῶν ἐντολῶν, νεκυδαίμων, ὅςτις ποτὲ εἶ, εἴτε ἄρ-
ρης εἴτε θήλεια, ἀλλ' ἔγειρέ μοι ςεαυτὸν καὶ ὕπαγε εἰς πᾶν
τόπον, εἰς πᾶν ἄμφοδον, εἰς πᾶςαν οἰκίαν, καὶ ἔνεγκόν μοι τὴν
δεῖνα ἣν ἔτεκεν ἡ δεῖνα.

---

22 ου --- ονομα om. W_1 ου omm. LP αι om. L ακουουςαι C : ακουςαντες LPM (in M post ονομα) το ονομα om. L **22** εξορκιζω W_2 γαρ post ςε add. W_2 **22-23** ορκιζω --- θηλεια om. M νε-κυδαιμων W_1 : νεκυς δαιμων C : νεκυδαιμον P : νεκυδαιμον Αντινοε L : om. W_2 post νεκυδαιμων add. οςτις ποτε ει C **23** ειτε αρςης ειτε θηλεια (αρρης---θηλυς P) CPW_1 : omm. LW_2 post του add. ενδοξου ονοματος W_2 ante μη add. ορκιζω ςε W_2 μου omm. LW_2 **24** των εντολων M : των ονοματων W_2 : των εντολων και των ονοματων post νεκυδαιμον transpos. P : omm. CLW_1 νεκυδαιμων MW_1 : νεκυς δαιμων C : νεκυδαιμον P : νεκυ-δαιμον Αντινοε L : om. W_2 **24-25** οςτις --- θηλεια (ειτε --- θηλεια omm. CW_1) MCW_1 : omm. LW_2 : ante και υπαγε transpos. P **24** ποτὲ : ποτ ουν (ποτ ⟦ου⟧ Daniel-Maltomini) W_1* **25** θηλυς P αλλ --- ςεαυτον om. C ἀλλ' : και W_1 εγειρον P : εξεγειρε W_2 μοι : μονον P : om. W_2 απο της εχουςης ςε αναπαυςεως post ςεαυτον add. P **25-27** και --- η δεινα om. W_1 **25** παν LMW_2 : παντα CP **26** και post τοπον et αμφοδον add. C **26-27** εἰς πᾶν --- ἡ δεῖνα : οπου εςτι Ματρωνα ην ετεκεν Ταγενη ης εχις την ουςιαν και απελθε προς αυτην W_2 **26** ενεγκον P : ενεγκε C : αγαγε L : καταδηςον M μοι om. M **26-27** την δεινα P : Ηρωνουν C : την Πτολεμαιδα L : Κοπριαν M **27** ην --- δεινα om. P ἡ δεῖνα : Πτολεμαις C : Αιας την θυγατερα Ωριγε-νους L : μητηρ Ταηςις ης εχις τας τριχας της κεφαλης Αιλουριωνι ω ετεκε μητηρ ονοματι Κοπρια M

ADDENDA

p. 1 n. 1: Daniel and Maltomini prefer a 2nd/3rd cent. date for this tablet and the parallel tablets (see pp. 131f.).

p. 4 n. 15: For other scenes of *psychostasia*, see E. Vermeule, *Aspects of Death in Early Greek Art and Poetry* (Berkeley and Los Angeles 1979) 160-62.

p. 5 n. 24: The precise title of this volume, which has now appeared, is *MAGICA HIERA: Ancient Greek Magic and Religion* (Oxford 1989).

p. 15: ἕτερον μέροϲ is rendered by Preisendanz "die andere Seite" and in *PGM Eng.* "the other side." Such translations are apparently based on a strict interpretation of ἕτερον which, as we have seen (below p. 59), is not necessary, especially in Greek of this period. The new Michigan tablet, which most likely reflects similar handbook instructions, shows that the phrase is best translated "another part."

p. 33: Fauth, however, admits the Seth-Yahweh synthesis for magical texts of the third cent. and later but denies it for *Pistis Sophia* and other gnostic literature. M. Tardieu (*Studies in Gnosticism and Hellenistic Religions* [Fest. Quispel, EPRO 91, edd. R. van den Broek, M.J. Vermaseren, Leiden 1981, 412-18] argues that Jesus *Aberamentho* reveals an underlying parallel between Jesus and Hermes-Thoth, whose name he finds in the θωου(θ) element of the palindrome.

p. 47: The same principle is, of course, illustrated by the above θεοῖϲ καταχθονίοιϲ (p. 34). For abundant illustration of that phrase, see Lattimore, *Epitaphs* 96 n. 70.

p. 52 n. 2: see below, on p. 84f.

p. 53: On ϲτέγειν (line 10) see F. Maltomini, *ZPE* 78 (1989) 95-97.

p. 57: μ[ὴ] | [ἐ]κ ἡ̣δ̣ο̣ν̣ῆ̣ϲ̣ Wortmann : μὴ | [λαι]καϲθ̣[ῇ] μήτε Jordan; the first is paleographically, the second linguistically, difficult. H.D. Jocelyn (*Proceedings of the Cambridge Philological Society* 206 [n.s. 26], 1980, 12-66) has sought to confirm the view of A.E. Housman that λαικάζειν means *fellare* but never *cunnum lingere*. Among the evidence he cites are the readings of C and L (cf. p. 20f.). In general I have reservations about Jocelyn's conclusions. His evidence does, however, prove to my satisfaction that λαικάζειν refers to a sexual act performed for a male by either a woman or another male, and thus Jordan's aor. passive is unlikely.

p. 61: H.D. Betz has called my attention to Jesus' declaration at the Last Supper, ἀμὴν λέγω ὑμῖν ὅτι οὐκέτι οὐ μὴ πίω ἐκ τοῦ γενήματοc τῆc ἀμπέλου ἕωc τῆc ἡμέραc ἐκείνηc ὅταν αὐτὸ πίνω καινὸν ἐν τῇ βαcιλείᾳ τοῦ θεοῦ (NT Mk. 14.25; cf. Mt. 26.29; esp. Lk. 22.16, 18, where he renounces both food and drink). J. Jeremias describes these sayings in terms of the Hebrew formula known as the *issar*, "vow of abstinence," and provides rich parallel material from Jewish and Christian sources (*Die Abendmahlsworte Jesu*, Göttingen[3] 1960, 199-210 [Eng. *The Eucharistic Words of Jesus*, Philadelphia 1977, 207-218]; the 4th German edition was not available to me).

p. 73: Lucan may be thinking of Homer's four-story universe, in which Tartarus is the lowest part, deep below Hades: τόccον ἔνερθ' Ἀΐδεω ὅcον οὐρανόc ἐcτ' ἀπὸ γαίηc (*Il.* VIII 16; cf. Aesch. *Pr.* 152ff.); cf. M.L. West's comment on Hes. *Theog.* 720f. (p. 338).

p. 81: There is, however, some controversey concerning the nature of *-ai* in Adonai (Eissfeldt in *Theological Dictionary of the Old Testament* I 63ff.).

p. 82, on line 18: W. Fauth (*Oriens Christianus* 73 [1973] 80-84) notes this etymology (basing it on Syriac), but expresses skepticism about it and other explanations of *bar-* and *mar-* forms, since they are subject to endless plays and often seem to be variations upon each other. In this connection he cites *nomina barbara* such as *barbariel*, *barbarioth*, *barbariao*, compared with *marmarel*, *marmarioth*, *marmaraoth/marmariao*, and notes that the name of the female aeon Βαρβελω has both βαρ- and μαρ- variants. It is my opinion that there is usually a discernable difference between such words which are standard and frequent, for which we may seek etymologies, and those which are plays upon them.

p. 82, on lines 18f.: ουcερβεντηθ also resembles Osiris names such as Οcερχενθε (*PGM* XIII 814; οθερ- pap.) and Οcερχενθεμενθει (815f.). K. Fr. W. Schmidt (*Philologische Wochenschrift* 41/42 [1935] 1183) interprets the latter word as wśir-ḫntj-ỉmntj.w, "Osiris, Erster der Westlichen (= Gestorbenen)." Cf. also *PGM* VII 445.

p. 84, on C: cf. ἕλκε τὴν Ματρῶνα, W_2 62f.; η > αι is not frequent, but occurs (Gignac I 247f., and cf. 111f. for omission of final ν). Daniel-Maltomini sugguest either ἕλκετε or ἕλκε τε (*Suppl. Mag.* p. 176). τε is possibly for δέ (cf. Mayser II 3. 156-158; Gignac I 80-83).

p. 84f., on W_2: Daniel and Maltomini interpret the supralinear strokes at the end of W_1 38 and W_2 25, 55, 56 as examples of a very rare method of indicating cancellation (thus ⟦ου⟧, W_1 38; μη⟦δε⟧|δ̣ὲ, W_2 25f.; ὕ⟦πν`ο´⟧|πνον, 55f.; βρο⟦το⟧|τον, 56f.; *Suppl. Mag.* pp. 200 and 209). Such strokes, however are a common means of writing ν at the end of lines, which makes good sense in all instances except perhaps W_2 25. Here, however, the stroke is not clear and could easily be a scratch (so Koenen; Wortmann and Jordan do not mention it). Even if the mark exists, it could be understood as superfluous ν (cf. Gignac I 112f.). Thus in W_2 the dittography remains uncorrected. In W_1 38f. we have ὅϲτιϲ ποτ' οὖν | [εἶ], for which cf. PGM IV 1240, 1244; Aud. 234. 1, 235.1, *al.* The οὖν further reenforces the indefiniteness of ὅϲτιϲ ποτ' ("hypercharakterisierend"; see Schwyzer 2.585). Cf. Aesch. *Supp.* 392f., μή τί ποτ' οὖν γενοίμαν ὑποχείριοϲ κράτεϲιν ἀρϲένων with KG 2.160.

p. 93: For bibliography on βαινχωωωχ see now Wm. Brashear, *ZPE* 78 (1989) 123 n. 3.

p. 104: J. Scherer, however, has proposed λο⟨γί⟩μων as a correction to μό-μων (*P. Phil.* p. 14 n. 1).

pp. 116 and 117: see above, on p. 84f.

LIST OF ABBREVIATIONS AND BIBLIOGRAPHY[1]

1. Books, Articles, and Reference Works

Abt, *Apol.*	Abt, A., *Die Apologie des Apuleius und die antike Zauberei* (RGVV IV 2), Giessen 1908
An. Ath.	Delatte, A., *Anecdota Atheniensia* I (*Bibliothèque de la Faculté de Philosophie et Lettres de l'Université de Liège* 36), 1927
AO	*Archiv Orientální*
ARW	*Archiv für Religionswissenschaft*
Aud.	Audollent, A., *Defixionum Tabellae*, Paris 1904 (cited by number of *defixio* unless otherwise indicated)
Barber	Barber, F., *A Linguistic Study of the Greek Magical Papyri* (M.A. Thesis, University of London, Birkbeck College), 1954
Baudissin, "Adonis"	Baudissin, W.W., "Adonis," *ZDMG* 70 (1916) 423ff.
Baudissin, "Iao"	*idem*, "Iao," *Studien zur semitischen Religionsgeschichte* I, Leipzig 1876, pp. 181ff.
Bauer	Bauer, W., *Griechisch-Deutsches Wörterbuch zu den Schriften des Neuen Testaments und der frühchristlichen Literatur*, 6., völlig neu bearbeitete Auflage herausgegeben von K. Aland und B. Aland, Berlin-New York 1988; translated and adapted by W.F. Arndt, F. W. Gingrich, and F.W. Danker, *A Greek-English Lexicon of the New Testament and Other Early Christian Literature* (on the basis of the 5th German edition of 1958), Chicago/ London[2] 1979

[1] Numbers following abbreviations in the text refer to pp. unless otherwise specified in this list. For abbreviations of papyrus editions, see Oates, J.F.; Bagnall, R.S.; Willis, W.H., *Checklist of Editions of Greek Papyri and Ostraca*. 3rd. ed., 1985 (an update appears on PHI Demonstration ROM #2, The Packard Humanities Institute 1988); I enter in this list abbreviations for volumes published since 1985.

BDB	Brown, B.; Driver, S.R.; Briggs, C.A., *A Hebrew and English Lexicon*, Boston/New York/Chicago 1906
BDR	Blass, F.; Debrunner, A.; Rehkopf, F., *Grammatik des neutestamentlichen Griechisch*, Göttingen[15] 1976
BIFAO	*Bulletin de l'Institut Français d'Archéologie Orientale*
Blau	Blau, L., *Das altjüdische Zauberwesen*, Berlin 1914
Bonner	Bonner, C., *Studies in Magical Amulets* (University of Michigan Studies, Humanistic Series 49), Ann Arbor 1950 (cited by page or amulet number, the latter indicated by #)
Bonnet	Bonnet, H., *Reallexikon der ägyptischen Religionsgeschichte*, Berlin 1952
Borghouts, *AEMT*	Borghouts, J.F., trans., *Ancient Egyptian Magical Texts* (NISABA 9), Leiden 1978 (usually by text and page number)
Budge, *Gods*	Budge, E.A.W., *The Gods of the Egyptians* I and II, London 1904
CCAG	*Catalogus Codicum Astrologorum Graecorum*, 1898ff.
CG	*Codex Cairensis Gnosticus*
Crum	Crum, W.E., *A Coptic Dictionary*, Oxford 1939
Cunn. Mem.	*Cunningham Memoirs* (pub. by Royal Irish Academy)
Daniel-Maltomini	see *Suppl. Mag.* I
Deissmann, *Bib. Stud.*	Deissmann, A., *Bible Studies*, transl. by A. Grieve, Edinburgh 1901
Delatte/Derchain	Delatte, A.; Derchain, P., *Les intailles magiques greco-égyptiennes*, Paris 1964 (cited by amulet number unless otherwise indicated)
Denniston	Denniston, J.D., *The Greek Particles*, Oxford[2] 1954
Dittenberger, *OGIS*	Dittenberger, G., *Orientis Graeci Inscriptiones Selectae* I and II, Leipzig 1903-05
Dittenberger, *Syll.*	Dittenberger, G., *Sylloge Inscriptionum Graecarum* I-IV, Leipzig[3] 1915-24

DMP	*The Demotic Magical Papyrus of London and Leiden*, edd. F.L. Griffith and H. Thompson, London 1904
Dodds, *Greeks and Irrat.*	Dodds, E.R., *The Greeks and the Irrational*, Berkeley/Los Angeles 1951
Dornseiff, *Alphabet*	Dornseiff, F., *Das Alphabet in Mystik und Magie* (ΣΤΟΙΧΕΙΑ VII), Leipzig[2] 1925
EPRO	Études Préliminaires aux Religions Orientales dans l'Empire Romain
Fauth	Fauth, W., *Oriens Christianus* 67 (1983) 63-103
GGA	*Göttingische gelehrte Anzeigen*
Gignac	Gignac, F.T., *A Grammar of the Greek Papyri of the Roman and Byzantine Periods*, I *Phonology*, II *Morphology* (Testi e documenti per lo studio dell'antichità LV 1 and 2), Milano 1976 and 1981
Gow	Gow, A.S.F., *Theocritus*, Cambridge[2] 1952
Griffiths, *Isis Book*	Griffiths, I.G., *The Isis Book, Apuleius Metamorphoses Book XI* (EPRO 39, Leiden 1975)
Griffiths, *Is. et Os.*	Griffiths, J.G., *Plutarch's De Iside et Osiride*, Univ. of Wales Press 1970
Gundel, H.G.,*Weltbild*	Gundel, H.G., *Weltbild und Astrologie in den griechischen Zauberpapyri* (Münch. Beitr. 53), 1968
Gundel, W., *Dekane*	*Gundel, W., Dekane und Dekansternbilder*, Glückstadt/Hamburg 1936
Harrauer, *Meliouchos*	Harrauer, C., *Meliouchos*, Arbeiten zur antiken Religionsgeschichte I (Wiener Studien, Beiheft 11), 1987
HDA	*Handwörterbuch des Deutschen Aberglaubens*
Heitsch	Heitsch, E., *Die griechischen Dichterfragmente der römischen Kaiserzeit*, Abhandlungen der Akademie der Wissenschaften in Göttingen, philol.-hist. Klasse, 3rd series 49, 1961
Helbing	Helbing, R., *Grammatik der Septuaginta*, Göttingen 1907
Henderson, *Muse*	Henderson, J., *The Maculate Muse*, New Haven/London 1975

Hopfner, *Is. et Os.*	Hopfner, T., *Plutarch über Isis und Osiris,* I and II (Monographien des Archiv Orientální 9), Prague 1940 and 1941
Hopfner, OZ	Hopfner, T., *Griechisch-ägyptischer Offenbarungszauber* I and II (Studien zur Palaeographie und Papyruskunde, ed. C. Wessely, XXI and XXIII, in Wessely's handwriting 1921 and 1924, repr. in typescript Amsterdam 1974 (I) and 1983 (II, pt. 1 only)
Horsley, *New Docs.* I-II	Horsley, G.H.R., *New Documents Illustrating Early Christianity* I (Maquarie 1981); II (1982)
HSCP	*Harvard Studies in Classical Philology*
HTR	*Harvard Theological Review*
ICS	*Illinois Classical Studies*
JANES	*Journal of the Ancient Near Eastern Society*
JEA	*Journal of Egyptian Archaeology*
Jordan, "Well"	Jordan, David, "Two Inscribed Lead Tablets from a Well in the Athenian Kerameikos," *MDAI*, Ath. Abt. 95, 1980, 225ff.
Kagarow	Kagarow, E., *Griechische Fluchtafeln*, Eus Supplementa 4, Leopoli 1929
Kapsomenakis	Kapsomenakis, S.G., *Voruntersuchungen zu einer Grammatik der Papyri der nachchristlichen Zeit,* (Münch. Beitr. 28), 1938
KB 1 and 2	Kühner, R.; Blass, F., *Ausführliche Grammatik der griechischen Sprache* I 1 and 2, Hannover 1890, 1892
KG 1 and 2	Kühner, R.; Gerth, B., *Ausführliche Grammatik der griechischen Sprache* II 1 and 2, Hannover/Leipzig 1898, 1904
Kopp	Kopp, U.Fr., *Palaeographica Critica* III and IV, Mannheim 1829
Kropp	Kropp, A.M., *Ausgewählte koptische Zaubertexte* I-III, Brussels 1930-31
Lampe	Lampe, G.W.H., *A Patristic Greek Lexicon*, Oxford 1971

Lattimore, *Epitaphs*	Lattimore, R., *Themes from Greek and Latin Epitaphs*, Urbana 1962
Lex. Äg.	*Lexikon der Ägyptologie*
Maas/Trypanis	Maas, P.; Trypanis, C.A., edd., *Sancti Romani Melodi Cantica*, Oxford 1963
Mandilaras	Mandilaras, B.G., *The Verb in the Greek Non-literary Papyri*, Athens 1973
Marganne	Marganne, M.-H., *Inventaire analytique des papyrus grecs de médecine*, Centre de Rech. d'Hist. et de Phil. de la IV Section de l'Ecole pratique des Hautes Etudes, III Hautes Etudes du Monde Gréco-Romaine, 12, Genève 1981
Massart, *Leid. Mag. Pap.*	Massart, A., *The Leiden Magical Papyrus* I 343 + I 345, Oudheidkundige Mededelingen uit het Rijksmuseum van Oudheden te Leiden 34, 1954
Mayser	Mayser, E., *Grammatik der griechischen Papyri aus der Ptolemäerzeit* I 2-3 (2nd ed.), II 1-3, Berlin/Leipzig 1926-38
Mayser/Schmoll	Mayser I 1, bearb. von H. Schmoll, Berlin[2] 1970
MDAI Ath. Abt.	*Mitteilungen des Deutschen Archäologischen Instituts*, Athenische Abteilung
Morenz, *Äg. Rel.*	Morenz, S., *Ägyptische Religion*, Stuttgart 1960; Eng. trans. Ithaca/London 1973
Münch. Beitr.	Münchener Beiträge zur Papyrusforschung und antiken Rechtsgeschichte
NHLib. Eng.	*The Nag Hammadi Library in English*, ed. J.M. Robinson, New York etc. 1977
Nock, *Essays*	Nock, A.D., *Essays on Religion and the Ancient World* I and II, Oxford 1972
Norden, *Aen. VI*	Norden, E., *P. Vergilius Maro Aeneis Buch VI*, Leipzig/Berlin 1916
Norden, *Ag. Th.*	Norden, E., *Agnostos Theos*, Leipzig/Berlin 1913
P. Münch.	*Die Papyri der Bayerischen Staatsbibliothek München*, I, Stuttgart[2] 1986 (corr. and supplem. by D.

	Hagedorn); II, Stuttgart 1986 (edd. A. Carlini *et al.*); III, Stuttgart 1986 (edd. U. and D. Hagedorn, R. Hübner, and J.C. Shelton)
Perdrizet	Perdrizet, P., "Amulette grecque trouvée en Syrie," *Revue des Études grecques* 41 (1928) 73ff.
Peterson, *EIC ΘEOC*	Peterson, E., *EIC ΘEOC* (Forschungen zur Religion und Literatur des Alten und Neuen Testaments, Neue Folge 24), Göttingen 1926
PGM	*Papyri Graecae Magicae* , 2 vols., ed. K. Preisendanz (2nd edition with additions by A. Henrichs), Stuttgart 1973-1974; photocopies of the proofs of vol. III (which never appeared) mainly containing the indices are available in many papyrological institutions. Pagan magical papyri are cited by text number in Roman numerals and line number in Arabic, Christian texts by Arabic text and line numbers; ostraca by text and line number, both in Arabics and preceded by "O"
PGM Eng.	*The Greek Magical Papyri in Translation* (vol. 1: Texts), ed. H.D. Betz, Chicago 1985
Pist. Soph.	Schmidt, C. ed., translated by V. MacDermot, *Pistis Sophia* (Nag Hammadi Studies 9), Leiden 1978
Pitra	Pitra, J.B., *Analecta Sacra Spicilegio Solesmensi* I, Paris 1876
Pradel	Pradel, F., *Griechische und süditalienische Gebete, Beschwörungen und Rezepte des Mittelalters*, RGVV III 3, Giessen 1907; cited by page and line number
Preisigke, *Fachwörter*	Preisigke, F., *Fachwörter des öffentlichen Verwaltungsdienstes Ägyptens*, Göttingen 1915
Preisigke, *Namenbuch*	*idem, Namenbuch*, Heidelberg 1922
Preisigke, *Wörterbuch*	*idem, Wörterbuch der griechischen Papyrusurkunden* I, II (completed by E. Kießling), III (ed. E. Kießling), Berlin 1925, 1927, and 1931; IV 1-4 (ed. E. Kießling), Berlin 1944 and Marburg 1958-1971
PSBA	*Proceedings of the Society of Biblical Archaeologists*
PTA	Papyrologische Texte und Abhandlungen

RAC	*Reallexikon für Antike und Christentum*
RE	*Paulys Real-Encyclopädie der classischen Altertumswissenschaft*, Stuttgart 1894-1980
Reitzenstein, *Poim.*	Reitzenstein, R., *Poimandres; Studien zur griechisch-ägyptischen und frühchristlichen Literatur*, Leipzig 1904
Renehan, *Gk. Text. Crit.*	Renehan, R., *Greek Textual Criticism*, Cambridge, Mass. 1969
RG	Morenz, S., *Religion und Geschichte des alten Ägyptens*, Köln/Wien 1975
RGVV	Religionsgeschichtliche Versuche und Vorarbeiten
Rh. Mus.	*Rheinisches Museum für Philologie*
Robinson, *Fest. Rand*	Robinson, D.M., "A Magical Text from Beroea in Macedonia," *Classical and Medieval Studies in Honor of E.K. Rand*, New York 1938, pp. 245ff.
Rohde, *Psyche*	Rohde, E., *Psyche* I and II, Tübingen 1907 (Eng. trans. 1925)
Roscher	Roscher, W.H., ed., *Ausführliches Lexikon der griechischen und römischen Mythologie*, Leipzig 1884-1937
SB	Preisigke, F., *et al.*, edd., *Sammelbuch griechischer Urkunden aus Ägypten*, Berlin/New York I-, 1915-
Scholem	Scholem, G.G., *Jewish Gnosticism, Merkabah Mysticism, and Talmudic Tradition*, New York 1965
Schwyzer	Schwyzer, E., *Griechische Grammatik* I, München 1939, and II (with A. Debrunner), 1950
Schwyzer, "Vulgärsprache	Schwyzer, E., "Die Vulgärsprache der attischen Fluchtafeln," *Neue Jahrbücher für das klassische Altertum* 5 (1900) 244ff.
SCO	*Studi Classici e Orientali*
Scriptiunculae	Youtie, H.C., *Scriptiunculae* I and II, Amsterdam 1973
Script. post.	Youtie, H.C., *Scriptiunculae posteriores* I and II, Bonn 1982

Stegemann	Stegemann, V., *Die koptischen Zaubertexte der Sammlung Papyrus Erzherzog Rainer in Wien*, Sitzungsberichte der Heidelberger Akademie der Wissenschaften, philos.-hist. Klasse, 24.1, 1934
Suppl. Mag. I	*Supplementum Magicum*, ed. with translations and notes by R.W. Daniel and F. Maltomini, I, Papyrologica Coloniensia XVI.1, Abh. d. Rhein.-Westf. Akademie der Wissensch., Opladen 1990.
TAPA	*Transactions of the American Philological Association*
TDNT	*Theological Dictionary of the New Testament*, Grand Rapids 1964-1976, translation of *Theologisches Wörterbuch zum Neuen Testament*, ed. G. Kittel
Test. Sol.	*The Testament of Solomon*, ed. C.C. McCown, Leipzig 1922
Thackeray	Thackeray, H.J., *A Grammar of the Old Testament in Greek* I, Cambridge 1909
Threatte	Threatte, L., *The Grammar of Attic Inscriptions* I, Berlin/New York 1980
Turner, *Syntax*	Turner, N., *Syntax*, vol. III of Moulton, J.H., *A Grammar of New Testament Greek*, Edinburgh 1963
Vanderlip	Vanderlip, V.F., *The Four Greek Hymns of Isidorus and the Cult of Isis* (American Studies in Papyrology 12), Toronto 1972
Veitch	Veitch, W., *Greek Verbs Irregular and Defective*, Oxford 1887
West, *Text. Crit.*	West, M.L., *Textual Criticism and Editorial Technique*, Stuttgart 1973
Wiemken	Wiemken, H., *Der griechische Mimus. Dokumente zur Geschichte des antiken Volkstheaters*, Bremen 1972
Wien. Stud.	*Wiener Studien*
Wolbergs	Wolbergs, Th., *Griechische religiöse Gedichte der ersten nachchristlichen Jahrhunderte* I, *Psalmen und Hymnen der Gnosis und des frühen Christentums*, Beitr. z. klass. Philologie 40, Meisenheim 1971

Wünsch	IG III, pars 3, Appendix, *Defixionum Tabellae*, ed. R. Wünsch, Berlin 1897 (cited by number of *defixo* unless otherwise indicated)
Youtie/Bonner, "Beisan"	Youtie, H.C.; Bonner, C., "Two Curse Tablets from Beisan," *TAPA* 68 (1937) 43ff. (*Script. post.* II, 609ff.). When cited, the *TAPA* and *Script. post.* pp. are separated by a slash.
ZÄS	*Zeitschrift für ägyptische Sprache und Altertumskunde*
ZDMG	*Zeitschrift der Deutschen Morgenländischen Gesellschaft*
ZPE	*Zeitschrift für Papyrologie und Epigraphik*

2. Abbreviations Pertaining to P. Mich. 757, the Parallel Texts[2], and Other Magical Texts

C = Cairo text	Edgar, C.C., "A Love Charm from the Fayoum," *Bulletin de la Société Archéologique d'Alexandrie* 21 (1925) 42ff. (*Suppl. Mag.* I 46; *SB IV* 7452; *SEG* 8 [1937] 574); from Hawaret el Maqta, Fayoum; 3rd cent. A.D. (Edgar), 2nd/3rd cent. A.D. (Daniel-Maltomini in *Suppl. Mag.*). Corrections by D.R. Jordan appeared in *ZPE* 72 (1988) 247 n. 4.
Edgar	C.C. Edgar's comments on C (q.v.).
Kambitsis	S. Kambitsis' comments on L (q.v.).
L = Louvre text	Kambitsis, S., "Une Nouvelle Tablette Magique d' Égypte," *BIFAO* 76 (1976) 213ff. (*Suppl. Mag.* I 47; Horsley, *New Docs.* I 8 [pp. 33ff.]; *SEG* 26 [1976/77] 1717); from Antinoopolis; 3rd/4th cent. A.D. (Kambitsis), 2nd/3rd cent. A.D. (Daniel -Maltomini in *Suppl. Mag.*).
M = Michigan text	P. Mich. 757 (*Suppl. Mag.* I 48); provenance unknown; 3rd/4th cent. A.D. (present editor), 2nd/3rd cent. A. D. (Daniel-Maltomini in *Suppl. Mag.*); for M_1, M_2 and M_3, see above pp. 86 and 89.

---

[2] On "the parallels" see above p. 6. The abbreviations of the texts are based on their present locations, except the two Wortmann tablets, which are at the University of Cologne.

P = Paris text (Bibliothèque Nationale	*PGM* IV 296-433; from Thebes; 4th cent. A.D.
W_1, and W_2 = Wortmann, texts 1 and 2	Wortmann, D., "Neue Magische Texte," *Bonner Jahrbücher* 168 (1968) 56-80, Nr. 1 and 2 (*Suppl. Mag.* I 49 and 50); from Oxyrhynchus; 3rd/4th cent. A.D. (Wortmann), 2nd/3rd cent. A.D. (Daniel-Maltomini in *Suppl. Mag.*); edition of W_1 by D.R. Jordan, *ZPE* 72 (1988) 245ff.; corrections on W_2 *ibid.* 246 n. 3.
W_3, W_4, W_6, and W_{12}	Wortmann, D., *loc. cit.*, 80-102, nos. 3 (*Suppl. Mag.* 51; Oxyrhynchus; 3/4th cent. A.D. [Wortmann], 2/3rd cent. A.D. [Daniel-Maltomini]) and 4 (*Suppl. Mag.* 45; Upper Egypt north of Assiut; 5th cent. A.D), pp. 104-105, no. 6 (*Suppl. Mag.* 2; Oxyrhynchus; 4th cent. A.D. [Wortmann], 3rd cent. A.D. [Daniel-Maltomini], and 108-109 (no. 12).
Wortmann	D. Wortmann's comments on the texts edited by him (see above).

3. Other Abbreviations

Eg.	Egyptian
Eng.	English
LXX	*Septuaginta*
MT	Masoretic Text
mw	magical word(s)
NT	New Testament
OT	Old Testament
tab.	tablet

INDICES

I. GREEK INDICES OF P. MICH. 757

Plain faced numbers refer to lines of sections J and K. Bold-faced numbers indicate page(s) in the commentary. Section symbols (§) followed by letters refer to the parts of the text besides J and K (see above p. 22). Letters A-G in parenthesis mean see/see also the appropriate section of this index. II A/B in parenthesis means see/see also the appropriate section of index II.

A. Names of Persons

B. Divine Names

C. *Logoi*

See also D for individual elements

D. *Nomina Barbara/Voces Magicae*

E. Palindromes

F. Vowels and *Characteres*

26-28, 29 **88**; §§ B, G, H, D, F **110f.**

G. General Index of Words

II. SUBJECT INDEX

A. English

B. Greek (see also I)

III. INDEX LOCORUM

For abbreviations used in this index, see List of Abbreviations (pp. 123ff.) or *ad loc.* The principle parallel texts (C L P W_1 W_2; see p. 6) are quoted at the beginning of each major section of the commentary and thus excluded from this index.

A. Magical Texts

1. GREEK AND LATIN

2. EGYPTIAN, DEMOTIC, COPTIC

B. Other Papyri and Inscriptions

1. PAPYRI

2. INSCRIPTIONS

C. Literature

1. GREEK

2. LATIN

D. Biblical and related Literature

1. OLD TESTAMENT

2. NEW TESTAMENT

E. Egyptian and Coptic Literatur

Plate

Due to an uneven surface, discoloration, and spots partly covered by lime deposits, we were unable to produce a readable photo. Close-ups of various parts of the tablet were no better. The present photo will at least allow the reader to discern the style of the hand.